CROSSROADS

TAL RONNEN
CROSSROADS

SCOT JONES and SERAFINA MAGNUSSEN
with JOANN CIANCIULLI

Photographs by LISA ROMEREIN

ARTISAN

NEW YORK

Library of Congress Cataloging-in-Publication Data

Ronnen, Tal.
  Crossroads / Tal Ronnen with Scot Jones and Serafina
Magnussen with JoAnn Cianciulli.
     pages cm
  Includes index.
  ISBN 978-1-57965-636-2
1. Cooking, Mediterranean. 2. Vegan cooking. I. Jones,
Scot. II. Magnussen, Serafina. III. Cianciulli, JoAnn. IV.
Title.
TX725.M35R66 2015
641.59'1822—dc23   2015010988

Design by Michelle Ishay-Cohen
Prop styling by Robin Turk
Lighting and digital technician: Matt "Primo" Harbicht

Artisan books are available at special discounts when
purchased in bulk for premiums and sales promotions
as well as for fund-raising or educational use. Special
editions or book excerpts also can be created to
specification. For details, contact the Special Sales
Director at the address below, or send an e-mail to
specialmarkets@workman.com.

Published by Artisan
A division of Workman Publishing Company, Inc.
225 Varick Street
New York, NY 10014-4381
artisanbooks.com

Published simultaneously in Canada by
Thomas Allen & Son, Limited

Printed in China

First printing, September 2015

10 9 8 7 6 5 4 3 2 1

to Lia

CONTENTS

Foreword by Michael Voltaggio   ix

Preface   x

Introduction   xiii

SNACKS AND SPREADS   1

SALADS   27

FLATBREADS   63

SOUPS   91

SMALL PLATES   113

PASTA   171

DESSERTS   211

COCKTAILS   247

BASICS   261

Acknowledgments   277

Index   278

FOREWORD

by Michael Voltaggio

When Tal asked me to write the foreword to this book, my first question was, why me? While my restaurant, ink, is down the street from Crossroads, Tal is a chef who is renowned for his unique take on plant-based dining, and I on the other hand include most animals (and their respective parts) in my menus. What do I know about vegan cuisine? I just know food that tastes good, and I appreciate and respect a chef who shares my passion for cooking and hospitality.

Like most people, I go out to dinner to celebrate special occasions, and I have realized that in several instances lately, I ended up craving not "vegan" food but the food Tal creates at Crossroads. Why? Because the food is simply delicious Mediterranean-based dishes that focus on seasonal vegetables, grains, legumes, flatbreads, and pastas. The dining room is warm and welcoming, and the cocktails are incredible.

Tal's food will surprise you: I indulge in oysters, Bolognese sauce, and a well-curated cheese plate. I eat fried calamari, caviar, fresh salads, and hearty pastas, and even desserts. But none of the food contains a trace of animal products. The "oysters" are made with oyster mushrooms that mimic the saline taste of the ocean, the fried "calamari" is made with battered and fried hearts of palm, and the cheese plate is crafted with Tal's own Kite Hill cheeses, which are nondairy and made from nut milks. The first time I ate at Crossroads, I thought, "Where the hell am I?" The dishes are thoughtful, playful, nourishing, satisfying, and yes . . . they happen to be vegan. And after a meal at Crossroads, I always feel satisfied, but I never feel heavy or as if I've overindulged.

I asked to meet the chef who has turned me into a vegan wannabe. A moment later, Tal was standing tableside wearing a clean, freshly pressed chef jacket, an apron, and black chef pants. I have to admit, I was ignorantly expecting a hippie with a T-shirt, a bandanna, and other casual clothing made from hemp and burlap. Nope; Tal is a professional chef with classic French culinary training who cooks some of the best-tasting food I have ever eaten. He is reinventing plant-based cuisine, and he is the only vegan chef who cooks for meat eaters—me included.

Tal and I soon realized that we are in fact very similar. We share some of the same guests, we have the same cooks rotating through our kitchens, we buy vegetables from the same farms, and we both work hard in our restaurants to deliver the best dining experience possible. Tal is a great neighbor and friend, an amazing chef, and perhaps a magician, because every time I eat his food, I find myself just wanting more and more, and I never miss the butter or bacon fat. If this is vegan cuisine, sign me up!

PREFACE

I opened Crossroads at the corner of Melrose and Sweetzer Avenues in Los Angeles in 2013. Crossroads is probably not what people picture when they think of a vegan restaurant. There are terrific vegetarian and vegan restaurants in Los Angeles, especially ethnic places where plant-based dishes are naturally part of the cuisine; however, the food and atmosphere tend to skew more casual. Crossroads redefines the concept of vegan dining, steering away from a sterile Zen-like atmosphere and a catering to more than a health-food crowd.

But the main thing that sets Crossroads apart is our menu, which is Mediterranean. Executive Chef Scot Jones and I met a few years ago when we worked together at Chrissie Hynde's restaurant VegiTerranean in Akron. Scot had stood at the helm of that city's best Italian restaurants for over a decade; we found a simpatico groove almost immediately, and to this day he's like my brother from another mother. Until we opened, most vegan restaurants in Los Angeles offered primarily an international mishmash of cuisines, serving dishes like black bean burritos, miso soup, tofu stir-fries, and dal curry. Scot and I stick to the Mediterranean food we know and love, like pastas and flatbreads, and shape them into plant-based equivalents. We refuse to dilute the menu with an eclectic spread of dishes that have little to do with one another . . . apart from the fact that they're all vegetarian. Since soybeans don't grow in the Mediterranean region, you won't find dishes featuring tofu or tempeh on our menu.

We are proud to serve mouthwatering Mediterranean meals in a refined environment that, frankly, hasn't been seen in LA before. The restaurant boasts a warm ambience and stylish décor, with deep banquettes and dramatic light fixtures; and we're the first plant-based restaurant in town to have a full bar with an inspired cocktail program. To finish off a meal, our desserts are the handiwork of Serafina Magnussen. You will find her sinfully delicious recipes in the dessert chapter (beginning on page 211).

We want to establish a sense of permanence, to make an impact with a timeless space that is an enduring part of the city. Service is paramount for us, and our staff both in the front and back of the house is committed to creating a unique dining experience for our guests. Crossroads has a convivial energy and serves wonderful food that one would expect from an upscale restaurant—with the only difference being that no animal products are used to prepare it. There are no obvious vegan cues, and most guests don't even make the connection that the menu is plant-based; they just know the restaurant is comfortable and the food is satisfying and delicious. Crossroads is defined not by what's missing, but by *what it is*.

The unqualified joy of being a chef in Los Angeles comes from the diners. Dining is a big deal here—people are food-savvy, with educated palates and an appreciation of fine food and wine. And we have been fortunate to connect with a diverse clientele. Crossroads has become a destination where doctors, housewives, punk rockers, icons of the adult film industry, foodies, and everyone in between come with an open mind to embrace the concept and share the experience. The positive response from the community and critics alike has been incredible, and the collective result of launching Crossroads has been an eye-opening revelation for us as well as for all types of diners—including non-vegetarians. The fact is, when treated with the same respect as any other cuisine, plant-based dining satisfies anyone who simply enjoys good food. I remain steadfast in my intention not to label the restaurant a vegan-only hangout, but instead to create a haven where all people feel relaxed and welcome.

Being a serious music aficionado, my business partner and friend Steve Bing suggested we name the restaurant Crossroads, drawing comparisons between Robert Johnson's legendary blues classic by the same name and our own road less traveled. Music critics speculate that the lyrics signify the spot where Johnson sold his soul to the Devil in exchange for his musical talents. The song title resonates with me. Crossroads marks a place we've all been in our lives at one point or another, where we examine the choices and encounters that shape our life experience. It makes me think about the journey and the individual efforts we make to meet at the same place. Our crossroads is an intersection where vegans, flexitarians, omnivores, and meat eaters can all cross paths to share a delicious meal and a good time. At Crossroads, we believe good food should be enjoyed by everyone.

INTRODUCTION

For many people, weaning themselves off animal products is a gradual process, but I dove into a vegetarian diet essentially overnight in my senior year of high school. In my twenties, I went all in and became vegan since I was eating nearly all plant-based foods already, and to this day I have never regretted my path. Back in the early 1990s, very few people were thinking about the serious downsides of being a carnivore, how it affects the environment or has ramifications on our health. Meat alternatives were limited then, and I was resigned to the notion that following a plant-based lifestyle involved a bit of a sacrifice. I remember that my only choice for a veggie burger in the grocery store came in the form of a boxed powdered mix that had to be combined with water. Restaurant options for vegans were almost nonexistent; when I dined out, the meat would be removed from the plate and I'd be served only the side dishes. The pitiful selections lacked substance and flair; white rice and steamed vegetables were standard, and I grew increasingly frustrated. I feared I'd be forever doomed to forgo taste and variety in favor of conscious eating. I hungered for the robust meals I used to love and became obsessed with creating plant-based dishes as delicious as anything I'd ever had as a meat eater.

As a lover of food, I realized it wasn't the animal products I actually longed for, but the texture, the flavor, the heartiness, and the satisfaction I feel when I indulge in a favorite food. What I really crave is the smoky paprika and fat in chorizo, not the pork itself; the richness of fresh pasta laced with a velvety, creamy sauce, not the eggs and butter; the smoky char of grilled steak, not the actual beef. The challenge in vegan cooking lies in not cheapening the food by making it feel like it's a knockoff of itself or a shadow of the original, but rather in making vegetables shine in their own right while still satisfying those cravings. I attended culinary school with the intention of learning classic French cooking techniques and applying them to plant-based foods. It's exciting to capture tradition untraditionally and to prepare food full of flavor, texture, and visual appeal—regardless of whether it is made with meat. By refocusing on what makes food rich and pleasurable to begin with, I realized I could create plant-based dishes that appeal to everyone, not just vegans.

The food at Crossroads is Mediterranean first and vegan second. Since I grew up in Israel, and Scot is classically trained in Northern Italian cooking, our combined influences translate to the creation of our pan-Mediterranean cuisine. California shares a similar climate to the region; the cuisine relies on seasonal produce, beans, and grains with an emphasis on straightforward preparation. Our menu represents the way many of us are eating today and easily translates to the home kitchen. Guests often ask for recipes, which brings us to writing this book.

There is flaky spanakopita, crispy polenta fries, stuffed ravioli bathed in garlic sauce, hearty flatbreads, and creative salads; not to mention decadent desserts, like chocolate cake, and tempting cocktails. Some dishes, such as Sweet Corn Risotto (page 165), are quick and simple to make for any weeknight dinner, and others, like Grilled Garden Vegetable Lasagna (page

201), require a little extra time in the kitchen and are great for a special meal. We want to inspire you to cook with a new appreciation for vegetables you probably already love, and at times to present them in a really dramatic fashion to unlock the wow factor. When prepared well and with imagination, vegetable-centric dishes can satisfy just as much as any piece of meat.

PHILOSOPHY

As I get older, my philosophy on cooking continues to grow and change. While I know creating exciting plant-based dishes will always be my focus, how I execute them keeps evolving. In the past, I composed plant-based dishes the same way I constructed any regular dish—with a balance of protein, vegetable, and starch. I largely took that approach as a personal challenge; colleagues said it couldn't be done, so, naturally, I wanted to prove otherwise. My approach has shifted through the years, and I'm sure it will continue to do so. What remains constant is that vegetables are always the jumping-off point.

A lot of people believe that eating a plant-based diet is restrictive and even boring. Untrue! Eating meatless opens up so many possibilities that I never think about the things I can't have. And the playing field is wide open. This type of cooking is relatively new, and there's so much more to create and explore with different flavors and textures. I'm constantly trying new ways to move plant-based cuisine forward, like turning nori from a sheet of seaweed into saltwater-tinged seasoning, cashews into cream, or yellow tomatoes into béarnaise sauce. You'll find new techniques throughout this cookbook. I want you to enjoy a great meal and improve your cooking techniques at the same time.

To be universally respected, plant-based cuisine has to appeal to the general population. This may sound obvious, but restaurants get it wrong all the time by serving fake meat that doesn't interest meat eaters or a vegan plate that's little more than an uninspired pile of vegetables. For instance, the portobello mushroom "burger" of yesterday and the cauliflower "steak" of today are examples of trendy executions that bastardize what I think superior vegan cuisine should be about. Just because there's an entire plate of grilled cauliflower doesn't make it a gratifying entrée. To be fair, there is a reason Crossroads is known for a dish called artichoke "oysters": oyster mushrooms are aptly named due to their resemblance in flavor and texture to the seafood—and I'm not the first person to identify that. Relying on portobello and cauliflower to mimic the flavor and texture of beef is another matter. Some still fall into the trap of thinking that vegetables or legumes need to be disguised as meat in order to be palatable. They don't.

With that said, I think there's a place for meat alternatives in the plant-based universe. At Crossroads we serve a couple of dishes, like scaloppini Marsala and Parmesan, specifically crafted as a gateway to satisfy the guys reluctantly pulled into the restaurant kicking and screaming. Including these crossover selections on the restaurant menu exposes people to new foods they likely would have never tried. We intentionally omitted those dishes from this book because they don't showcase the heart of what our Mediterranean food is about. In fact, only one recipe in the book—Pappardelle Bolognese—calls for a meat substitute, and it's used as an accent to the dish.

We know that most people are incorporating meatless meals into their diets more than ever before. With the popularity of Meatless Mondays, it's exciting to see the food trend moving in the direction of vegetables taking center stage. Many chefs today are starting to emphasize this shift, and vegetarian menus are popping up everywhere. Vegan cooking is finally taking its place as a respected form of cuisine in the culinary world, and one that's being celebrated as much by non-vegetarians as it is by vegetarians. It's incredibly gratifying not to be the odd man out in the chef community anymore.

COOKING CROSSROADS

Now that you understand my philosophy and how passionate I am about eating and living this way, I want you to get excited about cooking meat-, dairy-, and egg-free. Vegan food is not a radical departure from what you're likely already cooking at home: vegetables, grains, and legumes. The food in this book is not a trendy fad like a raw food diet, or Paleo, or even a collection of low-fat recipes attempting to extol the virtues of healthy eating. Nor is this a diet or gluten-free cookbook. Food is meant to nourish *and* satisfy. I don't believe in deprivation, so you will discover that some dishes are fried, others are fortified with nondairy butter, and some call for all-purpose flour. *Crossroads* takes "vegan" out of the equation and invites you to use it like every other cookbook on your shelf. My hope is that you open it often and get the pages dirty.

To be sure, *Crossroads* is not of the "easy, quick, five ingredients or less" cookbook variety, but the recipes aren't overwhelming, either. As with most meals, planning ahead will save you time getting dinner on the table, whether it's soaking cashews the night before to make cashew cream (which is essential to have on hand for many of the recipes in this book), roasting vegetables a couple of hours in advance, or keeping handmade pasta in your freezer. With few exceptions, most of the ingredients called for in the recipes are widely available at any well-stocked grocery store, Whole Foods Market being one of my favorites. You don't need to scour the Internet for hard-to-get ingredients or kitchen equipment, and recipes incorporating slightly out of the ordinary ingredients, such as nutritional yeast flakes and pomegranate molasses (pages 6 and 60), include notes on where to purchase the items and suggested substitutes. As with most dishes, the better the quality of the ingredients—whether olive oil or produce—you start with, the better the result. Farmers' markets are your friends. Eat local and in season when you can.

The wide range of options means you'll be able to find recipes for both casual weeknight suppers and special dinner parties. All of the Mediterranean dishes—snacks, soup, salad, pasta, small plates, desserts, and cocktail selections—work together and can be mixed and matched to create a satisfying meal. In addition to the recipes, I've included lots of basic cooking information and techniques to make you a better home cook. I hope that this book will expand your view of plant-based eating and inspire you to incorporate delicious vegan meals into your home repertoire.

A Few Words About Protein

Most of our ancestors ate meat, but it was in small amounts. It was eaten once a week as a treat, or it was served in small portions alongside grains and vegetables, but it was never the centerpiece. We've turned that around: today Americans eat animal protein three times a day, seven days a week. And many of us are afraid to follow pure vegetarian diets because we worry about not getting enough protein or eating "incomplete proteins" from plant sources. While I am not a registered dietitian or a doctor, I do have my finger on the pulse of what's going on. The fact is, we truly don't need to eat a complete protein in every bite of food or in every meal. Most Americans consume almost twice as much protein in their diet as people in any other country in the world. The idea that protein comes only from animal sources is an outdated myth that drives me crazy. Nearly all foods contain small amounts of protein, and it's very easy to obtain your daily protein requirements from beans, grains, nuts, and green vegetables. Do you know anyone in your life who is protein deficient? Doubtful. On the flip side, it is likely that someone you love suffers from diabetes, heart disease, cancer, or stroke. I think we need to worry more about eating enough vegetables than we do about whether we are getting enough protein.

SNACKS
AND
SPREADS

HARISSA POTATO CHIPS   4

SMOKED WHITE BEAN HUMMUS   6

MARINATED MEDITERRANEAN OLIVES
WITH ROSEMARY-FRIED ALMONDS   7

PICKLED VEGETABLES   10

LENTIL SKILLET BREAD   14

SPICY TOMATO-PEPPER JAM   18

LEEK PÂTÉ   19

BABA GANOUSH   20

PISTACHIO-KALAMATA TAPENADE   21

EGYPTIAN FAVA BEAN SPREAD   22

WARM KALE AND ARTICHOKE DIP   25

This chapter is loaded with a diverse collection of starters—whether you call them meze, tapas, or antipasti—inspired by the flavors of the Mediterranean: Middle Eastern Smoked White Bean Hummus (page 6) and savory Baba Ganoush (page 20), warm marinated olives Italian-style (see page 7), and French-influenced Leek Pâté (page 19), among others. My favorite Moroccan spice mix, harissa, takes homemade potato chips to the next level (see page 4), and the hearty Lentil Skillet Bread (page 14) is the perfect accompaniment for all kinds of dips.

These finger foods can be mixed and matched and make great party fare. Scot and I are complete opposites when it comes to entertaining. He creates elaborate menus and table settings. I like to keep things casual and stress-free. You can make it easy on yourself too with the recipes that follow, most of which can be made ahead and put together pretty quickly so you can enjoy your guests . . . and the food. (If you're making the spreads and dips in advance, remove them from the refrigerator 45 minutes before serving so they can come to room temperature.) And be sure to check out the cocktails in the chapter beginning on page 247 to serve alongside.

HARISSA POTATO CHIPS MAKES A BIG BOWL OF CHIPS (ABOUT 100)

2 large russet (baking) potatoes
(about 1 pound), scrubbed

Expeller-pressed canola oil,
for deep-frying

2 to 3 tablespoons harissa spice mix
(see Note)

Kosher salt

Smoked White Bean Hummus
(page 6), for serving (optional)

Homemade potato chips are easy to make, and the results can be amazing. I love spicy food; the dusting of peppery harissa spice mix gives these chips an extra kick. Serve with Smoked White Bean Hummus or your favorite dip.

Potato chips are best served right away, but once cool, they will keep covered at room temperature for up to 1 day. If stored longer, the chips become soggy.

Using a mandoline, slice the potatoes to about the thickness of a nickel; you should get about 50 slices per potato. Put the slices in a large bowl and add cool water to cover. Swish the potatoes around to remove the excess starch; this will make the chips super crispy. Drain the potatoes and repeat 2 or 3 times, until the water is no longer cloudy. Drain the potatoes really well in a colander.

Spread the potatoes out on a baking sheet and pat them dry with paper towels. Removing the excess moisture will prevent the oil from spattering.

Heat 3 inches of oil to 325°F in a deep fryer or deep pot. If you don't have a deep-fry thermometer, a good way to see if the oil is hot enough is to stick the end of a wooden spoon or chopstick in it; if bubbles circle around it, you're good to go.

Cook the potatoes in batches to avoid overcrowding and to keep the oil temperature constant: Put the potato slices in the fryer basket or a spider or other strainer and carefully lower into the hot oil, give them a stir to keep them from sticking together, and fry for 6 to 7 minutes, until golden brown and crispy. Remove the chips with the spider or a slotted spoon, allowing the excess oil to drain off, and transfer to a paper towel–lined platter to absorb any remaining oil.

Season the chips with the harissa and salt while they are still hot. Serve immediately, with Smoked White Bean Hummus if desired.

HARISSA SPICE MIX

A vibrant seasoning used in Moroccan cuisine, harissa is a spice blend made primarily from hot chilies, paprika, garlic, cumin, and coriander. The flavor is bright and smoky with a jolt of heat that elevates and complements other ingredients. I'm addicted to the stuff. It's terrific sprinkled on just about anything—soups, roasted vegetables, and dips (such as Egyptian Fava Bean Spread, page 22). You can find harissa in the dry spice aisle of most grocery stores. It comes as a paste too.

SMOKED WHITE BEAN HUMMUS MAKES 2 CUPS

1 cup dried cannellini beans, soaked overnight in cold water, or one 15-ounce can cannellini beans, drained and rinsed

2 tablespoons tahini (sesame seed paste)

2 tablespoons nutritional yeast flakes (see Note)

2 garlic cloves, coarsely chopped

½ shallot, coarsely chopped

Juice of 1 lemon

1 fresh thyme sprig, leaves stripped from the stem

1 teaspoon agave nectar

½ teaspoon freshly ground black pepper

1 teaspoon coarse smoked sea salt (optional; see headnote)

¼ cup extra-virgin olive oil

2 cups hickory or apple wood chips, soaked in water for 20 minutes and drained (optional; see headnote)

NUTRITIONAL YEAST FLAKES

Nutritional yeast may not sound like the most appetizing ingredient, but it has a cheesy, nutty, savory quality that gives any dish extra oomph. Just a tablespoon or two adds a creamy, salty richness to dips, soups, and sauces. Look for nutritional yeast flakes in the supplement section of the market or health food store. Be sure to select flakes instead of granules, which will deliver a bit of texture to whatever you add them to.

At Crossroads, we hot-smoke ingredients like corn and mushrooms (see pages 79 and 52), as well as the beans for this dip, to impart a rustic, earthy flavor. You can do the same by improvising a stovetop smoker at home; you will need a large pot with a steamer insert. Or you can simplify the recipe, by skipping this step and adding smoked sea salt to the beans.

Made with cannellini beans instead of the traditional chickpeas, this super-creamy hummus whips up beautifully and is far better than anything you can buy in the market. If using dried beans, you'll need to soak them overnight. Serve with Harissa Potato Chips (page 4) or good store-bought chips, pita, or crudités.

If using dried beans, drain and rinse the beans and transfer to a large pot. Add water to cover by 1 inch and bring to a boil, then simmer over medium-low heat until the beans are tender, about 1½ hours. Drain and rinse the beans. (The beans can be cooked a day ahead and refrigerated, covered.)

To smoke the beans: Open the windows and remove the battery from your smoke detector. Line a large pot that has a steamer insert with aluminum foil (this will keep the wood chips from scorching the bottom). Spread the wet wood chips on the foil. Cover the pot tightly with the lid and set over high heat.

Meanwhile, put the beans in the steamer basket. Once the chips begin to smoke, drop the steamer basket insert into the pot and cover tightly with the lid. Turn off the heat and allow the beans to soak up the smoke for 5 to 6 minutes—no peeking. Set the beans aside to cool. (The beans can be prepared a couple of hours in advance, covered, and held at room temperature.)

To make the hummus: Combine the beans, tahini, nutritional yeast flakes, garlic, shallot, lemon juice, thyme, agave, and pepper in a food processor. Add the smoked sea salt if you did not smoke the beans. Puree until the mixture is totally smooth, about 2 minutes. With the motor running, pour in the oil in a steady stream, making sure it directly hits the blade (this is the best way to distribute the oil and emulsify it evenly and quickly), and process until it is fully incorporated.

Store any leftover hummus covered in the refrigerator for up to 3 days.

MARINATED MEDITERRANEAN OLIVES
<small>WITH</small> ROSEMARY-FRIED ALMONDS <small>SERVES 4 TO 6 (MAKES ABOUT 3 CUPS)</small>

1 pound mixed unpitted black
 and green olives, such as
 Castelvetrano, Cerignola,
 Picholine, and Kalamata, drained

1½ cups extra-virgin olive oil

6 fresh thyme sprigs, leaves
 stripped from the stems and
 chopped (about 1½ teaspoons)

6 garlic cloves, thinly sliced (about
 2½ tablespoons)

Zest of 2 lemons, removed with
 a zester

1 shallot, thinly sliced (about
 2 tablespoons)

1½ teaspoons red pepper flakes

½ teaspoon kosher salt

¼ teaspoon freshly ground
 black pepper

Rosemary-Fried Almonds
 (recipe follows)

The inspiration for this rustic snack came from Scot, who spent some time cooking in Venice, Italy. Warming olives in olive oil infused with lemon and other aromatics intensifies their flavor and makes them really plump and juicy. While the process is simple, the result is transformative. I like using Castelvetrano and Cerignola olives for their big meaty bite and Picholine and Kalamata for their tart-fruity flavor. Be sure to purchase high-quality olives at an olive bar or a good market. The leftover oil is delicious for dipping bread or for dressing salads or roasted vegetables. Top the warm olives with Rosemary-Fried Almonds for an added crunch.

Put the olives in a heat-resistant bowl or container. Set aside.

Combine the oil, thyme, garlic, lemon zest, shallot, red pepper flakes, salt, and black pepper in a saucepan, set over low heat, and slowly warm the oil to infuse it with the aromatics, swirling the pan occasionally to prevent the oil from getting too hot, 5 to 7 minutes.

Pour the fragrant warm oil over the olives and let steep at room temperature, uncovered, for about 1 hour. Turn the olives over a few times to redistribute the aromatics.

To serve: Gently heat the olives in a small saucepan over low heat until warmed through, 2 to 3 minutes. Using a slotted spoon, scoop the olives and aromatics into a serving bowl and then pour a bit of the oil over the top. Serve warm, topped with the almonds.

ROSEMARY-FRIED ALMONDS

MAKES 2 CUPS

1 cup expeller-pressed canola oil

1 large fresh rosemary sprig, leaves
   stripped from the stem and
   coarsely chopped (about
   2 tablespoons)

2 cups whole Marcona almonds

1 teaspoon kosher salt

Popular in Spain, Marcona almonds are softer and sweeter than regular almonds and have a more rounded shape. Their rich, buttery flavor is due to the high oil and moisture content. Store the fried almonds in a sealed container at room temperature for up to 3 days or in the freezer for up to 3 months.

Put a cast-iron or other heavy skillet over medium-high heat. Pour in the oil, add the rosemary, and stir to infuse the flavor into the oil. Heat the oil to around 300°F. (You don't need a thermometer for this: Drop an almond into the oil. When it sinks a bit, then floats right back to the top and starts sizzling, the oil is hot enough.) Once the oil is ready to go, add half of the almonds and cook, stirring constantly, until they are fragrant and toasted, 10 to 20 seconds. Using a slotted spoon, remove the almonds from the oil and drain on paper towels. Sprinkle them with the salt while they are hot. Repeat with the remaining almonds. Use to top the marinated olives or serve as a snack.

PICKLED
VEGETABLES SERVES 6

BRINE

2 cups white vinegar

2 cups filtered water

¼ cup unrefined cane sugar

Pickling Spice (recipe follows) or
    2 tablespoons store-bought
    pickling spice mix

2 teaspoons kosher salt

SUGGESTED VEGETABLES

5 baby heirloom carrots, halved or
    quartered lengthwise

5 watermelon radishes (see Note)
    or regular radishes, thinly sliced
    on a mandoline

½ head of cauliflower, cut into
    small florets

4 scallions, white and light green
    parts only, cut into 1-inch pieces

2 Persian or Kirby cucumbers,
    quartered lengthwise

Scot and I share a passion for pickles from eating at Jewish delis as kids. Scot would skip school to go to Lou and Hy's Deli in Akron to feed his pickle craving. Every winter I would fly to Miami to visit my grandfather for a week or two. One of the necessary stops during my stay was the Rascal House. This deli was an institution, and the lines were out the door. But when you were finally seated, you'd be greeted with a stack of fresh rye bread, an assortment of homemade mustards, and a bowl of bright-green half-sour pickles. Heaven.

These are refrigerator pickles, so there's no hassle of canning, vacuum seals, or sterilized jars. You will need about 4 cups of vegetables total. Feel free to mix it up with other raw vegetables, such as okra or green beans. Keep in mind that vegetables with bold color, like beets, will bleed into the brine solution, so it's best to pickle them separately. If you like crisper pickles, chill the brine before pouring it over the vegetables. This recipe can easily be doubled if you want to prepare a bigger batch; the pickles keep well in the refrigerator.

To make the brine: Combine the vinegar, water, sugar, pickling spice, and salt in a medium saucepan and bring to a simmer over medium-low heat, stirring occasionally to dissolve the sugar.

Put the vegetables in a heatproof container and pour the hot liquid over them; they should be completely submerged. Cover and cool to room temperature, then chill for at least 24 hours, preferably 48.

The pickled vegetables will keep for up to 1 month covered in the refrigerator; be sure to keep them completely submerged in the liquid, adding vinegar if needed.

WATERMELON RADISHES

From the outside, watermelon radishes don't look like much—more like a turnip or an ordinary radish with a green hue—but inside they are a shade of vibrant raspberry pink that looks similar to watermelon. Watermelon radishes are crunchy and sweeter than other radishes. A mandoline is ideal for slicing these beauties super thin, but a sharp knife and steady hand will do.

PICKLING SPICE

MAKES 2 TABLESPOONS

2 bay leaves, crumbled

2 teaspoons mustard seeds

1 teaspoon coriander seeds

1 teaspoon whole black
   peppercorns

1 teaspoon red pepper flakes

Combine the bay leaves and spices in a small dry skillet and toast over medium-low heat for 1 to 2 minutes to release the fragrant oils, shaking the pan periodically so the spices don't scorch. Transfer the spice mixture to a jar with a tight-fitting lid. Store in a cool dark place for up to 3 months.

LENTIL SKILLET BREAD
MAKES 3 POUNDS DOUGH; 8 BREADS

¼ cup French green lentils (Puy),
   picked over and rinsed

¼ cup red or black quinoa, well
   rinsed and drained

One ¼-ounce envelope active dry
   yeast (2¼ teaspoons)

1 cup warm filtered water

1½ teaspoons agave nectar

1 cup vegan mayonnaise, such as
   Vegenaise, at room temperature

1½ teaspoons white balsamic or
   unfiltered apple cider vinegar

1 cup unsweetened plain
   almond milk

3 cups 7-grain flour, such as Great
   Rivers, plus more for dusting

1 cup whole wheat flour

½ cup bread flour

1 teaspoon baking powder

1 teaspoon fine sea salt

1 teaspoon ground coriander

1½ teaspoons garlic powder

Nonstick cooking spray

Flaked sea salt, such as Maldon

Freshly ground black pepper

Nutritional yeast flakes (see Note,
   page 6)

My dear friend chef Art Smith and I developed this recipe together. Packed with protein-rich lentils and quinoa, this naan-style bread has a nutty texture and flavor, but is also hearty and healthy. As you need only ½ cup each cooked lentils and quinoa, this is an excellent way to use leftovers. The bread pairs well with creamy spreads, especially the Pistachio-Kalamata Tapenade (page 21) and Egyptian Fava Bean Spread (page 22).

To prepare the lentils: Combine the lentils with 1 cup lightly salted filtered water in a small saucepan and bring to a boil. Reduce the heat to low and simmer, uncovered, until the lentils are just tender, 15 to 20 minutes. Drain the lentils and set aside to cool.

Meanwhile, prepare the quinoa: Combine the quinoa with 1 cup lightly salted filtered water in a small saucepan and bring to a boil. Cover, reduce the heat to low, and simmer until the water is absorbed and the quinoa has fluffed up, 10 to 12 minutes. The quinoa is done when you can see the curlicue popping out of each grain; drain off any excess water. Fluff the quinoa with a fork and set aside to cool.

To prepare the dough: Combine the yeast, warm water, and agave in a small bowl and stir gently to dissolve. Let stand until the yeast comes alive and starts to foam, 5 to 10 minutes.

Stir the vegan mayonnaise and vinegar together in a small bowl. Pour the almond milk into a saucepan and set over low heat. Stir in the mayonnaise mixture and heat gently, stirring occasionally, until the almond milk mixture reaches 100°F (about body temperature). Remove from the heat and stir in the yeast mixture. Set aside.

Whisk the flours, baking powder, fine sea salt, coriander, and garlic powder together in a large mixing bowl until blended. Make a well in the center and pour in the almond milk mixture. Using a wooden spoon, stir until all of the dry ingredients are moistened and a shaggy dough forms. Fold in the cooled quinoa and lentils until evenly distributed.

Turn the dough out onto a generously floured work surface and knead for 15 minutes, or until slightly firm and beginning to come together. The dough is really sticky, so it's best to flour your hands too.

PHOTOGRAPH ON PAGES 16–17

Divide the dough in half and shape into 2 balls. Cover with a clean towel and let rise in a warm spot until doubled in size, about 45 minutes. (Or wrap each ball of dough in plastic wrap and refrigerate for up to 1 day; this step will develop the bread's flavor further.)

To make the breads: Divide each ball of dough into 4 equal portions and shape into balls; they should be 6 ounces each and about the size of a tangerine. Cover 7 of the balls of dough with plastic wrap to prevent them from drying out.

On a lightly floured surface, press the remaining ball of dough out with your fingers into an 8-inch circle, about $\frac{1}{4}$ inch thick.

Coat a large cast-iron skillet with cooking spray and set over high heat. When the pan is smoking hot, lay the round of dough in the pan and coat the top with cooking spray. Cook until bubbles form on the top of the bread and there are golden spots on the bottom, 3 to 4 minutes. Flip the bread over with tongs and cook for 2 more minutes, or until the bread is firm and golden on the second side.

Transfer the bread to a cutting board. Sprinkle with flaked sea salt, black pepper, and nutritional yeast flakes and cut into 8 wedges. Cover and hold warm, and repeat with the remaining balls of dough. Serve the breads with your favorite dip or spread.

VARIATION

LENTIL CRACKERS

Preheat the oven to 450°F. Sprinkle a baking sheet lightly with flour.

On a lightly floured surface, with a floured rolling pin, roll the dough (you can use any amount) out into a rectangle about $\frac{1}{8}$ inch thick. Coat the dough with nonstick cooking spray and sprinkle with flaked sea salt, black pepper, and nutritional yeast flakes. Using a pizza cutter or a sharp knife, cut the dough into individual crackers roughly 1 inch by 2 inches. Alternatively, cut it into squares or diamonds, or use cookie cutters to cut out the crackers.

Using a dough scraper or a spatula, transfer the crackers to the prepared baking sheet. Prick the crackers with a fork to prevent them from puffing up during baking. Bake for 12 to 15 minutes, until the edges are golden brown. Transfer the crackers to a wire rack to cool. Once completely cool, the crackers can be stored in an airtight container at room temperature for up to 5 days.

SPICY TOMATO-PEPPER JAM MAKES 3 CUPS

4 large beefsteak tomatoes (about
   2 pounds), coarsely chopped,
   or one 28-ounce can whole
   tomatoes, preferably
   San Marzano
6 garlic cloves, thinly sliced
2 banana (Hungarian wax),
   Cubanelle, or Anaheim peppers,
   finely chopped
1 small onion, finely chopped
Juice of 3 limes
3 tablespoons light brown sugar
¼ cup fresh basil leaves, chopped
¼ cup fresh flat-leaf parsley
   leaves, chopped
2 tablespoons tomato paste
½ teaspoon kosher salt
¼ teaspoon freshly ground
   black pepper
Crackers or Lentil Skillet Bread
   (page 14), for serving

When Scot and I were working eighteen-hour days opening the restaurant VegiTerranean in Ohio, this homemade jam was our sustenance. Scot had an incredible garden filled with tomatoes, peppers, and herbs, and at the end of the summer, we'd cook a big batch of this intensely flavorful jam. A spreadable version of a spicy marinara sauce, it's a great sweet-and-sour match for crackers or flatbreads. We also use it as a base for Roasted Mushroom Flatbread (page 72). If you can't get banana peppers, substitute any long, pale-green chili pepper, such as Cubanelle or Anaheim (also known as California).

The key to developing the deep flavor and thick consistency of the jam is to not rush the cooking process. Take the time to let it gently simmer for at least 1 hour to allow the natural sugars of the tomatoes and peppers to reduce and caramelize. As the Beastie Boys say, "Slow and low, that is the tempo," and it is for the success of *this* jam too.

Put the tomatoes in a pot set over medium-high heat. Add the garlic, peppers, onion, lime juice, sugar, and herbs, stir together, and bring to a boil. Reduce the heat to low, stir in the tomato paste, and simmer, uncovered, for 1 to 1½ hours. As the tomatoes soften, smash and break them apart into chunky pieces with a wooden spoon. Season with the salt and pepper and let cool. The jam is done when the mixture has reduced and is very thick.

Serve the jam at room temperature or chilled with crackers or the skillet bread. The jam will keep for up to 5 days covered in the refrigerator—if it lasts that long.

PHOTOGRAPH ON PAGE 17

LEEK PÂTÉ

4 large leeks (about 1 pound), white
and pale green parts only

½ pound (2 sticks) Earth Balance
butter sticks, cut into chunks

1 cup dry white wine

1 cup Vegetable Stock (page 268) or
store-bought stock

Kosher salt and freshly ground
black pepper

Crackers or Lentil Skillet Bread
(page 14), for serving

Flaked sea salt, such as Maldon

There's nothing like the flavor and texture of classic pâté; this recipe uses braised leeks in place of liver. Leeks are not naturally spreadable, so they need to be cooked slow and low for a long time to break down the fibers and develop a rich flavor. Once the leeks are cooled and whipped in a food processor, they solidify into a texture similar to that of traditional pâté.

Halve the leeks lengthwise and then cut crosswise into ½-inch slices. You should have about 4 cups sliced leeks. Put the sliced leeks in a colander and rinse really well under cool water, checking for dirt between the layers. Drain well.

Put a large pot over medium heat and add the leeks, butter substitute, wine, and stock, stirring to combine. Bring the mixture to a simmer, then reduce the heat to medium-low and gently simmer, uncovered, stirring occasionally, until the leeks are butter-soft, about 40 minutes. Season with kosher salt and pepper.

Using a slotted spoon, carefully transfer the leek mixture to the bowl of a food processor. Pulse until coarsely pureed. If necessary, pour in some of the leek cooking liquid a little at a time, processing until the pâté is smooth. (The pâté will keep for up to 3 days covered in the refrigerator. Bring to room temperature to serve.)

Slather the pâté on crackers or the skillet bread, and top each with a pinch of flaked sea salt.

PHOTOGRAPH ON PAGE 16

BABA GANOUSH ^{MAKES 3 CUPS}

3 medium Italian eggplants (about
  3 pounds)

¼ cup tahini (sesame seed paste)

Juice of 1 lemon

4 garlic cloves, coarsely chopped

6 fresh flat-leaf parsley sprigs,
  coarsely chopped

2 tablespoons extra-virgin olive oil,
  plus more for serving

1 teaspoon kosher salt

1 teaspoon smoked paprika

½ teaspoon ancho chili powder

¼ teaspoon ground cumin

Lentil Skillet Bread (page 14) or pita
  wedges, for serving

The benefit of Mediterranean food is that so much of it is inherently vegan. Take baba ganoush. It's a Middle Eastern eggplant spread, and this recipe is close to my heart. My older sister Miki taught me to make it when I was staying at her incredible home overlooking the Western Wall in Jerusalem's Old City.

The secret to perfect baba ganoush is to cook the eggplant until it's done . . . and then cook it some more. The eggplant should be deeply charred and completely deflated, like a blown tire. I'm a spice lover, so I added smoked paprika and ancho chili powder to turn up the heat.

Prick the eggplants in a few places each with a fork, so the steam has somewhere to go when you cook them. Put one eggplant on a gas burner over high heat (if you do not have a gas stove, see Note). Char the eggplant, using tongs to turn it often, until the skin is deeply blistered and black and the eggplant is deflated and extremely soft, 10 to 15 minutes. Transfer it to a plate, cover it with plastic wrap, and let it steam for at least 10 minutes; this will make it easier to remove the flesh from the skin. Repeat with the remaining eggplants.

When the eggplants are cool enough to handle, carefully peel off the skins, dipping your fingers in water periodically—this helps to keep the burnt bits from sticking to your fingers and mixing in with the flesh.

Put the eggplant in the bowl of a food processor.

Add the tahini, lemon juice, garlic, parsley, oil, salt, paprika, chili powder, and cumin and pulse until the mixture has a fairly smooth texture but isn't totally pureed. Taste and adjust the seasoning as needed. (The baba ganoush will keep for up to 5 days covered in the refrigerator.)

Scrape the baba ganoush into a serving bowl and drizzle with oil. Serve with the skillet bread or pita wedges for dipping.

GRILLING OR ROASTING EGGPLANT

If you don't have a gas stove, you can grill the eggplants on a very hot oiled grill pan or outdoor grill, turning often, until the skins are wrinkled and black and the eggplants are shriveled and soft. Or, if you prefer, roast the eggplants on a baking sheet in a preheated 400°F oven for 30 minutes, turning occasionally.

PISTACHIO-KALAMATA TAPENADE MAKES 3 CUPS

2 cups pitted Kalamata olives, drained and rinsed

1 cup shelled pistachios, toasted

1 cup walnuts, toasted

4 fresh flat-leaf parsley sprigs, coarsely chopped

2 garlic cloves, coarsely chopped

1 shallot, coarsely chopped

½ teaspoon red pepper flakes

Juice of 1 lemon

½ cup extra-virgin olive oil

Kosher salt and freshly ground black pepper

Olive tapenade can be made from as many different olives as you can find, and there are so many ways to add texture and flavor. I used pistachios to lend a buttery, crunchy element. Serve it alongside Lentil Skillet Bread (page 14) or Lentil Crackers (page 15), or toss it with cooked pasta. The tapenade is also the base of Roasted Cauliflower Flatbread (page 75).

Combine the olives, nuts, parsley, garlic, shallot, red pepper flakes, and lemon juice in the bowl of a food processor and pulse to combine well, stopping to scrape down the sides of the bowl as needed. Then process until the mixture is coarsely pureed; you should still see bits of nuts throughout. With the motor running, pour in the oil in a steady stream, making sure it directly hits the blade (this is the best way to distribute the oil and emulsify it evenly and quickly), and process until it is fully incorporated, about 30 seconds. Taste and season with salt and black pepper.

The tapenade will keep for up to 5 days covered in the refrigerator.

EGYPTIAN FAVA BEAN SPREAD MAKES 3 CUPS

1 medium russet (baking) potato
(about ½ pound), peeled
and cubed

Kosher salt

2 tablespoons grapeseed oil

½ small sweet onion, such as
Vidalia, coarsely chopped
(about 1 cup)

6 garlic cloves, coarsely chopped
(about 2 tablespoons)

3 plum (Roma) tomatoes, cored and
coarsely chopped (1½ cups)

2 teaspoons za'atar (see Note)

1 teaspoon ground cinnamon

¼ teaspoon harissa spice mix
(see Note, page 4)

¼ teaspoon ground cumin

¼ teaspoon chili powder

⅛ teaspoon cayenne

2½ pounds whole fresh fava beans,
shelled and peeled (1½ cups;
see Note)

¼ cup Vegetable Stock (page 268)
or store-bought stock

Juice of ½ lemon

1 tablespoon dry sherry

4 fresh flat-leaf parsley sprigs,
coarsely chopped

Freshly ground black pepper

Crackers or Lentil Skillet Bread
(page 14) or cut-up raw
vegetables, for serving

The national dish of Egypt, *ful medames* is a fava bean stew traditionally served with rice or fluffy pita. *Ful* is a comfort food that reminds me of growing up in Israel. Here I've taken its basic ingredients—fava beans, sweet onion, and spices—and revamped them into a creamy spread. Za'atar is one of my all-star spices, and its zesty punch, along with the cumin and other spices, balances the richness of the fava beans.

Fresh fava beans are only available in the spring, so take advantage of the season and make this recipe often before they're gone.

To prepare the potato: Put the potato cubes in a saucepan and cover with cold water. Add ¼ teaspoon salt and bring to a boil, uncovered, over medium-high heat. Simmer until there is no resistance when a fork is inserted into a potato cube, about 20 minutes. Drain the potatoes well in a colander and set aside. (This step can be done up to 1 hour in advance.)

To prepare the spread: Put a large sauté pan over medium heat and add the oil. When the oil is hot, add the onion, cooked potato, and garlic and cook, stirring, until the onions begin to soften and turn golden, about 3 minutes. Stir in the chopped tomatoes, za'atar, cinnamon, harissa, cumin, chili powder, and cayenne and cook until the tomatoes begin to release their liquid, about 1 minute.

Add the fava beans, stock, lemon juice, and sherry and simmer, stirring occasionally, until the fava beans are tender, 4 to 5 minutes.

Carefully transfer the fava bean mixture to the bowl of a food processor. Add the parsley, season with salt and pepper, and puree until smooth. (The spread will keep for up to 5 days covered in the refrigerator. Serve at room temperature.)

Serve the spread with crackers or the skillet bread, or with cut-up raw vegetables.

PHOTOGRAPH ON PAGE 17

Za'atar is a wonderfully tangy Middle Eastern spice blend. Made primarily from a combination of sesame seeds, thyme, and sumac, it has deep nutty, woodsy accents. In the Old City of Jerusalem, merchants sell za'atar by the kilo and wrap it up in newspaper, ready for customers to dip hunks of fresh bread into. Za'atar can add a pop of flavor to almost anything, especially vegetables (see Shaved Brussels Sprouts, page 48), grains, and beans. You can find it in the spice aisle of good grocery stores.

FAVA BEANS

Also known as broad beans, fava beans are a sure sign of spring. When in their pods, fava beans look like overgrown sweet peas, but their flavor is smoother, sweeter, and richer. Fava beans have to be shelled and then peeled, which can make them a bit of a chore to prepare, but they are worth the extra effort.

To shell and peel fresh fava beans: First remove the beans from the pods by sliding your finger down one side of each one, opening the seam like a zipper, or just snap the pods apart in pieces. You'll notice that each bean has a thick whitish skin around it. The best way to remove the skins is to blanch the beans first. Bring a large pot of lightly salted filtered water to a boil and cook the beans for 1 minute. Drain the beans and plunge into an ice bath to "shock" them—i.e., stop the cooking process and cool them quickly. Blanching the beans loosens the skins so they're easier to remove. Slip off the skins by gently pinching each bean out into a bowl; discard the skins.

ARTICHOKE HEARTS

To prepare artichoke hearts, fill a large bowl halfway with water. Squeeze in the juice of 2 lemons, and toss the lemon halves into the water too. Working with one artichoke at a time, use a vegetable peeler to trim the tough outer part of the stem. Using a chef's knife, cut off the top 1 inch of the artichoke crown and then snap off or cut off all of the remaining leaves. Run a paring knife around the base of the artichoke to remove any tough green parts or bits of leaves. Cut the artichoke in half. Using a sharp spoon or a melon baller, scoop out the spiky purple center leaves and fuzzy choke inside and discard. Transfer the prepared artichoke hearts to the lemon water as you work, to keep them from oxidizing and turning brown.

WARM KALE ^{AND} ARTICHOKE DIP MAKES 4 CUPS

8 large artichoke hearts (see Note) or two 15-ounce cans artichoke hearts in water

2 tablespoons Earth Balance butter stick

2 shallots, minced

6 garlic cloves, minced

½ cup dry white wine

½ cup dry sherry

1 cup Cashew Cream (page 264)

1 cup Vegetable Stock (page 268) or store-bought stock

½ cup nutritional yeast flakes (see Note, page 6)

2 tablespoons fresh thyme leaves

6 cups baby kale, coarsely chopped

1 teaspoon kosher salt

½ teaspoon freshly ground black pepper

Harissa Potato Chips (page 4), Lentil Crackers (page 15), or sliced raw vegetables, for serving

Smoked paprika, for garnish

That retro classic, spinach and artichoke dip laden with cream cheese and sour cream, is transformed into a contemporary version that is still rich and creamy but allows the vegetables to shine. Kale's chewy texture and peppery kick make it a bold stand-in for spinach. When sautéing the artichokes, take care not to let them brown; you want the dip to keep its beautiful pale color. The cashew cream needs to be prepared a day in advance, so plan accordingly. Serve with Harissa Potato Chips, Lentil Crackers, or raw vegetables, or try putting it on baked potatoes or using it as a filling for stuffed pasta, such as cappellacci (page 197).

If using fresh artichoke hearts, bring a large pot of lightly salted water to a boil. Add the artichoke hearts and blanch for 10 minutes, or until slightly tender; a paring knife should slide in easily. Drain the hearts and plunge into an ice bath to "shock" them—i.e., stop the cooking and cool them quickly. Drain and coarsely chop. If using canned artichokes, simply drain and chop.

Put a large deep sauté pan over medium heat and add the butter substitute. When it has melted, add the shallots, garlic, and artichoke hearts and cook, stirring, until the vegetables are soft, 6 to 8 minutes.

Add the wine and sherry and cook for 1 minute to evaporate some of the alcohol. Add the cashew cream, stock, nutritional yeast flakes, and thyme, reduce the heat to medium-low, and gently simmer until thick, 35 to 40 minutes; stir occasionally to make sure the cream mixture doesn't stick and burn on the bottom of the pan.

Fold in the kale a few handfuls at a time and continue to simmer until the kale is soft and the artichokes have broken down slightly, about 10 minutes. Season with the salt and pepper. (The dip will keep for up to 3 days covered in the refrigerator. To serve, reheat over medium-low heat, stirring often.)

If the dip appears too thick, add a couple of tablespoons of stock or water.

Spoon the dip into a serving bowl, dust with smoked paprika, and serve with the potato chips, crackers, or sliced raw vegetables.

SALADS

SPRING CHOPPED SALAD WITH
WHOLE-GRAIN-MUSTARD VINAIGRETTE

BABY BEET SALAD WITH APPLES,
CANDIED WALNUTS, AND
BALSAMIC REDUCTION

SPICY MOROCCAN CARROT SALAD
WITH CHILI AND CUMIN

WATERMELON SALAD WITH PERSIAN
CUCUMBERS, CHERRY TOMATOES,
AND BALSAMIC REDUCTION

PEACH SALAD WITH BALSAMIC-
GLAZED CIPOLLINI ONIONS, TOASTED
HAZELNUTS, AND MINT VINAIGRETTE

MELON SALAD WITH WATERCRESS
AND OROBLANCO VINAIGRETTE

SHAVED BRUSSELS SPROUTS WITH
ZA'ATAR, LEMON, AND PINE NUTS

KALE SALAD WITH CURRANTS, PINE
NUTS, AND LEMON-THYME VINAIGRETTE

BLOOMSDALE SPINACH SALAD WITH
BLACK GARLIC VINAIGRETTE

ISRAELI COUSCOUS WITH CHAMPAGNE
GRAPES, HARICOTS VERTS, AND
MARCONA ALMONDS

BUTTERNUT SQUASH FARINATA WITH
ARUGULA SALAD AND POMEGRANATE
VINAIGRETTE

I'm a firm believer in eating what's good *when* it's good, and salads are the ultimate platform for showcasing produce at its finest any time of year.

Although some of the salads in this chapter feature greens, such as kale and my favorite type of spinach, others incorporate a wide range of vegetables with contrasting textures and flavors. Adding ingredients like fruits, nuts, and grains can turn a salad into one of the most satisfying parts of the meal.

Making your own vinaigrette is mandatory. The base of vinaigrette is acid and oil; all of the other components, like garlic and herbs, are yours for customizing. Be sure your oil is of high quality and hasn't been on the shelf (or, even worse, near the stove) for months, losing flavor and gradually turning rancid. Lastly, do not overdress or drown salads in vinaigrette; the dressing should serve as a subtle counterpoint to the ingredients in the salad itself.

Any of these salads can be served either as a prelude to a main course or as a light entrée. You can make the recipes that follow as written, but I urge you to use your imagination and to be flexible. Ultimately, let your local farmers' market lead you to ingredients that are seasonal, fresh, and at their peak.

SPRING CHOPPED SALAD WITH WHOLE-GRAIN-MUSTARD VINAIGRETTE SERVES 4

1 cup shelled fresh peas

½ pound sugar snap peas, strings removed and halved lengthwise

2 watermelon radishes (see Note, page 10) or 4 regular radishes, thinly sliced on a mandoline

4 celery stalks, thinly sliced

½ cup celery leaves

½ cup fresh flat-leaf parsley leaves

½ cup Whole-Grain-Mustard Vinaigrette (recipe follows)

Flaked sea salt, such as Maldon

Freshly ground black pepper

Pea tendrils, for garnish

As so often happens in a restaurant kitchen, this salad came together unintentionally. While prepping our spring menu one evening, Scot grabbed the freshest, best-looking ingredients and tossed them in a bowl, and this salad was born. The combination is a mix of textures and flavors—sweet peas, sharp radishes, soft and tender pea tendrils, and crunchy celery. Tart mustard vinaigrette is the right finish for the sweet vegetables.

Bring a small pot of salted water to a boil over high heat. Prepare an ice bath by filling a large bowl halfway with water and adding a tray of ice cubes.

Blanch the peas in the boiling water for only about 30 seconds; they will become tender very quickly. Drain the peas and plunge into the ice bath to shock them—i.e., stop the cooking process and cool them quickly; this procedure also sets the vibrant green color.

Drain the peas again and put in a mixing bowl. Add the snap peas, radishes, celery, celery leaves, and parsley. Drizzle the salad with the vinaigrette, season with flaked sea salt and pepper, and gently toss to coat the vegetables.

Divide the salad among chilled plates and top with pea tendrils.

WHOLE-GRAIN-MUSTARD VINAIGRETTE
MAKES ABOUT ¾ CUP

1 tablespoon whole-grain mustard

1 small shallot, minced

¼ cup white wine vinegar

1½ teaspoons agave nectar

½ cup extra-virgin olive oil

Kosher salt and freshly ground black pepper

Whole-grain mustard gives this vinaigrette texture and bite. Look for coarse-ground or stone-ground mustard if you can't find whole-grain.

Combine the mustard, shallot, vinegar, agave, and oil in a small mixing bowl or a Mason jar and season with salt and pepper. Whisk or shake vigorously to blend. Leftover vinaigrette can be kept covered in the refrigerator for up to 1 week.

BABY BEET SALAD WITH APPLES, CANDIED WALNUTS, AND BALSAMIC REDUCTION SERVES 4

4 fresh thyme sprigs

2 bay leaves

2 tablespoons white balsamic
vinegar

1 tablespoon agave nectar

1 teaspoon whole black
peppercorns

1 teaspoon kosher salt, plus more
for seasoning

16 baby rainbow beets, such as
golden, red, and candy stripe
(about 3 bunches total; about
1½ inches in diameter), rinsed
and tops trimmed

1 large Granny Smith apple

¼ cup Balsamic Reduction
(page 271)

½ cup Candied Walnuts
(recipe follows)

¼ cup Kite Hill almond ricotta

¼ cup micro arugula

Freshly ground black pepper

Extra-virgin olive oil

When buying beets, choose the younger, smaller ones—large, mature beets can have a bitter, almost dirty taste, whereas baby beets have a sweet, more concentrated flavor (you can even eat them raw). For this recipe, use a mix of rainbow baby beets, not just the familiar red ones. Not only are golden and candy-stripe beets (also known as Chioggia) gorgeous, each adds its own flavor. And don't discard the beet greens; they're wonderful simply sautéed in olive oil and garlic or tossed into a soup, stew, or risotto.

To prepare the beets: Pour 8 cups of filtered water into a medium pot and add the thyme, bay leaves, vinegar, agave, peppercorns, and salt. Add the beets and bring the liquid to a boil, then reduce the heat to low and simmer until the beets are tender, 30 to 40 minutes. To check for doneness, insert a paring knife into the center of a beet; it should slide in without any resistance.

Prepare an ice bath by filling a large bowl halfway with water and adding a tray of ice cubes.

Drain the beets and transfer to the ice bath to cool.

Once the beets are completely cool, drain them and rub off the skins with paper towels. If using red beets, it's wise to wear rubber gloves and put a piece of wax paper on your cutting board so everything doesn't get stained red! Cut the beets in half or into quarters, depending on size. Put them in a bowl and refrigerate until chilled. (The beets can be prepared a day in advance, covered, and refrigerated.)

To prepare the apple: Remove the stem and halve the apple from top to bottom. Using a mandoline or a very sharp knife, slice the apple lengthwise as thin as possible; cut each slice in half so you end up with half-moons. Trim the remaining core.

To serve: Dip a pastry brush in the balsamic reduction and paint a long stripe along the base of a platter or on each of four individual plates. Arrange the beets decoratively on top and nestle the apple slices in between them. Top the salad with the candied walnuts, dollops of the cheese, and the arugula. Season with salt and pepper, drizzle with olive oil, and serve.

PHOTOGRAPH ON PAGES 34–35

CANDIED WALNUTS
MAKES ABOUT 2 CUPS

1 cup raw walnut halves and pieces
½ cup unrefined cane sugar
2 tablespoons filtered water
½ teaspoon cayenne

These candied walnuts will add a spicy-sweet crunch to your salads. Take note that cooked sugar is stubborn to remove from even nonstick pans. To clean, while the candied walnuts are drying, add water to the empty skillet and bring to a boil to dissolve the baked sugar. Remove from the heat, let cool, and wipe the pan dry.

Put a large nonstick skillet over medium heat, add the nuts, and lightly toast them, shaking the pan from time to time to prevent burning, until they smell nutty and are light golden, about 8 minutes.

Sprinkle the sugar over the nuts and cook, tossing, until the sugar melts, about 5 minutes. Add the water and the cayenne and cook, stirring constantly, until the nuts are caramelized and well coated in the sugar syrup, about 5 minutes.

Transfer the candied walnuts to a baking sheet lined with a silicone mat or parchment paper, making sure that the pieces are not touching or sticking together. Set aside to cool for at least 10 minutes before serving. Leftover walnuts can be kept in an airtight container or resealable plastic bag for up to 1 week.

SPICY MOROCCAN CARROT SALAD
WITH CHILI AND CUMIN SERVES 4

1½ pounds small rainbow carrots
(about 24), tops trimmed

MARINADE

8 dried red chilies, such as guajillo,
stems removed

½ cup red wine vinegar

3 garlic cloves, coarsely chopped

1 teaspoon ground cumin

½ teaspoon kosher salt

½ teaspoon freshly ground
black pepper

½ teaspoon red pepper flakes

½ cup extra-virgin olive oil

¼ cup micro greens, such as Hearts
on Fire (see Note)

¼ cup Rosemary-Fried Almonds
(page 9) or toasted Marcona
almonds, smashed with a mallet
or heavy pan

Flaked sea salt, such as Maldon

HEARTS ON FIRE

Hearts on Fire is a variety of micro greens with garnet-colored veins and stems. They not only give stunning color to a dish but also add a vibrant tart, citrusy flavor, reminiscent of sorrel.

This recipe has sentimental meaning for me—it is an ode to my childhood nanny, Sol. Both of my parents worked full-time, so for the first eight years of my life, my sisters and I were like Sol's adopted children. Sol came to Israel from Morocco in the mid-1950s, and years later, thankfully, she found her way to the Ronnen household. Her cooking was so different from the food we knew. Sol's was laced with chilies and spices, and her carrot salad was a mainstay on the table.

She made this dish with sliced carrots and a type of chili pepper that, sadly, isn't available outside Israel. So I restructured her killer recipe using whole rainbow carrots and guajillo chilies.

To prepare the carrots: Bring a large pot of lightly salted water to a boil over high heat. Prepare an ice bath by filling a large bowl halfway with water and adding a tray of ice cubes.

Blanch the carrots in the boiling water until tender when pierced with a knife, about 3 minutes. Drain the carrots and plunge into the ice bath to shock them—i.e., stop the cooking and cool them quickly; this procedure also locks in the carrots' bright color.

Drain the carrots again. You want them to be relatively uniform in size, so if any of them are large, cut them lengthwise in half.

To prepare the marinade: Put a small dry skillet over low heat, add the chilies, and toast for 1 or 2 minutes; shake the pan so they don't scorch. Break up the chilies and put them in a food processor. Pulse the chilies to a coarse powder; you should have about ½ cup.

Put the chili powder in a mixing bowl, add the vinegar, garlic, cumin, kosher salt, black pepper, and red pepper flakes, and whisk until blended. While whisking, slowly pour in the oil in a stream until emulsified.

Put the carrots in a mixing bowl and pour in the chili mixture, tossing to coat. Marinate for 1 to 2 hours, tossing periodically.

To serve: Crisscross the carrots on a platter. Scatter the micro greens and almonds on top and season with flaked sea salt.

WATERMELON SALAD ^{WITH} PERSIAN CUCUMBERS, CHERRY TOMATOES, ^{AND} BALSAMIC REDUCTION

SERVES 4

¼ cup Kite Hill almond ricotta

4 Persian cucumbers (4 inches long), ends trimmed and skin peeled off in strips to create a striped effect

2 tablespoons white wine vinegar

½ small seedless yellow watermelon (about 1½ pounds)

½ small seedless red watermelon (about 1½ pounds)

¼ cup Balsamic Reduction (page 271)

16 cherry tomatoes

¼ cup pistachios, toasted and smashed with a mallet or heavy pan

¼ cup micro basil

Flaked sea salt, such as Maldon

Freshly ground black pepper

Extra-virgin olive oil

Watermelon, cucumbers, and tomatoes are all at their peak at around the same time in the summer, so it only makes sense to combine them in a salad. Each fruit and vegetable is purposefully cut large here—I want each piece to be its own perfect bite of summer, followed by another, so that moving from vegetable to vegetable on the plate is like eating a four-course tasting menu. The almond ricotta and the slight sweetness of the balsamic reduction are what tie the whole dish together.

Scoop the ricotta into a fine-mesh sieve and place it over a bowl. Let it drain for 20 minutes. Discard the water.

Put the cucumbers in a bowl, add the vinegar, and cover with cold water. Set aside for 10 to 15 minutes while you prepare the watermelon.

To prepare the watermelon: Trim off the rind and discard. Cut each watermelon half horizontally into four 1-inch-thick slabs. Lay the slabs on the cutting board and slice into 1-inch-wide strips. Square off the ends and lay the melon pieces horizontally on the board. Holding the knife blade at a 45-degree angle, cut a 1-inch-long piece from one end of the strip. Move the knife about 1 inch and make a cut straight down, so you have another piece with a flat end and an angled end. Repeat the process with all of the watermelon strips; you should have 16. Set aside.

Drain the cucumbers and cut them in the same way you did the watermelon, so you have 16 pieces.

To serve: Dip a pastry brush in the balsamic reduction and paint a long stripe along the base of a platter or on each of four individual plates. Arrange the red and yellow watermelon and cucumbers decoratively on top, standing the pieces upright on their flat ends. Nestle the tomatoes in between. Top the salad with the pistachios, ricotta, and basil. Season with flaked sea salt and pepper, drizzle with oil, and serve immediately.

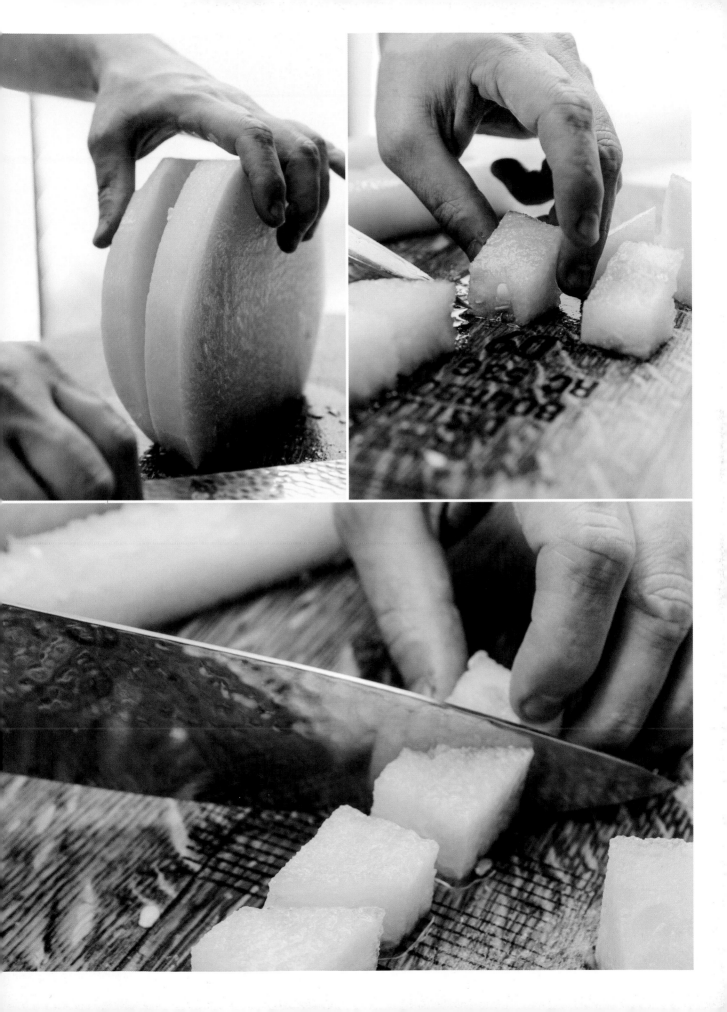

PEACH SALAD ^{WITH} BALSAMIC-GLAZED CIPOLLINI ONIONS, TOASTED HAZELNUTS, ^{AND} MINT VINAIGRETTE ^{SERVES 4}

½ pound cipollini onions (see Note, page 44) or 8 shallots

2 tablespoons extra-virgin olive oil

1 cup balsamic vinegar

Kosher salt and freshly ground black pepper

2 bunches watercress, stems trimmed (about 8 cups lightly packed)

4 ripe yellow peaches, halved, pitted, and cut into 8 slices each

About ¼ cup Mint Vinaigrette (recipe follows)

¼ cup hazelnuts, toasted and crushed (see Note, page 44)

Flaked sea salt, such as Maldon

Stone fruit, especially peaches, are one of my favorite gifts of summer. Here, the sweetness of juicy peaches plays off the savory roasted onions and the sharp watercress. Toasted hazelnuts add a necessary crunch and a bit of fat to round out this light salad.

To prepare the onions: Bring a large pot of lightly salted water to a boil over high heat. Prepare an ice bath by filling a large bowl halfway with water and adding a tray of ice cubes.

Blanch the onions in the boiling water for about 1 minute. Drain the onions and plunge into the ice bath to shock them—i.e., stop the cooking process and cool them quickly. Drain the cooled onions in a colander and peel them.

Put the onions in a mixing bowl and drizzle with the oil. Pour in the vinegar, season with kosher salt and pepper, and turn the onions over so they are well coated. Set the onions aside for 10 minutes to soak up the vinegar.

Preheat the oven to 400°F.

Transfer the onions, along with the vinegar, to a small baking pan. Roast for 45 minutes, or until the onions are tender and deep purple. Set aside to cool. Cut the cooled onions into quarters.

To serve: Put the watercress in a large salad bowl. Add the peach segments and roasted onions and spoon on enough vinaigrette to coat lightly. Divide among four chilled small salad bowls, distributing the peaches and onions evenly. Top with hazelnuts and sprinkle with flaked sea salt.

MINT VINAIGRETTE

MAKES ABOUT 1 CUP

1½ cups fresh mint leaves,
   coarsely chopped
1 tablespoon fresh flat-leaf
   parsley leaves
¼ cup white balsamic vinegar
2 garlic cloves, coarsely chopped
1 small shallot, coarsely chopped
1 teaspoon light brown sugar
½ teaspoon kosher salt
½ teaspoon freshly ground
   black pepper
¾ cup grapeseed oil

For this light summer vinaigrette, I prefer white balsamic vinegar for its golden color and clean aftertaste. It complements summer fruits and delicate greens, such as butter lettuce.

Combine the mint, parsley, vinegar, garlic, shallot, sugar, salt, and pepper in the bowl of a food processor and process for about 1 minute, until smooth and green. With the motor running, pour in the oil in a steady stream, making sure it directly hits the blade (this is the best way to distribute the oil and emulsify it evenly and quickly). Pour the vinaigrette into a container or jar, cover, and shake it well just before using. Leftover vinaigrette can be kept covered in the refrigerator for up to 5 days.

CIPOLLINI ONIONS

Pronounced "chip-oh-LEE-nee," cipollini are sweet flattened flying saucer–shaped onions originally from Italy. Blanching the onions makes it much easier to peel these little guys. Cipollini are becoming much more widely available; Melissa's is one of my favorite brands. If they are not available, you can substitute shallots.

TOASTING HAZELNUTS

Spread the hazelnuts on a baking sheet and roast in a 350°F oven for 10 to 12 minutes, until fragrant and golden brown. If there are skins on the hazelnuts, wrap the warm nuts snugly in a kitchen towel and rub them together to loosen the skins. Then put in a colander and shake to sift off the skins.

To crush the nuts, when they have cooled, put them in a resealable plastic bag and smash them with a mallet or heavy pan.

MELON SALAD
<small>WITH</small> WATERCRESS <small>AND</small> OROBLANCO VINAIGRETTE <small>SERVES 4</small>

1 ripe canary or honeydew melon
(about 2 pounds; see Note)

2 Oroblanco or other seedless
white grapefruits

½ cup fresh mint leaves, cut into
chiffonade

½ cup finely diced Kite Hill truffle,
dill, and chive soft fresh almond
milk cheese (optional)

½ cup watercress, stems trimmed

¼ cup Oroblanco Vinaigrette
(recipe follows)

Flaked sea salt, such as Maldon

Freshly ground black pepper

CANARY MELON

The bright-yellow canary melon gets its name from the color of the tiny bird. The flesh is actually light green, with a sweet flavor that is slightly tangier than that of honeydew. If canary melon is not available, substitute honeydew.

When it comes to grapefruit, the Oroblanco is the best. Developed by scientists at the University of California, this hybrid is a cross between a white grapefruit and an acidless pomelo. It has a distinctively citrusy, floral aroma and is less abrasive on the palate than regular grapefruit. Ripe summer melon adds subtle sweetness to the salad, while peppery watercress and fresh mint are the perfect partners for the mild tartness of the Oroblanco. This salad is a lovely start to any summer meal.

To prepare the melon: Slice a small disk off the bottom of the melon so it can stand upright on a cutting board. Cut the melon down the middle to halve it and scoop out the seeds and membranes with a tablespoon. Halve the melon pieces again, so you have four ½-inch-thick slabs. Lay the slabs on the cutting board and, using a 1-inch round cutter, punch out 5 circles from each slab. Set aside. Discard the rind.

To suprême (segment) the grapefruits: First slice off the top and bottom of each one and stand upright on a cutting board. Use a paring knife to cut off the skin and bitter white pith of the fruit in strips from top to bottom, following the natural round shape and turning the grapefruit as you go. Trim off any white pith that remains. Hold each grapefruit over a bowl to catch the juices and carefully cut along the membranes on both sides of each segment to free it, letting the pieces drop into the bowl. Squeeze the juice from the grapefruit membranes into the bowl; you'll need the juice for the vinaigrette.

To serve: Arrange 5 melon rounds on each plate. Strew the mint ribbons over them. Scatter the grapefruit segments, cheese, if using, and watercress on top. Drizzle with the vinaigrette and season with flaked sea salt and pepper.

OROBLANCO VINAIGRETTE

MAKES ABOUT 1 CUP

½ shallot, minced

2 garlic cloves, minced

4 fresh basil leaves, finely chopped

Pinch of red pepper flakes

¼ cup fresh Oroblanco grapefruit
    juice (reserved from salad)

¼ cup white balsamic vinegar

¼ cup extra-virgin olive oil

¼ cup grapeseed oil

Kosher salt and freshly ground
    black pepper

To keep the vinaigrette light, I use a combination of olive oil and neutral-flavored grapeseed oil. Olive oil alone would overwhelm the delicate flavor of the grapefruit juice.

Combine the shallot, garlic, basil, and red pepper flakes in a small mixing bowl or a Mason jar. Add the juice, vinegar, and oils, season with salt and black pepper, and whisk or shake vigorously to blend. Leftover vinaigrette can be kept covered in the refrigerator for up to 1 week.

SHAVED BRUSSELS SPROUTS WITH ZA'ATAR, LEMON, AND PINE NUTS SERVES 4

1 pound Brussels sprouts
    (about 30), tough outer
    leaves discarded and stem
    ends trimmed
4 baby rainbow carrots
Finely grated zest and juice of
    2 lemons
1 tablespoon za'atar (see Note,
    page 23)
3 tablespoons extra-virgin olive oil
Kosher salt and freshly ground
    black pepper
¼ cup pine nuts, toasted

With only a handful of ingredients, this unusual salad couldn't be easier. People often cook Brussels sprouts until they are a mushy, bitter mess. When shaved raw, these badass cabbage buds are an entirely different beast. Delicate and hearty at the same time, this is one of those make-ahead salads where the flavors get even better if it is allowed to stand.

Prepare an ice bath by filling a large bowl halfway with water and adding a tray of ice cubes.

Using a mandoline or a very sharp knife, slice the Brussels sprouts and carrots as thin as possible. Put them in the ice bath for 5 minutes to crisp them up.

Drain the sprouts and carrots and dry well in a salad spinner, or drain in a colander and pat dry. Transfer to a mixing bowl. Add the lemon zest and juice, za'atar, and oil; season with salt and pepper, and toss with your hands to coat. Sprinkle in the pine nuts and toss again to combine.

If you have time, allow the salad to stand for 15 minutes. Serve the salad on a platter or divide among four individual plates.

BLACK KALE

Once you've tried black kale, you might not ever go back to the more conventional curly variety. Also known as Tuscan or lacinato kale, or cavolo nero, this Italian specialty has long, spiky, ruffled deep green leaves. It's less bitter than curly kale and has an earthier taste. And kale is one of the most nutritious vegetables on the planet to boot.

KALE SALAD WITH CURRANTS, PINE NUTS, AND LEMON-THYME VINAIGRETTE SERVES 4

2 bunches (about 1½ pounds) black
    kale (aka Tuscan or lacinato kale
    or cavolo nero; see Note)
½ cup dried currants
½ cup pine nuts, toasted
¼ cup Lemon-Thyme Vinaigrette
    (recipe follows)
Kosher salt and freshly ground
    black pepper

Raw kale can be tough, so it has to be treated right. Yet all of the talk about "massaging" kale to make the leaves tender and palatable is nonsense. The key to achieving a melt-in-your-mouth texture is to cut the robust green leaves into a fine chiffonade, resembling strands of confetti. Once the kale is shredded, you don't have to chew it endlessly to break down the tough leaves. But be sure to dress the salad with the vinaigrette about 10 minutes before serving, so it has a chance to soak into the kale and soften it a bit.

One at a time, lay each kale leaf upside down on a cutting board and use a paring knife to cut down both sides of the center rib to remove it. Stack a few leaves at a time, roll them into a tight cigar shape, and cut crosswise into thin ribbons (no more than ⅛ inch). You should have about 6 cups shredded kale.

Put the shredded kale in a colander or salad spinner and rinse well with cold water. Drain and dry well.

Combine the kale, currants, and pine nuts in a salad or mixing bowl. Drizzle the salad with the vinaigrette and season with salt and pepper. Gently toss with your hands to dress the salad evenly, and let stand for about 10 minutes.

Serve the salad in the salad bowl or divide among four individual plates.

LEMON-THYME VINAIGRETTE
MAKES 1 CUP

½ small shallot, minced
1 garlic clove, minced
2 fresh thyme sprigs, leaves
    stripped from the stems
¼ cup white balsamic vinegar
Finely grated zest and juice of
    1 lemon
1 tablespoon agave nectar
½ cup extra-virgin olive oil
Kosher salt and freshly ground
    black pepper

You will want to keep this light, tangy, and faintly sweet vinaigrette in the refrigerator as your go-to salad dressing.

Combine the shallot, garlic, thyme, balsamic, lemon zest and juice, agave, and oil in a small mixing bowl or a Mason jar and season with salt and pepper. Whisk or shake vigorously to blend. Leftover vinaigrette can be kept covered in the refrigerator for up to 1 week.

BLOOMSDALE SPINACH SALAD
WITH BLACK GARLIC VINAIGRETTE SERVES 4

SMOKED MUSHROOMS

1 pound mixed cremini and shiitake
   mushrooms, stemmed, wiped of
   grit, and thinly sliced

2 tablespoons extra-virgin olive oil

3 tablespoons sherry vinegar

Kosher salt and freshly ground
   black pepper

1 teaspoon smoked sea salt
   (optional; see headnote)

2 tablespoons maple syrup

2 cups hickory or apple wood chips,
   soaked in water for 20 minutes
   and drained (optional;
   see headnote)

SALAD

1 pound Bloomsdale spinach,
   stems trimmed (about 6 cups)

¼ cup Black Garlic Vinaigrette
   (recipe follows), warmed

Flaked sea salt, such as Maldon

Freshly ground black pepper

½ cup Kite Hill almond ricotta

½ cup Crispy Shallots (page 71)

I'm not a huge fan of regular spinach—I find the leaves to be a little flat, and they give my tongue a weird, fuzzy finish. Bloomsdale spinach has a much heartier texture and a cleaner flavor. And because it doesn't wilt as easily as some greens, it can stand up to a warm vinaigrette.

This twist on the classic spinach salad with bacon comes from our sous-chef Duane Taguchi, who turned it into a savory vegan version that's rich in umami. The fried shallots contribute a crispy bite, and the smoked mushrooms impart a flavor redolent of bacon. To smoke the mushrooms, you will need a large pot with a steamer insert. Or you can simply skip that step and add smoked sea salt to the mushrooms instead.

To roast the mushrooms: Preheat the oven to 450°F.

Put the mushrooms in a mixing bowl, drizzle with the oil, and toss to coat. Add the vinegar, season the mushrooms with kosher salt and pepper, and toss to coat evenly.

Spread the mushrooms out in a single layer on a baking sheet and roast for 25 to 30 minutes, turning them over with a spatula from time to time to prevent them from burning, until they lose their moisture and shrink. The mushrooms should be dark brown; feel dry to the touch, almost dehydrated; and be crispy. You should have about 1 cup. Set aside to cool (be sure the mushrooms are still in a single layer), air-dry, and firm up.

If you are not smoking the mushrooms, sprinkle them with the smoked sea salt. Set aside.

To smoke the mushrooms: Open the windows and remove the battery from your smoke detector. Line a large pot that has a steamer insert with aluminum foil (this will keep the wood chips from scorching the bottom). Spread the wet wood chips out on the foil. Cover the pot tightly with the lid and heat over high heat.

CONTINUED

BLACK GARLIC

Black garlic is one of those mysterious ingredients that can take a dish from good to great. It's a staple in Asian cuisine that originated in Korea. Because of black garlic's molasses-like richness, this unique ingredient translates beautifully to Mediterranean cuisine. Basically candied garlic, black garlic is aged in a special fermentation process during which it develops its rich ebony color, flavor, and jelly-like consistency; the taste is sweet and syrupy, with hints of balsamic vinegar. Thankfully, black garlic is becoming more widely available at supermarkets, either as whole bulbs or peeled cloves, and it keeps for at least 6 months in the fridge. A little tip: slicing black garlic can be sticky business, so take care to dip your fingers in warm water as you cut to wash away any residue.

Meanwhile, put the mushrooms in the steamer basket. Once the chips begin to smoke, drop the steamer basket insert into the pot and cover tightly with the lid. Turn off the heat and allow the mushrooms to soak up the smoke for 5 to 6 minutes—no peeking. Set the mushrooms aside to cool.

Toss the cooled mushrooms with the maple syrup. (The mushrooms can be prepared a couple of hours in advance, covered, and held at room temperature.)

To prepare the salad: Combine the spinach, mushrooms, and warm vinaigrette in a mixing bowl, season with flaked sea salt and pepper, and toss to coat the spinach evenly. Arrange the salad on a platter or divide among four individual plates. Top with the almond ricotta and crispy shallots and serve immediately.

BLACK GARLIC VINAIGRETTE
MAKES 1 CUP

½ cup white balsamic vinegar

¼ cup fresh flat-leaf parsley leaves, coarsely chopped

6 black garlic cloves (see Note)

2 fresh thyme sprigs, leaves stripped from the stems

1 shallot, coarsely chopped

1 teaspoon agave nectar

½ teaspoon kosher salt

⅛ teaspoon freshly ground black pepper

Pinch of red pepper flakes

¾ cup extra-virgin olive oil

This is my favorite vinaigrette; you can taste all of the ingredients working together to hit the right notes of tart, smoky, and sweet. The real highlight comes from the black garlic, which has a complex umami flavor. Serve warm.

Combine the vinegar, parsley, black garlic, thyme, shallot, agave, salt, black pepper, and red pepper flakes in the bowl of a food processor and process for a few seconds, until the garlic is completely incorporated with the rest of the ingredients. With the motor running, pour in the oil in a steady stream, making sure it directly hits the blade. (This is the best way to distribute the oil and emulsify it evenly and quickly.) The vinaigrette will be smoky brown in color and somewhat thick.

When ready to serve, warm the vinaigrette over low heat. Leftover vinaigrette can be kept covered in the refrigerator for up to 5 days.

ISRAELI COUSCOUS WITH CHAMPAGNE GRAPES, HARICOTS VERTS, AND MARCONA ALMONDS SERVES 4

1 cup Israeli couscous

1 cup filtered water

3 tablespoons extra-virgin olive oil

½ pound haricots verts (thin French green beans), cut into ⅛-inch pieces

½ cup champagne grapes or quartered red seedless grapes

4 fresh flat-leaf parsley sprigs, leaves stripped from the stems and minced (about 2 tablespoons)

4 fresh mint springs, leaves stripped from the stems and minced (about 2 tablespoons)

Juice of 1 lemon

Kosher salt and freshly ground black pepper

Pinch of red pepper flakes

¼ cup Rosemary-Fried Almonds (page 9) or toasted Marcona almonds, smashed with a mallet or heavy pan

¼ cup micro basil, or regular basil leaves, minced

Israeli couscous, a pearl-like pasta, is a versatile foundation for many combinations of flavors. Traditional couscous salads often include raisins, but here I use champagne grapes for their sweetness and mere hint of tartness. This summer salad is finished with crisp green beans, minced fresh herbs, and crunchy Marcona almonds. While any green beans will do, I'm a fan of French haricots verts. Serve with a chilled rosé.

Put a small saucepan over medium-low heat, add the couscous, and toast, stirring frequently, until it smells nutty and is golden brown, about 5 minutes. Pour in the water, cover, and simmer until the couscous is just tender, 10 to 12 minutes; drain if necessary. Set the couscous aside to cool.

Toss the couscous with 1 tablespoon of the oil to prevent the grains from sticking together. (The couscous can be prepared up to a day in advance, covered, and refrigerated.)

When ready to serve, combine the cooled couscous, green beans, grapes, parsley, and mint in a large mixing bowl. Drizzle the lemon juice and then the remaining 2 tablespoons oil over the couscous and season with salt, black pepper, and the red pepper flakes. Toss gently with your hands to coat and distribute the ingredients evenly.

Mound the couscous salad on a platter or individual plates. Sprinkle the almonds over the top and garnish with the basil.

FARRO

Farro is similar to wheat berries but better all around, as far as I'm concerned. I'm crazy about its hearty nuttiness and firm but chewy texture. Popular since the golden days of ancient Rome, this healthful whole grain stands up to everything from salads to soups. It is a rich source of vitamins and nutrients, as well as protein and fiber. Farro is available in most grocery stores and health food stores. Look for the semi-pearled variety, which allows for speedier cooking. Toasting farro in a dry pan before cooking makes the flavor extra nutty. I cook farro just like pasta, uncovered, in plenty of boiling salted water, and then drain. Some packages call for cooking farro like rice, tightly covered in a measured amount of water until the water is absorbed, but I find this method makes it a bit mushy.

BUTTERNUT SQUASH FARINATA ^{WITH} ARUGULA SALAD ^{AND} POMEGRANATE VINAIGRETTE^{SERVES 8}

FARINATA

1½ cups chickpea (or garbanzo bean) flour, such as Lucini or Bob's Red Mill

2 cups filtered water, at room temperature

5 tablespoons extra-virgin olive oil

4 fresh thyme sprigs, leaves stripped from the stems and chopped (about 1 teaspoon)

2 fresh flat-leaf parsley sprigs, leaves stripped from the stems and chopped (about 2 tablespoons)

¾ teaspoon kosher salt, plus more to taste

¼ teaspoon freshly ground black pepper, plus more to taste

1 tablespoon Earth Balance butter stick

2 cups finely diced butternut squash

1 shallot, minced

SALAD

8 lightly packed cups baby arugula

2 cups cooked farro (see Note)

½ cup Pomegranate Vinaigrette (recipe follows)

Kosher salt and freshly ground black pepper

Farinata is a rustic Italian bread made from chickpea flour that is often enjoyed as street food in Tuscany and Liguria. Typically baked in a hot cast-iron skillet, farinata has a golden, crisp outside and a soft, cakey center.

My friend Renee Frigo, who makes the award-winning Lucini olive oil, introduced me to farinata when she launched her Cinque e' Cinque brand of chickpea flour. When I tasted it, I realized that farinata is much more than a simple bread—it can be a nutty-tasting canvas for endless toppings: here a hearty winter salad of farro and arugula, dressed with a tart pomegranate vinaigrette.

When you make the farinata, letting the batter rest results in a more complex flavor and less gritty texture. But if you're in a hurry, just let it sit while you preheat the oven and prepare the rest of the ingredients. Chickpea (or garbanzo bean) flour can be found in Italian markets and some grocery stores (Lucini's Cinque e' Cinque is available at Whole Foods). If you will be storing the flour for more than a month, keep it in the freezer to prevent it from turning rancid.

To prepare the farinata: Whisk together the flour and water in a mixing bowl until smooth and free of lumps. Add 3 tablespoons of the oil, the thyme, parsley, salt, and pepper and whisk until the mixture is the consistency of pancake batter. Cover and let the batter stand for at least 1 hour at room temperature, or up to 2 hours if you have the time.

When ready to bake the farinata, preheat the oven to 425°F.

Whisk the batter again to bring it back together. Put a 10-inch cast-iron or other heavy ovenproof skillet over medium heat and add the butter substitute and the remaining 2 tablespoons oil, swirling the pan to coat. When all the butter substitute has melted, add the squash and shallot and cook, stirring, until soft, about 4 minutes. Season with salt and pepper.

CONTINUED

Spread the squash and shallot evenly in the skillet and pour the batter over it. Carefully transfer to the hot oven and bake for 30 minutes, or until the farinata is no longer wet in the center and the edges are browned and pulling away from the sides of the pan. Remove the farinata from the oven and cool in the pan for 10 minutes.

To serve: Flip the farinata onto a cutting board and cut into 8 wedges.

Combine the arugula and farro in a mixing bowl. Drizzle with the vinaigrette, season with salt and pepper, and toss gently with your hands.

Place a wedge of farinata in the center of each salad plate. Top with the salad, making sure to distribute the pomegranate seeds evenly. Spoon any extra vinaigrette on top so it soaks into the farinata.

POMEGRANATE VINAIGRETTE
MAKES 1 CUP

¼ cup pomegranate molasses
(see Note)
½ shallot, minced
Finely grated zest and juice of
1 lemon
Kosher salt and freshly ground
black pepper
½ cup extra-virgin olive oil
1 tablespoon finely chopped
fresh mint
1 tablespoon finely chopped fresh
flat-leaf parsley
2 tablespoons pomegranate seeds

This sweet-tangy vinaigrette marries well with peppery greens like dandelion. Leftovers will keep for 4 days covered in the refrigerator.

Whisk together the pomegranate molasses, shallot, and lemon zest and juice in a small bowl. Season with salt and pepper. Slowly whisk in the oil until emulsified. Stir in the mint, parsley, and pomegranate seeds.

POMEGRANATE MOLASSES

Pomegranate molasses is a thick reduced syrup of pomegranate juice that has a tart and fruity flavor. A gorgeous deep reddish purple, the molasses is found in Mediterranean and Middle Eastern markets, and it keeps almost indefinitely in the refrigerator. If pomegranate molasses is not available, pour 2 cups pure pomegranate juice into a small pot, put over medium-low heat, and boil until the juice has reduced to ¼ cup and is thick and syrupy, about 20 minutes. Let cool.

FLATBREADS

FLATBREAD DOUGH 66

ROASTED SPRING ROOT VEGETABLE
FLATBREAD WITH LEEK PÂTÉ AND
CRISPY SHALLOTS 69

ROASTED MUSHROOM FLATBREAD
WITH SPICY TOMATO-PEPPER JAM
AND CARAMELIZED ONIONS 72

ROASTED CAULIFLOWER FLATBREAD
WITH PISTACHIO-KALAMATA
TAPENADE AND FRISÉE 75

CHARRED OKRA FLATBREAD WITH
SWEET CORN PUREE AND
CHERRY TOMATOES 78

BUTTERNUT SQUASH–PUREE
FLATBREAD WITH MUSTARD GREENS
AND FRIED BRUSSELS SPROUT LEAVES 82

TAGINE FLATBREAD WITH
EGGPLANT AND MINTED SPINACH 86

Flatbreads have always been a staple on the Mediterranean and Middle Eastern table, but in recent years, they have become a great canvas for creativity. Flatbread dough is thinner, lighter, and not as filling as pizza dough, leaving you more room to play with interesting toppings. Varying the choice of vegetables, as well as their texture and temperature, adds loads of dimension to the crust. Do so, or (pardon the pun) your flatbreads will taste flat.

When building flatbreads, I like to start with a thin layer of a vegetable puree or a flavorful spread, like tapenade (see page 21), leek pâté (see page 19), or tomato jam (see page 18) to add the creaminess that traditionally comes from cheese. And I like to change the toppings with the seasons—charred okra in the summer (see page 78), sweet butternut squash in the fall (see page 82), roasted cauliflower in the winter (see page 75), and vibrant root vegetables in the spring (see page 69).

You don't need a special oven to make great flatbread, although I recommend purchasing a pizza stone from your local kitchen store to ensure a crispy, crunchy crust. You can buy a stone for around $25, and it will more than pay off as you use it over and over again. A pizza paddle is also handy for transferring flatbreads into and out of the oven. If you don't have a stone, though, just flip over a baking sheet or use a rimless cookie sheet and dust it heavily with cornmeal to ensure that the flatbreads slide off easily. If you're using a baking sheet, you won't need a paddle, either, because you can just slide the sheet right out of the oven.

Flatbreads are meant for sharing and make great starters. Or serve a flatbread or two with a big salad for a satisfying light meal.

FLATBREAD
DOUGH MAKES 1½ POUNDS

½ teaspoon active dry yeast

1 cup plus 2 tablespoons warm
   filtered water

1 teaspoon unrefined cane sugar

2¾ cups bread flour, plus more
   for dusting

2 teaspoons extra-virgin olive oil,
   plus more for the bowl

1 teaspoon kosher salt

1 teaspoon freshly ground
   black pepper

Nonstick cooking spray if storing
   the dough

This leavened dough, which is similar to pizza dough, can be made in less than an hour with basic pantry ingredients.

While you don't *need* a stand mixer with a dough hook to prepare this dough, it certainly speeds things up. If you choose to go the route of making the dough entirely by hand, the kneading process will take twice as long—but you'll also get a good workout. Use flour judiciously to keep the dough from sticking to your hands and the work surface as you knead.

In the bowl of a stand mixer fitted with the dough hook, combine the yeast, water, and sugar, stirring gently to dissolve the yeast and sugar. Let the mixture stand until the yeast comes alive and starts to foam, 5 to 10 minutes.

Turn the mixer to low speed and slowly add the flour in 3 batches. When the dough starts to come together, increase the speed to medium and add the oil, salt, and pepper. Knead the dough in the mixer, stopping the machine periodically to scrape the dough off the hook, until the dough has come together and is no longer sticky, about 10 minutes.

Turn the dough out onto a lightly floured work surface and knead for a few minutes with floured hands: To knead, fold the dough over itself and push it out, not down, with the heel of your hand. Then rotate it a quarter turn and repeat. Continue until you can stretch the dough without it tearing; when you press on the dough with your fingertips, it should spring back quickly.

Form the dough into a round and place in a large oiled bowl. Cover the bowl with plastic wrap or a damp towel and let rise in a warm place until doubled in size, about 30 minutes. Test the dough by pressing two fingers into it: if the indents remain, the dough is ready.

Divide the dough into four 6-ounce portions and shape into balls. If you are not going to bake all 4 balls, tightly wrap each ball of dough in a few layers of plastic wrap (lightly coat the first layer with non-stick cooking spray). The dough will keep in the refrigerator for up to 5 days or can be frozen for up to 1 month. Defrost the dough overnight in the refrigerator before rolling out and baking.

ROASTED SPRING ROOT VEGETABLE FLATBREAD
WITH LEEK PÂTÉ AND CRISPY SHALLOTS SERVES 8; MAKES 4 FLATBREADS

1 celery root (celeriac; about
  1 pound)

Extra-virgin olive oil

Kosher salt and freshly ground
  black pepper

½ pound fingerling potatoes (about
  6), scrubbed and finely diced

2 large carrots, finely diced

1 fennel bulb, trimmed, halved,
  cored, and finely diced

Four 6-ounce balls Flatbread Dough
  (page 66)

Unbleached all-purpose flour,
  for dusting

Cornmeal, for dusting

2 cups Leek Pâté (page 19)

Crispy Shallots (recipe follows)

Leek pâté is used as the creamy base of this flatbread, which I use in place of the traditional layer of cheese. Celery root is added to increase the depth of flavor. It's sharp and clean, like celery, but has the texture of a root vegetable.

Preheat the oven to 450°F.

To prepare the root vegetables: Celery root needs to be peeled, and you need to be aggressive when you do it. Don't try to use a vegetable peeler, which will probably just break. Instead, lay the celery root on its side and use a sharp chef's knife to lop off the knobby roots at the bottom. Cut off the top. Stand the celery root upright so it is stable and cut the remaining skin off in vertical strips, from top to bottom, following the shape of the root and turning as you go. Cut the celery root into ½-inch-thick slabs, cut into strips, and then cut crosswise into medium dice.

Put the celery root on a large rimmed baking sheet. Drizzle with oil, toss to coat, and spread out in a single layer. Season generously with salt and pepper. Roast, shaking the pan from time to time, for about 20 minutes, until the celery root has begun to shrink and is lightly browned.

Add the potatoes, carrots, and fennel to the pan, tossing to combine with the celery root. Return the pan to the oven and roast for about 20 minutes longer, until all of the vegetables are tender when pierced with a knife and charred on the edges. Set the vegetables aside to cool. (The roasted vegetables can be prepared a couple of hours in advance, covered, and held at room temperature.)

To prepare the flatbread: At least 20 minutes before baking, put a pizza stone or a baking sheet on the middle oven rack and preheat the oven to 450°F.

On a lightly floured surface, with a floured rolling pin, roll one ball of dough into an oval about 8 inches long, 6 inches wide, and ¼ inch thick. With a docker or a fork, prick the surface of the flatbread to

prevent air bubbles from forming during baking. Dust a pizza paddle with cornmeal and slide it under the dough. (If you don't have a paddle, flip over a baking sheet and use it.) Lightly brush the dough with oil to give a sheen to the crust.

Smear ½ cup of the leek pâté over the dough, leaving a ½-inch border all around. Distribute one-quarter of the roasted vegetables evenly over the pâté. Repeat with the remaining dough, pâté, and vegetables.

Working in batches, slide the prepared flatbreads onto the hot pizza stone or pan and bake for 10 to 15 minutes, until the crust is nicely browned. Using tongs, pull the flatbreads onto a cutting board. Scatter the crispy shallots on top and cut the flatbreads into wedges with a sharp knife or pizza cutter. Serve warm.

PHOTOGRAPH OPPOSITE (TOP RIGHT)

CRISPY SHALLOTS
MAKES ABOUT 2 CUPS LOOSELY PACKED

4 large shallots
1 tablespoon hot sauce, such
   as Tabasco
Kosher salt and freshly ground
   black pepper
¼ cup cornstarch
Expeller-pressed canola oil, for
   shallow-frying (about 2 cups)

Fried shallots add a crunch to this flatbread and to Bloomsdale Spinach Salad (page 52). This recipe makes plenty for snacking too—you'll thank me later.

Slice the shallots as thin as possible, using a mandoline or a very sharp knife. Put the sliced shallots in a colander and separate into rings. Set the colander over a bowl or in the sink and season the shallots with the hot sauce, salt, and pepper, tossing to coat. Sprinkle on the cornstarch and toss the shallot rings, shaking the colander, to coat them evenly.

Pour ½ inch of oil into a large sauté pan or cast-iron skillet set over medium-high heat. When the oil is hot, add the shallots in batches and fry, stirring constantly to keep them from clumping together, until crisp and light golden brown, about 30 seconds. Using a slotted spoon, transfer the fried shallots to a paper towel–lined plate to drain. Season with salt and pepper. Serve warm or at room temperature.

ROASTED MUSHROOM FLATBREAD WITH SPICY TOMATO-PEPPER JAM AND CARAMELIZED ONIONS SERVES 8; MAKES 4 FLATBREADS

1 pound mixed cremini and shiitake
   mushrooms, stemmed, wiped of
   grit, and thinly sliced

Extra-virgin olive oil

3 tablespoons sherry vinegar

Kosher salt and freshly ground
   black pepper

1 sweet onion, such as Vidalia,
   halved lengthwise and
   thinly sliced

1 teaspoon unrefined cane sugar

Unbleached all-purpose flour,
   for dusting

Four 6-ounce balls Flatbread Dough
   (page 66)

Cornmeal, for dusting

2 cups Spicy Tomato-Pepper Jam
   (page 18)

½ cup Kite Hill almond ricotta

1 head of frisée, torn into
   small pieces (about 2 cups
   lightly packed)

The base of many flatbreads is tomato sauce; here, the Spicy Tomato-Pepper Jam is used for a more rustic flavor. Seasoning the mushrooms in sherry vinegar—a Spanish vinegar with a strong umami component—before roasting helps to develop a deeper flavor before they get added to the flatbread.

Preheat the oven to 450°F.

To prepare the mushrooms: Put the mushrooms in a mixing bowl and drizzle with a couple of tablespoons of oil, tossing to coat. Add the vinegar, season with salt and pepper, and toss the mushrooms to coat evenly.

Spread the mushrooms out in a single layer on a baking sheet. Roast for 15 to 20 minutes, until the mushrooms have released their moisture and shrunk; turn them over with a spatula from time to time. Make sure the mushrooms don't burn. Set aside. (The roasted mushrooms can be prepared a couple of hours in advance, covered, and held at room temperature.)

To prepare the caramelized onions: Put the onions in a bowl and toss with a couple of tablespoons of oil, the sugar, and salt and pepper to taste. Put a sauté pan over medium-high heat. Add the onions and cook, stirring, until soft and lightly browned, about 10 minutes. Remove from the heat.

To prepare the flatbread: At least 20 minutes before baking, put a pizza stone or a baking sheet on the middle oven rack and preheat the oven to 450°F.

On a lightly floured surface, with a floured rolling pin, roll one ball of dough into an oval about 8 inches long, 6 inches wide, and ¼ inch thick. With a docker or a fork, prick the surface of the flatbread to prevent air bubbles from forming during baking. Dust a pizza paddle with cornmeal and slide it under the dough. (If you don't have a paddle, flip over a baking sheet and use it.) Lightly brush the dough with oil to give a sheen to the crust.

Smear ½ cup of the tomato-pepper jam over the dough, leaving a ½-inch border all around. Distribute one-quarter of the caramelized onions and roasted mushrooms evenly over the jam. Repeat with the remaining dough, jam, and vegetables. Dollop the almond ricotta over the top.

Working in batches, slide the prepared flatbreads onto the hot pizza stone or pan and bake for 10 to 15 minutes, until the crust is nicely browned. Using tongs, pull the flatbreads onto a cutting board. Scatter the frisée on top. Cut the flatbreads into wedges with a sharp knife or pizza cutter. Serve warm.

PHOTOGRAPH ON PAGE 70 (CENTER LEFT)

ROASTED CAULIFLOWER FLATBREAD WITH PISTACHIO-KALAMATA TAPENADE AND FRISÉE

SERVES 8; MAKES 4 FLATBREADS

1 head of cauliflower (1½ pounds), stem and core removed, florets chopped into pea-size pieces

Extra-virgin olive oil

2 garlic cloves, minced

1 shallot, minced

1 teaspoon smoked paprika

⅛ teaspoon red pepper flakes

Kosher salt and freshly ground black pepper

Unbleached all-purpose flour, for dusting

Four 6-ounce balls Flatbread Dough (page 66)

Cornmeal, for dusting

1 cup Pistachio-Kalamata Tapenade (page 21)

1 head of frisée, torn into small pieces (about 2 cups lightly packed)

¼ cup fresh flat-leaf parsley leaves

¼ teaspoon flaked sea salt, such as Maldon

2 tablespoons Balsamic Reduction (page 271)

Cauliflower is an excellent candidate for roasting because its mellow flavor deepens with a bit of time in a hot oven. Here the sharp edge of the Pistachio-Kalamata Tapenade adds a subtle saltiness, and the smoked paprika and balsamic reduction are used for the kind of deep flavor you might traditionally get from pancetta.

Preheat the oven to 450°F.

To prepare the cauliflower: Put the cauliflower in a large mixing bowl and drizzle with a couple of tablespoons of oil, tossing to coat. Add the garlic, shallot, paprika, and red pepper flakes, season with kosher salt and black pepper, and toss the cauliflower to coat evenly.

Spread out the cauliflower in a single layer on a large baking sheet. Roast the cauliflower for 30 to 35 minutes, shaking the pan from time to time, until tender and slightly charred. Set aside. (The roasted cauliflower can be prepared a couple of hours in advance, covered, and held at room temperature.)

To prepare the flatbread: At least 20 minutes before baking, put a pizza stone or a baking sheet on the middle oven rack and preheat the oven to 450°F.

On a lightly floured surface, with a floured rolling pin, roll one ball of dough into an oval about 8 inches long, 6 inches wide, and ¼ inch thick. With a docker or a fork, prick the surface of the flatbread to prevent air bubbles from forming during baking. Dust a pizza paddle with cornmeal and slide it under the dough. (If you don't have a paddle, flip over a baking sheet and use it.) Lightly brush the dough with oil to give a sheen to the crust.

Smear ¼ cup of the tapenade over the dough, leaving a ½-inch border all around. Distribute one-quarter of the roasted cauliflower evenly over the tapenade. Repeat with the remaining dough, tapenade, and cauliflower.

CONTINUED

Working in batches, slide the prepared flatbreads onto the hot pizza stone or pan and bake for 10 to 15 minutes, until the crust is nicely browned.

While the flatbreads are baking, toss the frisée and parsley with 1 tablespoon olive oil, the flaked sea salt, and black pepper to taste in a mixing bowl.

Using tongs, pull the flatbreads onto a cutting board. Scatter the frisée mixture on top and drizzle with the balsamic reduction. Cut the flatbreads into wedges with a sharp knife or pizza cutter. Serve warm.

Kite Hill

I'm thrilled to be part of the team developing Kite Hill artisan almond milk cheeses. Unlike other nut cheeses, our cheeses are made the same way as dairy milk cheeses.

Regular cheese is made from milk, which is coagulated as a curd forms; that curd is then cut and drained. The other nut cheeses that are available, largely because of the raw-food movement, are made from cashews that are ground into a paste, soured, and then pressed into molds; in some instances, these are aged. Because Kite Hill is crafted in the same manner as dairy cheese, it is the first brand of almond milk cheese to be sold in the main Whole Foods cheese shops, not segregated in their nondairy alternative section. The quest to create Kite Hill cheeses has been a labor of love, drawing on the time-honored techniques of traditional artisanal cheese making and a bit of science.

The journey started when I was on my first book tour in 2009, teaching workshops on vegan cooking at every Le Cordon Bleu campus in the United States. Chef Monte Casino, the artisan-cheese instructor at the school in Boston, attended one of my signings and, in turn, I sat in on his cheese class. Monte and I became fast friends, and we joined forces to try to create cheeses from cashew milk. Cheese making at its most elemental involves acidifying milk, souring it, and then adding an enzyme to thicken it. We knew that nut milk has the same four basic components as dairy milk—sugar, protein, fat, and water—and, hypothetically, should thicken in the same way. Wrong. After much research and experimentation, we learned that cashew milk does not have enough protein to form a curd.

Around the same time Monte and I were trying to develop cashew cheese, a friend of mine, Stanford University biochemist Dr. Patrick Brown, was working on creating a nut cheese that followed classic cheese-making techniques without using gums and starches, as most vegan cheeses do. He systematically tested twenty-seven different nuts, using them to make pure nut milks, and then determined how much fat and protein each contained to see which was the closest to dairy milk and, therefore, should form a curd.

Months later, we discovered that a particular almond varietal from San Joaquin Valley produced an almond milk that was the closest to dairy, with enough protein and fat to form a curd. Patrick created the almond milk in his lab in California, perfecting it over months of recipe testing, and shipped it to Monte in Boston to make cheese, until we finally had a prototype that could be produced in volume for the consumer. Based on that successful experiment, we started Kite Hill.

To help us build and design our production facility, I brought in Jean Prevot, former director of operations for Laura Chenel Chèvre. Once we had the team and facility, we were ready to introduce Kite Hill to the marketplace.

Cathy Strange, the global cheese buyer for Whole Foods and former president of the American Cheese Society, tasted our Kite Hill lineup a couple of years ago and loved it instantly. As a result of that tasting, we launched retail distribution throughout Whole Foods markets across the country.

CHARRED OKRA FLATBREAD ^{WITH} SWEET CORN PUREE ^{AND} CHERRY TOMATOES SERVES 8; MAKES 4 FLATBREADS

16 fresh or frozen okra, rinsed under
  cool water to thaw if frozen,
  halved lengthwise

Extra-virgin olive oil

Kosher salt and freshly ground
  black pepper

¼ pound (about 3) fingerling
  potatoes, scrubbed and diced

16 cherry tomatoes, halved

Unbleached all-purpose flour,
  for dusting

Four 6-ounce balls Flatbread Dough
  (page 66)

Cornmeal, for dusting

Sweet Corn Puree (recipe follows)

2 cups lightly packed baby arugula

Juice of ½ lemon

Trust me, even okra haters will love this sweet and savory flatbread. If you scoop out the innards and char it at high heat, okra crisps beautifully. In fact, Scot was once an okra skeptic, but I convinced him to give this surefire method a try, and now this flatbread is one of his favorites. The corn puree and cherry tomatoes that round out the topping make this a flatbread to serve during the height of summer.

Preheat the oven to 450°F.

To prepare the okra and vegetables: Run a demitasse spoon, teaspoon, or a small melon baller down the inside of each piece of okra from top to bottom to remove the seeds and membranes; the hollowed-out halves should look like canoes.

Put the okra on a baking sheet, drizzle with 1 tablespoon oil, and toss to coat. Spread out in a single layer and season generously with salt and pepper. Repeat the process with the potatoes and the cherry tomatoes, arranging them on two separate small baking sheets.

Roast the vegetables for 15 to 20 minutes, shaking the pans from time to time, until the okra and potatoes are lightly charred and the tomatoes have collapsed. Set the vegetables aside to cool. (The roasted vegetables can be prepared a couple of hours in advance, covered, and held at room temperature.)

To prepare the flatbread: At least 20 minutes before baking, put a pizza stone or a baking sheet on the middle oven rack and preheat the oven to 450°F.

On a lightly floured surface, with a floured rolling pin, roll one ball of dough into an oval about 8 inches long, 6 inches wide, and ¼ inch thick. With a docker or a fork, prick the surface of the flatbread to prevent air bubbles from forming during baking. Dust a pizza paddle with cornmeal and slide it under the dough. (If you don't have a paddle, flip over a baking sheet and use it.) Lightly brush the dough with oil to give a sheen to the crust.

Smear ¼ cup of the corn puree over the dough, leaving a ½-inch border all around. Distribute one-quarter of the roasted potatoes, okra, and tomatoes evenly over the puree. Repeat with the remaining dough, puree, and vegetables.

Working in batches, slide the prepared flatbreads onto the hot pizza stone or pan and bake for 10 to 15 minutes, until the crust is nicely browned.

While the flatbreads are baking, toss the arugula with 1 tablespoon olive oil, the lemon juice, and salt and pepper to taste in a mixing bowl. Set aside.

Using tongs, pull the flatbreads onto a cutting board. Scatter the arugula on top. Cut the flatbreads into wedges with a sharp knife or pizza cutter. Serve warm.

PHOTOGRAPH ON PAGE 70 (CENTER RIGHT)

SWEET CORN PUREE
MAKES ABOUT 1 CUP

2 ears of corn, husked and kernels cut from the cobs, or 2 cups thawed frozen corn kernels

1 large leek, white and pale green parts only

2 tablespoons Earth Balance butter stick

3 garlic cloves, coarsely chopped

1 shallot, coarsely chopped

¼ cup dry sherry

½ cup Cashew Cream (page 264)

¼ cup Vegetable Stock (page 268) or store-bought stock

1 teaspoon smoked sea salt (optional; see headnote)

2 cups hickory or apple wood chips, soaked in water for 20 minutes and drained (optional; see headnote)

Hot-smoking corn pumps up its flavor and balances its natural sweetness. You will need a large pot with a steamer insert. If you want to skip the smoking step, though, you can add smoked sea salt to the puree instead. This creamy, comforting puree also makes a sweet filling for ravioli.

Note that the cashew cream for the puree needs to be prepared a day in advance.

To smoke the corn: Open the windows and remove the battery from your smoke detector. Line a large pot that has a steamer insert with aluminum foil (this will keep the wood chips from scorching the bottom). Spread the wet wood chips out on the foil. Cover the pot tightly with the lid and heat over high heat.

Meanwhile, put the corn kernels in the steamer basket. Once the chips begin to smoke, drop the steamer basket insert into the pot and cover tightly with the lid. Turn off the heat and allow the corn to soak up the smoke for 5 to 6 minutes—no peeking. Set the corn aside

to cool. (The corn can be prepared a couple of hours in advance, covered, and held at room temperature.)

To prepare the corn puree: Halve the leek lengthwise and then cut crosswise into ½-inch slices. You should have about 1 cup sliced leeks. Put the sliced leeks in a colander and rinse really well under cool water, checking for dirt between the layers. Drain well.

Put a large saucepan over medium heat and add the butter substitute. When it has melted, add the leeks, garlic, and shallot and cook, stirring, until soft, about 10 minutes. Deglaze the pan with the sherry and cook for 1 minute to evaporate some of the alcohol. Add the cashew cream, stock, and corn kernels. Add smoked sea salt if you did not smoke the corn. Reduce the heat to medium-low and gently simmer, uncovered, stirring occasionally to make sure the cream mixture doesn't stick and burn on the bottom of the pan, until it is thick, 20 to 25 minutes.

Using a slotted spoon, carefully transfer the corn mixture to the bowl of a food processor. Pulse until coarsely pureed. The puree should have a slightly chunky texture. Set aside to cool slightly and thicken up. The corn puree will keep covered in the refrigerator for up to 3 days.

BUTTERNUT SQUASH– PUREE FLATBREAD WITH MUSTARD GREENS AND FRIED BRUSSELS SPROUT LEAVES

SERVES 8; MAKES 4 FLATBREADS

1 butternut squash (about 2 pounds), halved lengthwise and seeds and membranes removed

Extra-virgin olive oil

1 sweet onion, such as Vidalia, halved lengthwise and thinly sliced

4 tablespoons (½ stick) Earth Balance butter stick

4 garlic cloves, coarsely chopped

1 shallot, coarsely chopped

2 fresh thyme sprigs, leaves stripped from the stems

¼ cup sweet Marsala

¼ cup sweet Madeira

¼ cup Vegetable Stock (page 268) or store-bought stock

Kosher salt and freshly ground black pepper

½ pound Brussels sprouts (about 15)

Expeller-pressed canola oil, for deep-frying

¼ teaspoon unrefined cane sugar

Unbleached all-purpose flour, for dusting

Four 6-ounce balls Flatbread Dough (page 66)

Cornmeal, for dusting

½ cup Kite Hill almond ricotta

2 cups baby mustard greens

Juice of 1 lemon

¼ cup toasted pumpkin seeds (pepitas)

I find butternut squash to be a little sweet, so adding spice with cayenne or black pepper—and in this case, a peppery mustard green—helps to balance the sweetness. I add the crispy fried Brussels sprouts for crunch.

To prepare the squash: Preheat the oven to 450°F.

Put the squash cut side down in a 9-by-13-inch baking dish. Pour ½ inch of water into the dish around the squash halves to create steam as the squash cooks. Roast for about 1 hour, until the squash is golden and is tender when pierced with a knife. Set aside to cool. (The squash can be prepared a couple of hours in advance, covered, and held at room temperature.)

Meanwhile, prepare the caramelized onions: Put a large sauté pan over medium-high heat and coat with 2 tablespoons olive oil. Add the onions and cook, stirring, until soft and light brown, about 10 minutes. Set aside.

Put a medium saucepan over medium heat. Add the butter substitute, garlic, shallot, and thyme and sauté until the shallot and garlic are soft, about 3 minutes. Pour in the Marsala, Madeira, and stock and simmer until the liquid is reduced by half, about 5 minutes. Remove from the heat.

When the squash is cool enough to handle, scoop the flesh out with a spoon and put it in the bowl of a food processor. With the motor running, carefully pour in the wine sauce a little at a time and puree until smooth. Season with salt and pepper.

To prepare the Brussels sprouts: Cut off the stem ends of the sprouts. Peel off the outer leaves of each sprout until you get to the hard heart and can't peel off any more; discard the hearts. You

should have about 3 cups leaves. Pat the leaves really dry with paper towels; you don't want them to spatter in the oil.

Pour 1 inch of canola oil into a wide pot and set over medium-high heat. When the oil is hot, add the Brussels sprout leaves, in batches, using the lid of the pot to shield and protect your hands from popping oil, and fry, stirring constantly to keep the leaves from burning, until crispy and brown, about 30 seconds. Use a long pair of tongs or a slotted spoon to remove the sprouts from the hot oil, transfer to a paper towel–lined plate to drain, and season with the sugar and salt and pepper.

To prepare the flatbread: At least 20 minutes before baking, put a pizza stone or a baking sheet on the middle oven rack and preheat the oven to 450°F.

On a lightly floured surface, with a floured rolling pin, roll one ball of dough into an oval about 8 inches long, 6 inches wide, and ¼ inch thick. With a docker or a fork, prick the surface of the flatbread to prevent air bubbles from forming during baking. Dust a pizza paddle with cornmeal and slide it under the dough. (If you don't have a paddle, flip over a baking sheet and use it.) Lightly brush the dough with olive oil to give a sheen to the crust.

Smear ½ cup of the butternut squash puree over the dough, leaving a ½-inch border all around. Distribute one-quarter of the almond ricotta evenly over the puree. Repeat with the remaining dough, puree, and ricotta.

Working in batches, slide the prepared flatbreads onto the hot pizza stone or pan and bake for 10 to 15 minutes, until the crust is nicely browned.

While the flatbreads are baking, toss the mustard greens with 1 tablespoon olive oil, the lemon juice, and salt and pepper to taste in a mixing bowl.

Using tongs, pull the flatbreads onto a cutting board. Scatter the caramelized onions, mustard greens, fried Brussels sprout leaves, and pumpkin seeds on top. Cut the flatbreads into wedges with a sharp knife or pizza cutter. Serve warm.

TAGINE FLATBREAD WITH EGGPLANT AND MINTED SPINACH

SERVES 8; MAKES 4 FLATBREADS

1 large Italian eggplant
   (about 1 pound), unpeeled,
   ends trimmed, and cut into
   ¼-inch cubes

Extra-virgin olive oil

Kosher salt and freshly ground
   black pepper

Unbleached all-purpose flour,
   for dusting

Four 6-ounce balls Flatbread Dough
   (page 66)

Cornmeal, for dusting

1 cup Tagine Sauce (recipe follows)

2 cups lightly packed baby
   spinach leaves

¼ cup Mint Vinaigrette (page 44)

¼ teaspoon flaked sea salt,
   such as Maldon

This flatbread was inspired by a trip I took to Marrakesh with my restaurant partner, feature film producer Steve Bing. He invited me to join him on location while he was shooting the movie *Rock the Casbah*.

Tagine is one of the signature dishes of Morocco; it's a slow-cooked stew made with spices and dried fruits and baked in a conical clay pot. The spices are complex and boldly balanced. I took very specific notes so I could re-create my own tagine sauce.

I found the majority of markets in Marrakesh to be nothing more than tourist traps, dangling dainty little bags of stale spices. Spices are the defining point of Moroccan cooking, so you'd think the good stuff would be easy to find! On a mission, I asked our local driver, "Where would your mother go to buy ingredients for *her* tagine?" He pointed me to a hole-in-the-wall corner store, with bins of colorful spices right next to other essentials, like dish soap. I filled a suitcase with huge bags of aromatic spices—turmeric, ginger, and cumin—and put this dish on the menu at Crossroads as soon as I got home.

Preheat the oven to 450°F.

To prepare the eggplant: Put the eggplant in a mixing bowl. Drizzle with 1 tablespoon oil and season with kosher salt and pepper, tossing thoroughly to evenly coat. Spread the eggplant out in a single layer on a baking sheet. Roast for 25 to 30 minutes, turning the pieces over with a spatula from time to time to prevent them from burning, until the eggplant shrinks and is well charred. Set aside to cool. (The roasted eggplant can be prepared a couple of hours in advance, covered, and held at room temperature.)

To prepare the flatbread: At least 20 minutes before baking, put a pizza stone or a baking sheet on the middle oven rack and preheat the oven to 450°F.

On a lightly floured surface, with a floured rolling pin, roll one ball of dough into an oval about 8 inches long, 6 inches wide, and ¼ inch thick. With a docker or a fork, prick the surface of the flatbread to prevent air bubbles from forming during baking. Dust a pizza paddle with cornmeal and slide it under the dough. (If you don't have a paddle, flip over a baking sheet and use it.) Lightly brush the dough with oil to give a sheen to the crust.

Smear ¼ cup of the tagine sauce on the dough, leaving a ½-inch border all around. Distribute one-quarter of the roasted eggplant evenly over the sauce. Repeat with the remaining dough, sauce, and eggplant.

Working in batches, slide the prepared flatbreads onto the hot pizza stone or pan and bake for 10 to 15 minutes, until the crust is nicely browned.

While the flatbreads are baking, toss the spinach with the vinaigrette in a mixing bowl and season with flaked sea salt and pepper. Set aside.

Using tongs, pull the flatbreads onto a cutting board. Scatter the spinach on top. Cut the flatbreads into wedges with a sharp knife or pizza cutter. Serve warm.

PHOTOGRAPH ON PAGES 88–89

TAGINE SAUCE

MAKES 1 CUP

2 tablespoons extra-virgin olive oil

2 shallots, chopped

½ cup (3 ounces) dried Turkish apricots, finely chopped

6 garlic cloves, chopped

Kosher salt and freshly ground black pepper

½ teaspoon ground cinnamon

½ teaspoon ground ginger

½ teaspoon paprika

½ teaspoon turmeric

½ teaspoon harissa spice mix (see Note, page 4)

¼ teaspoon ground cumin

4 plum (Roma) tomatoes, cored and diced (about 1½ cups)

1½ cups Vegetable Stock (page 268) or store-bought stock, plus more if needed

This bold sauce is not only terrific on flatbread, it also gives new life to ordinary roasted potatoes or stewed chickpeas.

Put a medium saucepan over medium heat and add the oil. When the oil is hot, add the shallots and cook, stirring, until softened, about 2 minutes. Add the apricots, garlic, ½ teaspoon salt, ¾ teaspoon pepper, cinnamon, ginger, paprika, turmeric, harissa, and cumin and cook, stirring, until the apricots begin to soften and the spices smell fragrant, about 2 minutes.

Add the tomatoes and stock, increase the heat to high, and bring to a boil. Reduce the heat to low and gently simmer, stirring occasionally, until the tomatoes break down and the sauce is thick, about 45 minutes; add more stock if needed if the sauce thickens too much.

Season with salt and pepper. Let cool. The sauce will keep covered in the refrigerator for up to 5 days.

SOUPS

SUMMER MINESTRONE WITH BASIL PESTO   94

TOMATO AND WATERMELON GAZPACHO   97

CREAM OF FAVA BEAN AND PEA SOUP   98

CAULIFLOWER BISQUE WITH
FRIED CAPERS   100

MUSHROOM FARRO SOUP   104

FRENCH LENTIL SOUP WITH CRISPY KALE   107

VEGETABLE BOUILLABAISSE
WITH ROUILLE   108

The majority of soups found on restaurant menus can be off-limits if you're avoiding animal products; they're often made with beef or chicken stock, cream, and butter. On the flip side, traditional vegan soups can be one-dimensional, lacking the savory elements and body we love in soup in the first place. But the soups in this chapter are guaranteed to leave you satisfied. If you're in the mood for a big bowl of something brothy, try the delicate, saffron-scented Vegetable Bouillabaisse with Rouille (page 108). If you're craving something warm and creamy, turn to the Cauliflower Bisque (page 100); it is made with Cashew Cream (page 264). If you want something hearty, try the Mushroom Farro Soup (page 104).

All of the soups in this chapter can be made a day ahead; in fact, the flavors will benefit and deepen with time. Each soup is a meal on its own, but if you wish, serve a soup with one of the salads in the chapter beginning on page 27 to make a casual weeknight dinner.

SUMMER MINESTRONE WITH BASIL PESTO

SERVES 8; MAKES 8 CUPS

½ head of escarole
  (about ½ pound), halved
  lengthwise
3 tablespoons extra-virgin olive oil
1 onion, chopped
1 celery stalk, chopped
1 carrot, chopped
½ fennel bulb, cored and
  thinly sliced
4 garlic cloves, chopped
2 bay leaves
Kosher salt and freshly ground
  black pepper
1 yellow squash, halved lengthwise
  and thinly sliced
One 28-ounce can crushed
  tomatoes
4 cups Vegetable Stock (page 268)
  or store-bought stock
One 15-ounce can cannellini beans,
  drained and rinsed
1 cup farro (see Note,
  page 58), rinsed
6 fresh basil leaves, chopped
About 1 cup Basil Pesto (page 272)

When Scot was chef/owner of Grappa's in Akron, minestrone was a mainstay for family meal—the restaurant ritual where the kitchen team has dinner together before the doors open to guests. To have a little fun with the staff, he'd play a game where the person who got the bay leaf in his or her soup would have to do all the dishes. After Scot moved to Los Angeles to open Crossroads with me, he put minestrone on the menu to remind him of his roots.

Cut the escarole crosswise into ½-inch-wide strips. You should have about 6 cups escarole. Dunk it in a large bowl of cold water and swish the water around, letting the sand fall to the bottom of the bowl. Lift the escarole out and spread it on a kitchen towel to dry.

Put a soup pot over medium heat and add the oil. When the oil is hot, add the onion, celery, carrot, fennel, garlic, and bay leaves, season with salt and pepper, and cook, stirring, until the vegetables are softened but not browned, about 10 minutes.

Stir in the squash and escarole and cook and stir for 1 minute. Add the tomatoes, stock, and beans and bring the soup to a boil. Reduce the heat to medium-low and simmer, stirring occasionally, until slightly thickened, 20 to 25 minutes.

Meanwhile, put a dry nonstick skillet over medium-high heat, add the farro, and toast, shaking the pan periodically, until golden, about 5 minutes. Remove from the heat.

Bring a medium pot of salted water to a boil over high heat. Add the toasted farro, give it a couple of good stirs with a wooden spoon, and reduce the heat to medium. Simmer, uncovered, until the farro is tender and the grains have split open, about 20 minutes. Drain well in a sieve and rinse with cool water to stop the cooking.

Remove the bay leaves. Stir the farro and basil into the soup and simmer for 8 to 10 minutes.

Ladle the soup into bowls. Top each with a generous tablespoon of pesto and serve with garlic bread and a big leafy green salad.

TOMATO AND WATERMELON GAZPACHO SERVES 4 TO 6; MAKES 8 CUPS

2 cups cubed seedless watermelon

4 large beefsteak tomatoes (about
   2 pounds), coarsely chopped

1 small red bell pepper, cored,
   seeded, and coarsely chopped

1 small green bell pepper, cored,
   seeded, and coarsely chopped

½ English cucumber, halved
   lengthwise, seeded, and
   coarsely chopped

1 shallot, coarsely chopped

Juice of 2 limes

Juice of 1 lemon

½ cup extra-virgin olive oil

½ cup tomato juice

1 teaspoon cayenne

Kosher salt and freshly ground
   black pepper

GARNISHES

Finely diced green bell pepper

Finely diced red bell pepper

Finely diced shallot

Almond Greek Yogurt (page 263)

Gazpacho is essentially a salad transformed into a refreshing cold soup. Actually, when I first tried gazpacho, I thought it tasted more like a huge bowl of salsa. The addition of watermelon completely changes the game, imparting a sweetness that pairs beautifully with the tomatoes and other vegetables. As with most Mediterranean dishes, this is a simple recipe, so the quality of the ingredients is important. The garnish of diced bell peppers and shallots reinforces the flavors in the soup and adds texture at the same time. Top each bowl with a small dollop of the Almond Greek Yogurt, and serve as a starter or a light lunch—especially good when it's hot outside.

Put the watermelon in a blender or food processor. Add the tomatoes, along with their juice, bell peppers, cucumber, shallot, and lime and lemon juices and puree on high speed until completely smooth, about 5 minutes. With the motor running, pour in the oil in a steady stream, making sure it directly hits the blade. Process until fully incorporated.

Pour the vegetable mixture into a large bowl. Stir in the tomato juice, cayenne, and salt and pepper to taste until thoroughly combined. Refrigerate the soup for at least 2 hours, or, even better, overnight, until very well chilled; the flavors will develop as it sits.

Season the gazpacho again with salt and pepper. Serve in chilled bowls or a chilled tureen and top with the desired garnishes.

CREAM OF FAVA BEAN
AND PEA SOUP   SERVES 4; MAKES 4 CUPS

1 tablespoon grapeseed oil

1 tablespoon Earth Balance
  butter stick

1 shallot, minced

2½ pounds whole fresh fava beans,
  shelled and peeled (1½ cups; see
  Note, page 23)

1 cup shelled fresh peas

2 cups Vegetable Stock (page 268)
  or store-bought stock

1 cup Cashew Cream (page 264)

1 bunch spinach, stems trimmed
  (about 2 cups), lightly packed

Kosher salt and freshly ground
  black pepper

Almond Greek Yogurt
  (page 263; optional)

If all you know about fava beans is that Hannibal Lecter enjoyed them with "a nice Chianti," then you're in for a pleasant surprise. Fava beans are a spring staple of Mediterranean and Middle Eastern cooking; they're smoother, sweeter, and meatier than most other fresh beans, and they have a nutty taste and buttery texture all their own. I'm not going to lie—fava beans take a bit of work to shell and peel, but the result is well worth the effort. Serve the soup hot or chilled. Note that the cashew cream needs to be prepared a day in advance.

Put a large saucepan over medium heat and add the oil and butter substitute. When the butter substitute has melted, add the shallot and sauté until soft but not browned, about 2 minutes. Add the fava beans and peas, pour in the stock, and bring to a boil. Reduce the heat to medium-low and simmer, uncovered, until the beans and peas are tender, about 15 minutes. Add the cashew cream, stirring to incorporate, and simmer until heated through and thickened, about 2 minutes.

Working in batches, carefully ladle the soup into a blender, filling it no more than halfway each time and adding a handful of the spinach to each batch. (If you have an immersion blender, this is a great time to use it.) Puree the soup for a few seconds, until completely smooth and emerald green (be sure to hold down the lid with a kitchen towel for safety), and transfer to a saucepan or bowl. Season with salt and pepper.

Divide the soup among four soup bowls, dollop with the yogurt, if desired, and serve.

CAULIFLOWER BISQUE WITH FRIED CAPERS

SERVES 6 TO 8; MAKES 8 CUPS

1 head of cauliflower (1½ pounds),
　　stem and core removed, florets
　　chopped into 1-inch pieces

4 garlic cloves, coarsely chopped

2 leeks, white and light green parts
　　only, halved lengthwise, coarsely
　　chopped, and well rinsed

1 onion, coarsely chopped

3 tablespoons extra-virgin olive oil

Kosher salt and freshly ground
　　black pepper

4 tablespoons (½ stick) Earth
　　Balance butter stick

2 bay leaves

4 cups Vegetable Stock (page 268)
　　or store-bought stock

1 cup Cashew Cream (page 264)

4 fresh thyme sprigs, leaves
　　stripped from the stems
　　(about 1 tablespoon)

Fried Capers (recipe follows)

Roasting the cauliflower imparts a caramelized flavor and winter-white color to this soothing fall soup. After roasting, the vegetables are pureed, giving the soup a silky mouthfeel without it being too rich. The cashew cream needs to be prepared a day in advance, so plan accordingly.

Preheat the oven to 425°F.

Put the cauliflower, garlic, leeks, and onion in a large mixing bowl. Add the oil, season with salt and pepper, and toss to coat evenly. Spread the vegetables out in a single layer on a large baking sheet and roast for 30 to 40 minutes, shaking the pan from time to time, until tender and slightly charred. Set aside. (The roasted vegetables can be prepared a couple of hours in advance, covered, and held at room temperature.)

Put a soup pot over medium heat and add the butter substitute. When it has melted, add the bay leaves and stir until fragrant, about 1 minute. Add the roasted vegetables, turning them over with a wooden spoon to coat. Pour in the stock and bring to a boil over medium-high heat. Reduce the heat to medium and simmer the soup, stirring occasionally, until slightly reduced, about 20 minutes.

Reduce the heat to medium-low, pour in the cashew cream, and gently simmer until slightly thickened, about 5 minutes. Remove from the heat and discard the bay leaves.

Working in batches, carefully ladle the soup into a blender, filling it no more than halfway each time and adding some of the thyme and salt and pepper to taste to each batch. (If you have an immersion blender, this is a great time to use it.) Puree the soup for a few seconds, until completely smooth (be sure to hold down the lid with a kitchen towel for safety), and transfer to a saucepan or bowl. If desired, pass the soup through a fine-mesh strainer, pushing down on the solids with the back of a wooden spoon; discard the solids.

Divide the soup among soup bowls, scatter the fried capers on top, and serve.

PHOTOGRAPH ON PAGE 103

FRIED CAPERS

MAKES ½ CUP

Expeller-pressed canola oil,
    for frying
½ cup capers, drained and
    dried well

Crispy and briny, these little blossoms of goodness add unexpected dimension to even the simplest dishes. Try scattering them over salads, sliced ripe tomatoes, or Marinated Mediterranean Olives (page 7). It's important to drain the capers well and squeeze out as much of the brine as possible before frying.

Heat approximately ¼ inch of oil in a small sauté pan until very hot but not smoking. Carefully add the dried capers to the hot oil (they may spit and bubble) and gently stir until the capers bloom and become crisp, 30 to 45 seconds. Remove the capers with a slotted spoon and transfer to a plate lined with paper towels. The fried capers can be kept in a tightly covered container at room temperature for up to 2 hours.

MUSHROOM FARRO SOUP
SERVES 6 TO 8; MAKES 8 CUPS

Mushroom stock is a versatile staple to keep on hand—its deep, rich flavor and color make it a great substitute for beef stock. We save the scraps of vegetables from the soup—peels, ends, and stems—to fortify the stock, so nothing goes to waste. If you have it, you can substitute 4 cups Roasted Vegetable Stock (page 269).

STOCK

1½ cups reserved vegetable trimmings from the soup (onion, celery, carrot, mushrooms, and garlic)

1 ounce dried shiitake mushrooms, rinsed

8 cups filtered water

SOUP

2 tablespoons grapeseed oil

1 tablespoon Earth Balance butter stick

1 onion, finely chopped

1 celery stalk, finely chopped

1 carrot, finely chopped

1 pound mixed mushrooms, such as cremini and shiitake, stemmed, wiped of grit, and sliced

2 garlic cloves, minced

6 fresh thyme sprigs

1 fresh rosemary sprig

Kosher salt and freshly ground black pepper

½ cup sweet Madeira

1 tablespoon sherry vinegar

½ cup farro (see Note, page 58), rinsed

Truffle salt (optional)

To prepare the stock: Combine the vegetable trimmings and dried shiitake mushrooms in a medium saucepan, pour in the water, and bring to a boil over medium heat, then reduce the heat to low and simmer, covered, for 30 minutes. Remove the lid and simmer the stock for 30 minutes more.

Carefully pour the stock through a fine-mesh strainer into a heat-proof container and use the back of a wooden spoon to press on the solids to extract as much flavor as possible; discard the solids. You should have about 4 cups mushroom stock.

To prepare the soup: Put a soup pot over medium heat and add the oil and butter substitute. When the butter substitute has melted, add the onion, celery, and carrot and cook, stirring, until the vegetables begin to soften, about 2 minutes. Add the mushrooms, garlic, thyme, and rosemary, season with salt and pepper, and turn the vegetables over with a wooden spoon, and cook until tender, about 5 minutes. Pour in the wine and vinegar and stir until almost evaporated. Add the stock and simmer, uncovered, until slightly reduced, about 20 minutes.

Meanwhile, prepare the farro: Put a dry nonstick skillet over medium-high heat, add the farro, and toast, shaking the pan periodically, until golden, about 5 minutes. Remove from the heat.

Bring a medium pot of salted water to a boil over high heat. Add the toasted farro, stir with a wooden spoon, and reduce the heat to medium. Simmer, uncovered, until the farro is tender, about 20 minutes. Drain well in a sieve and rinse with cool water to stop the cooking.

Stir the farro into the soup and simmer for 8 to 10 minutes. Remove the thyme and rosemary sprigs.

Ladle the soup into bowls, sprinkle with truffle salt, if using, and serve.

FRENCH LENTIL SOUP WITH CRISPY KALE

SERVES 6 TO 8; MAKES 8 CUPS

3 tablespoons grapeseed oil

1 onion, finely chopped

1 celery stalk, finely chopped

1 carrot, finely chopped

½ fennel bulb, cored and
finely chopped

2 garlic cloves, finely chopped

1 turnip, peeled and diced

1 Yukon Gold potato, peeled and
finely chopped

8 fresh thyme sprigs

2 bay leaves

Kosher salt and freshly ground
black pepper

¼ teaspoon red pepper flakes

1¼ cups (¾ pound) French green
lentils (Puy), picked over
and rinsed

1 kale leaf, tough center rib
removed, leaf hand-torn

4 cups Vegetable Stock (page 268)
or store-bought stock

4 cups filtered water

Crispy Kale (recipe follows)

1 bunch kale (about 1 pound), rinsed
and dried well

3 tablespoons extra-virgin olive oil

Nutritional yeast flakes (see Note,
page 6)

Flaked sea salt, such as Maldon

I love this homey soup for its many layers of flavor and texture: the earthiness of the lentils, the sweetness of the onions and carrots, and the crunch of crispy kale. Lentils love to absorb other flavors, making them the ultimate base for a soup. This one is made with French green lentils (Puy), which hold their shape and thicken the soup without turning it into sludge, the fate of too many lentil soups.

Put a soup pot over medium heat and add the oil. When the oil is hot, add the onion, celery, carrot, and fennel and cook, stirring, until they begin to soften, about 2 minutes. Add the garlic and stir to combine. Add the turnip, potato, thyme, and bay leaves, season with salt, black pepper, and the red pepper flakes, and turn the vegetables over with a wooden spoon to coat. Cook until the vegetables are tender, about 5 minutes.

Stir in the lentils and torn kale. Pour in the stock and water and bring to a boil over high heat, then reduce the heat to medium-low and simmer, stirring occasionally, until the lentils are tender, about 30 minutes. Add more water as necessary if the soup becomes too thick. Remove the thyme sprigs and bay leaves.

Ladle into soup bowls and scatter the crispy kale on top.

CRISPY KALE

MAKES ABOUT 2½ CUPS

The secret to getting the kale leaves crisp is to dry them well. Spread the kale out in a single even layer on the baking sheet so the leaves can dry out and crisp. This makes a terrific snack.

Preheat the oven to 300°F.

Remove the tough center ribs of the kale. Tear the leaves into large bite-size pieces. You should have about 8 cups leaves.

Toss the leaves with the oil and spread in a single layer on a large baking sheet. Bake for 30 minutes, tossing the kale every 10 minutes as it begins to shrink, until crisp on the edges and slightly browned.

Sprinkle the crispy kale with nutritional yeast flakes and salt while hot. The kale keeps for up to 3 days, uncovered, at room temperature.

8 cups filtered water

4 Sencha green tea bags
(see Note, page 111)

Two 6-inch sheets dried kombu,
wiped of grit (see Note, page 111)

2 tablespoons grapeseed oil

1 onion, cut into chunks

1 celery stalk, cut into chunks

3 garlic cloves, coarsely chopped

2 bay leaves

2 fresh thyme sprigs

½ teaspoon whole black peppercorns

Kosher salt and freshly ground
black pepper

½ cup dry white wine, such as
Sauvignon Blanc

SOUP

1 teaspoon saffron threads

1½ pounds oyster and lobster
mushrooms, stems trimmed,
wiped of grit, and halved if large

4 artichoke hearts (see Note,
page 24), or one 15-ounce can
artichoke hearts in water, chopped

One 15-ounce can diced tomatoes

2 leeks, white and light green parts
only, halved lengthwise,
well rinsed, and chopped

1 fennel bulb, trimmed, halved,
cored, and chopped

3 garlic cloves, minced

4 fresh flat-leaf parsley sprigs,
chopped

Finely grated zest and juice of
2 seedless oranges

2 tablespoons Pernod

1 teaspoon herbes de Provence

Kosher salt and freshly ground
black pepper

Rouille (recipe follows)

Toasted crusty baguette slices,
for serving

VEGETABLE BOUILLABAISSE WITH ROUILLE

SERVES 6 TO 8; MAKES 8 CUPS

Bouillabaisse, the most famous soup in the South of France, is typically prepared with an array of seafood. But reincarnating the soup as an equally hearty vegan meal is simple. This version honors all of the familiar flavors and textures of classic bouillabaisse: Redolent of the ocean, Sencha green tea and Japanese kombu seaweed (see Notes, page 111) anchor the soup and provide a base for the garlic, orange, and tomato. The firm mushrooms and feathery artichoke hearts mimic the contrasting textures of the different fish.

To prepare the stock: Bring the water to a boil in a saucepan over high heat. Add the tea and kombu, turn off the heat, and steep for 15 minutes to infuse the water, which should turn light brown. Remove the tea bags and kombu and discard. Set the tea-kombu stock aside.

Put a soup pot over medium heat and add the oil. When the oil is hot, add the onion and celery and cook, stirring, until they begin to soften, about 2 minutes. Add the garlic, bay leaves, thyme, and peppercorns and stir to combine, then season with salt and pepper and cook, stirring, until fragrant, about 2 minutes. Pour in the wine and stir until almost evaporated, about 1 minute.

Pour in the tea-kombu stock and simmer, uncovered, until slightly reduced, about 20 minutes. Carefully pour the stock through a fine-mesh strainer into another pot to remove the solids. You should have about 6 cups stock. (The stock can be prepared ahead and kept covered in the refrigerator for about a week or frozen for a couple of months.)

To prepare the soup: Bring the stock to a simmer in a medium pot over medium heat. Stir in the saffron to dissolve. Add the mushrooms, artichoke hearts, tomatoes, leeks, fennel, garlic, and parsley, then stir in the orange zest and juice and Pernod and season with the herbes de Provence, salt, and pepper. Simmer, stirring occasionally, until the vegetables are tender, 40 to 45 minutes. Taste and season as needed.

Ladle the bouillabaisse into soup bowls and dollop the rouille on the toasted baguette for dunking.

ROUILLE

MAKES 1 GENEROUS CUP

½ cup vegan mayonnaise,
   such as Vegenaise

1 jarred roasted red bell pepper,
   rinsed and coarsely chopped

3 garlic cloves, coarsely chopped

One 3-inch piece baguette, crust
   removed and torn into pieces

1 tablespoon Dijon mustard

Juice of ½ lemon

¼ cup extra-virgin olive oil

Kosher salt and freshly ground
   black pepper

Pinch of cayenne

The orange color of this creamy sauce comes from roasted red peppers and cayenne, which gives it its name—*rouille* is French for "rust."

Combine the vegan mayonnaise, roasted pepper, garlic, bread, mustard, and lemon juice in a food processor and pulse, scraping down the sides as necessary, until well combined. With the motor running, drizzle in the oil in a steady stream, making sure it directly hits the blade, and process until emulsified and thick. Season with salt, pepper, and the cayenne.

Transfer the rouille to a tightly covered bowl or jar and refrigerate until ready to use. It can be stored for up to 3 days.

SENCHA GREEN TEA

Sencha is a variety of green tea from Japan. Although it certainly doesn't have a Mediterranean heritage, the tea adds a savory umami flavor and deep jade color to the bouillabaisse. You can find Sencha green tea at Asian markets and most fine grocery stores; Eden Foods and Harney & Sons are terrific brands that are widely available.

KOMBU

A member of the kelp/seaweed family, kombu is a sea vegetable. Mildly salty and subtly sweet, and packed with nutrients and minerals, it gives this bouillabaisse a deep, oceany flavor. Dried kombu can be found in Asian markets and health food stores. The sheets are often covered with a white powder from natural salts. Just give them a quick rinse before cooking, or your stock will be super salty. Store kombu in an airtight container away from sunlight and moisture.

SMALL
PLATES

HEARTS OF PALM CALAMARI
WITH COCKTAIL SAUCE AND
LEMON-CAPER AÏOLI 117

KALE SPANAKOPITA WITH
HARISSA SAUCE AND MINT OIL 120

BALSAMIC-ROASTED
MUSHROOMS WITH
SHALLOTS AND TOASTED
MARCONA ALMONDS 124

RAPINI WITH BLACK GARLIC,
SHERRY VINEGAR, AND
TOASTED HAZELNUTS 127

SPICED CHICKPEAS 128

ARTICHOKE OYSTERS WITH
TOMATO BÉARNAISE AND
KELP CAVIAR 131

OVEN-ROASTED OKRA WITH
CALABRESE PEPPERS AND
PICKLED SCALLIONS 137

PAPAS ARRUGADAS (SPANISH
WRINKLED POTATOES) WITH
PARSLEY VINAIGRETTE 138

SWEET POTATO LATKES WITH
SPIKED APPLESAUCE 141

SPAGHETTI SQUASH
NOCE MOSCATA 144

ROASTED FENNEL WITH
CLEMENTINE BEURRE BLANC
AND TOASTED BUCKWHEAT 147

CAULIFLOWER WITH OLIVES
AND SUN-DRIED TOMATOES 151

OVEN-ROASTED ROMANESCO
WITH ONION AGRODOLCE AND
GRAPPA-SOAKED RAISINS 152

ITALIAN BUTTER BEANS WITH
PAN-ROASTED KALE, SHERRY
AGLIO OLIO, AND TOASTED
PUMPKIN SEEDS 157

ROASTED BABY PARSNIPS
WITH SHERRY-MAPLE GLAZE
AND CHANTERELLES 158

CREAMY POLENTA WITH
ROASTED CORN AND PORCINI
MUSHROOM–BORDELAISE SAUCE 161

SWEET CORN RISOTTO WITH
BUTTERED LEEKS, CHERRY
TOMATOES, AND TOMATO-
SHERRY CREAM SAUCE 165

FIG CAPONATA WITH
POLENTA FRIES 167

Simply put, the food at Crossroads is Mediterranean first and vegan second. A plant-based lifestyle isn't about deprivation or compromising taste, as the dishes that follow demonstrate. They run the gamut to offer whatever type of food you may be craving: When you want something light and crunchy, there's Kale Spanakopita (page 120) or crispy fried Hearts of Palm Calamari (page 117). If you're looking for something comforting, there's Creamy Polenta with Roasted Corn and Porcini Mushroom–Bordelaise Sauce (page 161). If you're celebrating and want to serve an elegant dish, there's Artichoke Oysters with Tomato Béarnaise and Kelp Caviar (page 131).

Variety is inherent in the plant and grain world, and the endless possibilities in these small plates may surprise you. I think small plates are the perfect place for experimenting with creative combinations of vegetables and grains. These dishes are where I get to present Mediterranean favorites in unfamiliar ways. For meat eaters and vegetarians, the recipes are also a great way to incorporate new flavors and vegan ideas.

At the restaurant, people like to sample a bunch of small plates, mixing and matching dishes, and share them around the table. This way of eating is both fun and gratifying, especially if you're serving a group of people. Some of these small plates are light, some are more filling, but all are damn delicious.

HEARTS OF PALM CALAMARI WITH COCKTAIL SAUCE AND LEMON-CAPER AÏOLI SERVES 4

BATTER

1 cup Cashew Cream (page 264)

2 tablespoons filtered water

1 tablespoon toasted nori flakes, finely ground

½ teaspoon kosher salt

¼ teaspoon freshly ground black pepper

Two 14-ounce cans hearts of palm (12), drained and rinsed

1 cup finely ground yellow cornmeal or polenta

1 cup rice flour

1 tablespoon Old Bay seasoning, plus more to taste

½ teaspoon kosher salt, plus more to taste

¼ teaspoon freshly ground black pepper, plus more to taste

Expeller-pressed canola oil, for frying

Cocktail Sauce (recipe follows)

Lemon-Caper Aïoli (recipe follows)

Much of the Crossroads philosophy is about taking classic, familiar dishes and giving them new soul as plant-based renditions. Here hearts of palm are sliced into rounds that look like rings of calamari. They are lightly coated in a batter seasoned with Old Bay and nori seaweed and fried to golden perfection. The cooked palm rings look like calamari and taste like calamari, and if you tell your guests the dish is fried calamari, they'll likely believe you.

The cashew cream for the batter needs to be prepared a day in advance, but all of the components can be made ahead of time, so frying and serving happen quickly. The cocktail sauce and lemon-caper aïoli are dipping sauces typically served with calamari. For an Italian spin, you could also serve Scoty's Marinara Sauce (page 275). After hollowing out the hearts of palm, you can cut up the unused centers and toss into a salad, such as the Melon Salad with Watercress and Oroblanco Vinaigrette (page 45).

To prepare the batter: Put the cashew cream in a bowl and add the water, ground nori, salt, and pepper. Stir the batter to combine; it should be smooth and not gloppy in the slightest. Set aside at room temperature to let the flavors meld while you prepare the hearts of palm.

To prepare the hearts of palm calamari: Trim both ends of each heart of palm to expose the center; this will make it easier to see and remove. Working from the narrow end, gently push out the insides of each cylinder, using your pinkie or a chopstick. Some pieces will be easier to gut than others—don't worry if a few split. (Reserve the insides for another use—see the headnote.)

Using a paring knife, carefully cut each hollow spear into four 1-inch-wide rings. You should end up with about 48 pieces.

CONTINUED

Add the hearts of palm to the cashew cream batter, gently turning the pieces over with your hands until thoroughly coated. Set aside.

Put the cornmeal in a food processor and process to a fine powder. Transfer to a large mixing bowl, add the rice flour, Old Bay seasoning, salt, and pepper, and toss to distribute the ingredients evenly.

Using a slotted spoon, working in batches, scoop the hearts of palm from the batter, letting the excess drip back into the bowl, add to the cornmeal mixture, and toss with your hands until evenly coated on all sides. Transfer the breaded hearts of palm to a strainer set over a bowl, or work over the sink, and shake off the excess cornmeal. This is a key step to ensure that the cornmeal crust is light and not clumpy whatsoever. (All of this can be prepared up to 2 hours in advance. Arrange the breaded hearts of palm in a single layer on a baking sheet and refrigerate, uncovered. Allow the hearts of palm to come to room temperature before frying.)

To deep-fry the hearts of palm calamari: Heat 2 inches of oil to 325°F in a cast-iron skillet or heavy saucepan. Working in batches, add the hearts of palm to the hot oil and fry, carefully turning with tongs, until golden brown and crispy on all sides, 2 to 3 minutes. Remove the cooked pieces to a paper towel–lined platter to drain. Season the hearts lightly with salt, pepper, and a sprinkle of Old Bay seasoning while still hot.

Pile the hearts of palm on a large platter and serve with the cocktail sauce and lemon-caper aïoli for dipping.

COCKTAIL SAUCE

MAKES 1 CUP

1 cup organic ketchup

1 to 2 tablespoons prepared
   horseradish, or more if you
   like it hot

Juice of 1 lemon

1 teaspoon vegan Worcestershire
   sauce, such as Wizard

This couldn't-be-simpler cocktail sauce is so much better than store-bought, you will never buy bottled again.

Combine the ketchup, horseradish, lemon juice, and Worcestershire in a small bowl. Gently whisk until well combined. Cover and chill for at least 30 minutes.

The flavor of the cocktail sauce gets better as it sits, and it keeps in the refrigerator for up to 1 week.

LEMON-CAPER AÏOLI

MAKES 1½ CUPS

1 cup vegan mayonnaise,
   such as Vegenaise

Juice of 1 lemon

2 tablespoons fresh flat-leaf parsley
   leaves, chopped

1 tablespoon capers, drained and
   finely chopped

2 garlic cloves, finely chopped

3 tablespoons extra-virgin olive oil

Kosher salt and freshly ground
   black pepper

Aïoli is chef code for souped-up mayo. Try this as a dip with grilled artichokes or as a savory sandwich spread.

Put the vegan mayonnaise, lemon juice, parsley, capers, and garlic in a small bowl and gently whisk until combined. While whisking, slowly drizzle in the oil until the aïoli is thickened and smooth. Season with salt and pepper. Cover and chill for at least 30 minutes.

The flavor of the aïoli gets better as it sits, and it keeps in the refrigerator for up to 1 week. Stir in 1 tablespoon water or lemon juice to thin it if needed.

KALE SPANAKOPITA ^{WITH} HARISSA SAUCE ^{AND} MINT OIL SERVES 4 TO 6; MAKES 36 PIECES

3 tablespoons grapeseed oil

1 large onion, chopped

4 garlic cloves, minced

2 pounds kale, washed, dried,
   tough center ribs removed,
   and leaves finely chopped

½ teaspoon red pepper flakes

Kosher salt and freshly ground
   black pepper

2 cups (about 14 ounces) crumbled
   Kite Hill almond ricotta

½ cup finely chopped fresh dill

½ cup finely chopped fresh mint

8 tablespoons (1 stick) Earth
   Balance butter stick, melted

Half of a 1-pound package filo
   dough, such as Athens
   (eighteen 9-by-14 inch sheets),
   thawed but kept refrigerated

Harissa Sauce (recipe follows)

¼ cup Mint Oil (recipe follows)

Traditional Greek spanakopita consists of a flaky filo crust filled with spinach and feta cheese, flavored with garlic, onion, and herbs. But anything spinach can do, kale can do better. Its hearty texture and mildly sweet flavor take spanakopita to another level.

Spanakopita is usually formed into delicate little triangles. When I was growing up, my nanny used to make Moroccan "cigars," with a spicy ground beef filling hand-rolled in crisp, flaky filo wrappers. I took that as my inspiration and form my spanakopita into fat cigars—which are better for dipping and hold together better anyway.

While I don't recommend refrigerating the assembled spanakopita (it becomes soggy), it can be made ahead and frozen: Arrange the spanakopita in a single layer on a baking sheet, cover with plastic wrap, and freeze until solid. Transfer to a resealable plastic bag and store in the freezer for up to 2 months. You do not need to thaw the spanakopita before baking.

Put a large sauté pan over medium-high heat and add the grapeseed oil. When the oil is hot, add the onion and garlic and sauté until very soft, about 4 minutes. Add the kale in handfuls, folding the leaves over with a spoon until each batch is wilted before adding more. Once all the kale is in the pan, season with the red pepper flakes, salt, and black pepper.

Transfer the kale mixture to a colander set over a bowl or in the sink. Using the back of a spoon, gently press out all of the excess liquid. Spread the kale out on a baking sheet and set aside to cool; the kale needs to be completely cool to prevent the dough from becoming soggy. (The kale can be prepared a couple of hours in advance, covered, and refrigerated.)

Transfer the cooled kale to a cutting board and coarsely chop. Then transfer to a mixing bowl and stir in the almond ricotta, dill, and mint until well combined. Season with salt and black pepper.

Preheat the oven to 375°F. Brush two baking sheets with some of the melted butter substitute.

Unroll the filo dough and lay one sheet on a work surface. (Keep the remaining filo covered with a damp—not wet—towel as you work to prevent it from drying out and becoming brittle.) Brush the sheet with melted butter substitute. Stack a second sheet of filo on top and brush with melted butter substitute, then repeat the process with another sheet of filo, so you have three buttered layers.

With a sharp knife or pizza cutter, cut the sheets lengthwise into 3-inch-wide strips. Cut the pieces crosswise in half, so you end up with 6 pieces. Place a heaping tablespoon of the kale-ricotta filling near the bottom of one filo strip. Fold the sides over, then fold the bottom up to encase the filling. Tightly roll up the filo away from you, to form a cigar-shaped spanakopita. Place on one of the prepared baking sheets, seam side down, and cover with plastic wrap while you fill and roll the remaining strips. Repeat the process until all of the filo sheets are layered, cut, filled, and rolled.

Brush the tops of the spanakopita cigars with the remaining melted butter substitute. Bake for 20 to 30 minutes, until crisp and golden. Serve hot or warm, with the harissa sauce, dotted with the mint oil, on the side for dipping.

HARISSA SAUCE

MAKES 1½ CUPS

Harissa gives this fresh tomato sauce a vibrant kick, without being overly hot or spicy.

2 tablespoons Earth Balance
    butter stick

2 pints cherry tomatoes, stemmed

1 shallot, chopped

2 garlic cloves, chopped

Kosher salt and freshly ground
    black pepper

¾ cup dry white wine

2½ tablespoons nutritional yeast
    flakes (see Note, page 6)

2 tablespoons harissa spice mix
    (see Note, page 4)

Put a large sauté pan over medium heat and add the butter substitute. When it has melted, add the tomatoes, shallot, and garlic, season with salt and pepper, and cook, stirring, until the tomatoes soften and collapse, 8 to 10 minutes.

Pour in the wine and cook until the liquid is almost evaporated, about 2 minutes. Stir in the nutritional yeast flakes and remove from the heat.

Working in batches, carefully ladle the mixture into a blender, filling it no more than halfway, and adding half the harissa spice mix and a pinch of salt and pepper to each batch. (If you have an immersion blender, this is a great time to use it.)

CONTINUED

Puree the sauce for a few seconds, until completely smooth (be sure to hold down the lid with a kitchen towel for safety). Pour the sauce through a fine-mesh strainer to remove the solids.

The sauce keeps covered in the refrigerator for up to 5 days; reheat gently before serving.

MINT OIL
MAKES ½ CUP

1 cup fresh mint leaves with
  tender stems
½ cup extra-virgin olive oil
⅛ teaspoon kosher salt

Herb-infused oils are a quick way to add flavor to a dish. Blanching and shocking the mint first helps it retain its vibrant color. This recipe also works well with fresh basil or parsley.

Bring a medium pot of water to a boil over high heat. Prepare an ice bath by filling a large bowl halfway with water and adding a tray of ice cubes.

Blanch the mint in the boiling water for about 20 seconds and then, using a slotted spoon, transfer to the ice bath to cool quickly. Drain again, wrap the mint in cheesecloth or a dish towel, and twist it tightly to wring out the excess liquid.

Put the mint in a blender and pour in the oil. Puree until well blended and dark green, about 2 minutes. Pour the oil through a fine-mesh strainer into a bowl or container, pressing down on the mint with the back of a wooden spoon to extract as much flavor as possible; discard the leaves. Season the herb oil with the salt.

BALSAMIC-ROASTED MUSHROOMS WITH SHALLOTS AND TOASTED MARCONA ALMONDS SERVES 4

MUSHROOMS

2 pounds mixed mushrooms,
    such as cremini and shiitake,
    stemmed, wiped of grit,
    and quartered
4 large shallots, halved
    lengthwise and cut crosswise
    into large slices
3 tablespoons extra-virgin olive oil
¼ cup Balsamic Reduction
    (page 271)
¼ teaspoon red pepper flakes
Kosher salt and freshly ground
    black pepper

1 tablespoon extra-virgin olive oil
1 shallot, minced
4 garlic cloves, minced
½ cup dry sherry
2 tablespoons Balsamic Reduction
    (page 271)
¼ cup fresh mint leaves, hand-torn,
    plus more for garnish
¼ cup fresh flat-leaf parsley leaves,
    hand-torn, plus more for garnish
4 fresh dill sprigs, hand-torn, plus
    more for garnish
4 fresh chives, sliced into 1-inch
    pieces, plus more for garnish
Kosher salt and freshly ground
    black pepper
¼ cup toasted Marcona almonds
    or Rosemary-Fried Almonds
    (page 9), smashed with a mallet
    or heavy pan

Roasted mushrooms alone can be satisfying, but adding a balsamic reduction and fresh herbs makes them special. Full of earthy flavor and umami, the mushrooms soak up the rich flavor of the vinegar, which becomes even more concentrated as they roast. Serve this as a main course or a hearty side.

To prepare the mushrooms: Preheat the oven to 400°F.

Put the mushrooms and shallots in a mixing bowl and drizzle with the oil. Pour in the balsamic reduction, season with the red pepper flakes, salt, and black pepper, and turn the mushrooms and shallots over so they are well coated. Spread the vegetables out in a single layer on a baking sheet and roast for 20 to 25 minutes, until they are tender and deep brown. Set aside. (The roasted mushrooms and shallots can be prepared a couple of hours in advance, covered, and held at room temperature.)

Put a large sauté pan over medium heat and coat with the oil. When the oil is hot, add the roasted mushrooms and shallots, toss in the minced shallot and garlic, and cook, stirring, until the shallot and garlic soften, about 1 minute. Add the sherry and balsamic reduction and cook, stirring, until the liquid has evaporated, about 2 minutes. Remove from the heat and add the mint, parsley, dill, and chives, tossing to distribute them evenly. Season with salt and black pepper.

Transfer to a serving bowl or individual plates and scatter the almonds on top. Top with more herbs and serve warm.

RAPINI WITH BLACK GARLIC, SHERRY VINEGAR, AND TOASTED HAZELNUTS SERVES 4

3 tablespoons grapeseed oil

6 black garlic cloves (see Note, page 54), sliced

2 garlic cloves, minced

½ shallot, minced

½ teaspoon red pepper flakes

Kosher salt and freshly ground black pepper

2 bunches (about 2 pounds) rapini (broccoli rabe), stems trimmed, or broccolini (see headnote)

¼ cup sherry vinegar

¼ cup Vegetable Stock (page 268) or store-bought stock

Juice of ½ lemon

¼ cup hazelnuts, toasted (see Note, page 44) and chopped

Zest of 1 lemon, removed with a zester

Rapini, also known as broccoli rabe, is one of those vegetables that you either love or hate. Scot and I are huge fans of the green's slightly bitter edge, which begs to be balanced with other bold ingredients, such as black garlic. If you can't get your hands on rapini, broccolini or regular broccoli will work well in this dish too. Rather than serve the rapini on its own, you could toss it with dried or fresh linguine (see page 159) for a main course. Serve with a cold glass of Pinot Grigio.

Put a large sauté pan over medium heat and add the oil. When the oil is hot, add the black garlic, minced garlic, and shallot, season with the red pepper flakes, salt, and black pepper, and cook, stirring, until fragrant, about 1 minute. Add the rapini and toss until it begins to wilt and is evenly coated with the garlic mixture. Pour in the vinegar, stock, and lemon juice and cook and toss until the rapini is tender and the liquid is reduced to a thin sauce, 1 to 2 minutes.

Transfer the rapini to a serving bowl, garnish with the nuts and strands of lemon zest, and serve.

SPICED
CHICKPEAS SERVES 4

2 cups dried chickpeas
(garbanzo beans), soaked
overnight in cold water, or
two 15-ounce cans chickpeas,
drained and rinsed

1 teaspoon ground cumin

1 teaspoon red pepper flakes

½ teaspoon cayenne

½ teaspoon kosher salt

½ teaspoon freshly ground
black pepper

6 tablespoons grapeseed oil

½ shallot, minced

2 garlic cloves, minced

Juice of ½ lemon

1 tablespoon dry sherry

1 cup Scoty's Marinara Sauce
(page 275) or store-bought sauce

Chopped fresh flat-leaf parsley,
for garnish

With high levels of fiber and protein, there's no question that chickpeas are good for you. Sadly, though, they often fall short in the flavor department, ending up bland or, even worse, mealy. Scot and I are huge lovers of spicy food, so we tinkered around with ideas until we produced this dish, which packs a powerful punch of cumin, cayenne, and red pepper flakes. The marinara sauce added at the end gives the chickpeas a terra-cotta hue.

These spiced chickpeas pair well with flatbreads, rice, and even potato dishes. For a crunchy snack, season the chickpeas as directed and roast until dry on the outside and slightly tender in the middle, 30 to 35 minutes. If you are using dried chickpeas, which I recommend, you will need to soak them overnight.

If using dried chickpeas, drain and rinse them and transfer to a large pot. Add water to cover by 1 inch and bring to a boil, then simmer over medium-low heat until the chickpeas are tender, about 1½ hours. Drain and rinse. (The chickpeas can be cooked a day ahead and refrigerated, covered.)

Preheat the oven to 425°F.

Combine the chickpeas, cumin, red pepper flakes, cayenne, salt, and black pepper in a mixing bowl, drizzle with ¼ cup of the oil, and toss to coat. Spread the chickpeas out on a baking sheet in a single layer and roast, shaking the pan from time to time, for 20 to 25 minutes, until the chickpeas are firm and dry. Set aside to cool. (The roasted chickpeas can be prepared a couple of hours in advance, covered, and held at room temperature.)

Put a large sauté pan over medium heat and add the remaining 2 tablespoons oil. When the oil is hot, stir in the shallot and garlic and cook, stirring, until soft, about 2 minutes. Add the chickpeas, tossing to heat through. Stir in the lemon juice, sherry, and marinara sauce and cook, stirring, until the chickpeas are well coated and the sauce is hot, about 2 minutes.

Mound the chickpeas in a shallow serving bowl, top with chopped parsley, and serve warm.

ARTICHOKE OYSTERS WITH TOMATO BÉARNAISE AND KELP CAVIAR SERVES 4 TO 6

2 lemons, halved

4 large artichokes
(about 3 pounds), rinsed

1 tablespoon Earth Balance
butter stick

1 shallot, chopped

1 garlic clove, minced

Kosher salt and freshly ground
black pepper

¾ cup Vegetable Stock (page 268)
or store-bought stock

½ cup dry white wine

½ cup Cashew Cream (page 264)

¼ cup nutritional yeast flakes
(see Note, page 6)

Rock or ice cream salt, for serving

Fried Oyster Mushrooms
(recipe follows)

Tomato Béarnaise (recipe follows)

2 tablespoons Cavi-art black
seaweed caviar (see Note,
page 132)

1 ounce dried seaweed salad mix,
such as SeaSnax, or a mix of
wakame, agar, and suginori,
reconstituted, for garnish

Without question, artichoke oysters are *the* signature dish of Cross-roads. This tongue-in-cheek dish evokes the appearance and flavor of oysters on the half shell. We incorporate the entire artichoke: The base of the dish is bright-green artichoke leaves, used in lieu of oyster shells, which are plated on a bed of rock salt to simulate the classic raw bar presentation. The leaves are dolloped with a whipped artichoke heart puree and topped with crispy nori-scented oyster mushrooms that stand in for the oysters. For complete decadence, the dish is bathed in yellow tomato béarnaise and garnished with jet-black seaweed caviar. Visually, texturally, and flavor-wise, this is definitely a conversation starter.

While there are several different components, the dish isn't difficult to pull off, though it does take time to prepare. (The cashew cream needs to be prepared a day in advance, for example.) Your guests will be blown away.

To prepare the artichoke hearts: Fill a large bowl halfway with water. Squeeze in the lemon juice, and toss the lemon halves into the water too. Remove and discard the small artichoke leaves at the base of each artichoke and then the tough outer leaves. Using a chef's knife, cut off the top 1 inch of each artichoke crown. Then snap off or cut off all of the remaining large leaves with kitchen shears and put them in the lemon water. You should have 20 to 24 large leaves. These leaves are your "oyster shells." Set aside.

Working with one artichoke at a time, use a vegetable peeler to trim off the tough outer part of the stem, to reveal the tender inside. Cut off the stem, coarsely chop it, and put in the lemon water. Run a paring knife around the base of the artichoke to remove any tough green parts or bits of leaves. Cut the artichoke in half. Using a sharp spoon or a melon baller, scoop out the spiky purple center leaves and fuzzy choke inside and discard. Transfer the prepared artichoke hearts to the lemon water as you work to keep them from oxidizing and turning brown.

CONTINUED

Bring a pot of lightly salted water to a boil over high heat. Add the artichoke leaves and simmer until tender, about 10 minutes. Drain and set aside in the refrigerator.

Meanwhile, remove the prepared artichokes from the lemon water, pat dry, and coarsely chop.

Put a small pot over medium heat and add the butter substitute. When it has melted, add the chopped artichoke hearts and stems, shallot, and garlic and cook until tender but without any color, about 10 minutes. Season with salt and pepper.

Add the stock, wine, cashew cream, and nutritional yeast flakes and simmer, stirring frequently, until the liquid is reduced by half, about 8 minutes.

Carefully transfer the artichoke mixture to a food processor and process until chunky-smooth. Season with salt and pepper. Cover to keep warm.

To serve: Spread the rock salt on a serving platter. Arrange the artichoke leaves decoratively on the salt. Spoon a small dollop of the artichoke puree on the meaty end of each leaf, then set a fried oyster mushroom on the puree and pour some tomato béarnaise on top. Garnish each artichoke oyster with a small dollop of the caviar and some seaweed. Serve immediately.

SEAWEED CAVIAR

Formulated to resemble Beluga caviar, Cavi-art, or seaweed caviar, is a seaweed-based delicacy that looks and tastes like the real thing. The tiny black beads burst with a clean, briny flavor and texture that "pops" in your mouth, much like fish eggs. Cavi-art is available online and in gourmet markets.

FRIED OYSTER MUSHROOMS

MAKES ABOUT 2 CUPS

BATTER

½ cup Cashew Cream (page 264)

2 tablespoons filtered water

1 tablespoon toasted nori flakes,
    finely ground

1 teaspoon kosher salt

½ teaspoon freshly ground
    black pepper

6 ounces oyster mushrooms
    (about 28), stems trimmed, wiped
    of grit, and cut into 1-inch pieces

1 cup yellow cornmeal or polenta
    (not quick-cooking)

1 cup rice flour

½ teaspoon kosher salt, plus more
    to taste

¼ teaspoon freshly ground
    black pepper, plus more to taste

Expeller-pressed canola oil, for
    deep-frying

With a meaty texture like oysters, these little mushroom bites are also good for snacking. Serve with Cocktail Sauce (page 119) for dipping. The cashew cream needs to be prepared a day in advance, so plan accordingly.

To prepare the batter: Put the cashew cream in a bowl and add the water, ground nori, salt, and pepper. Stir the batter to combine; it should be smooth and not gloppy in the slightest. If you have time, set aside for 10 minutes to let the flavors meld.

Add the mushrooms to the batter, gently turning the pieces over with your hands until thoroughly coated. Set aside.

Put the cornmeal in a food processor and process to a fine powder. Transfer to a large mixing bowl, add the rice flour, salt, and pepper, and toss to distribute the ingredients evenly.

Using a slotted spoon, working in batches, scoop the mushrooms from the batter, letting the excess drip back into the bowl, add to the cornmeal mixture, and toss with your hands until evenly coated on all sides. Transfer the breaded mushrooms to a strainer set over a bowl, or work over the sink, and shake off the excess cornmeal. This is a key step to ensure that the cornmeal crust is light and not clumpy whatsoever. (All of this can be prepared up to 2 hours in advance. Arrange the breaded mushrooms in a single layer on a baking sheet and refrigerate, uncovered. Allow the mushrooms to come to room temperature before frying.)

Heat 2 inches of oil to 325°F in a deep cast-iron skillet or a heavy saucepan. Working in batches, add the mushrooms to the hot oil and fry, carefully turning with tongs, until golden brown and crispy on all sides, about 2 minutes. Remove the cooked mushrooms to a paper towel–lined platter to drain. Season lightly with salt and pepper while still hot and serve.

TOMATO BÉARNAISE

MAKES 2 CUPS

2 large yellow tomatoes, cored

Extra-virgin olive oil

Kosher salt and freshly ground
  black pepper

½ cup dry white wine

3 tablespoons white wine vinegar

1 shallot, chopped

2 tablespoons minced
  fresh tarragon

½ teaspoon whole black
  peppercorns

¼ cup Cashew Cream (page 264)

1 tablespoon nutritional yeast flakes
  (see Note, page 6)

⅛ teaspoon Kala Namak salt, such
  as Frontier (see headnote)

2 tablespoons cold Earth Balance
  butter stick, cut into chunks

"Don't get saucy with me, Béarnaise" is one of my favorite lines from Mel Brooks's *History of the World*. If you haven't seen it, you must. The key to this "eggy" béarnaise is Indian Kala Namak salt, which is high in sulfur, so it smells and tastes curiously like eggs. The cashew cream needs to be prepared a day in advance.

Preheat the oven to 350°F.

Put the tomatoes in a small baking pan, drizzle with oil, and season generously with kosher salt and pepper. Cover the pan tightly with aluminum foil. Roast the tomatoes for 20 to 25 minutes, until soft. Set aside. (The roasted tomatoes can be prepared a couple of hours in advance, covered, and held at room temperature.)

Combine the wine, vinegar, shallot, tarragon, and peppercorns in a small saucepan, bring to a simmer over medium heat, and cook until the liquid is reduced by half, about 10 minutes. Pass the wine reduction through a fine-mesh strainer to remove the solids. You should have about ¼ cup.

Transfer the wine reduction to a blender and add the roasted tomatoes, cashew cream, nutritional yeast flakes, Kala Namak salt, 2 teaspoons oil, and the butter substitute. Blend on low speed to break down the tomatoes, then increase the speed to high and blend until the sauce is thick enough to coat the back of a spoon; add 1 teaspoon water if the sauce becomes too thick. Strain the sauce to remove any bits of tomatoes and give it a smooth texture. Season with kosher salt and pepper and serve, or set aside, covered, in a warm spot until needed.

OVER-ROASTED OKRA ^{WITH} CALABRESE PEPPERS ^{AND} PICKLED SCALLIONS

OVEN-ROASTED OKRA WITH CALABRESE PEPPERS AND PICKLED SCALLIONS SERVES 4

1 pound fresh or frozen okra
(about 32), rinsed under cool
water to thaw if frozen,
halved lengthwise

3 tablespoons grapeseed oil

Kosher salt and freshly ground
black pepper

Pinch of red pepper flakes

1 shallot, minced

2 garlic cloves, minced

3 jarred Calabrese peppers packed
in oil (see Note), such as Frutto
d'Italia, stemmed, halved
lengthwise, seeded, and chopped

Pinch of unrefined cane sugar

2 tablespoons sherry vinegar

3 pickled scallions (page 10), sliced

¼ cup Rosemary-Fried Almonds
(page 9) or toasted Marcona
almonds, smashed with a mallet
or heavy pan

I love okra: pickled, fried, and, especially, roasted. Oven-roasting okra changes its texture completely and adds a charred flavor. By hollowing out the centers of the okra before you roast it, you do away with the seeds and membranes, the culprits for the slimy texture. To finish the dish, pickled scallions and almonds add brine and crunch.

Preheat the oven to 450°F.

Run a demitasse spoon, a teaspoon, or a small melon baller down the inside of each piece of okra from top to bottom to remove the seeds and membranes; the hollowed-out halves should look like canoes.

Put the okra on a large baking sheet, drizzle with 2 tablespoons oil, and toss to coat. Spread out in a single layer and season with salt, black pepper, and the red pepper flakes. Roast, shaking the pan from time to time, for 15 to 20 minutes, until the okra is lightly charred. Set aside. (The roasted okra can be prepared a couple of hours in advance, covered, and held at room temperature.)

Put a large sauté pan over medium heat and coat with the remaining tablespoon oil. When the oil is hot, add the shallot and garlic and cook, stirring, until tender, about 1 minute. Add the roasted okra, chopped peppers, and sugar, tossing to coat. Remove from the heat and stir in the vinegar and pickled scallions.

Transfer the okra to a platter and scatter the almonds on top. Serve warm.

CALABRESE PEPPERS

Long, red chili peppers from Calabria, Italy, these add a fiery edge to any dish. Spicy, fruity, and subtly smoky, they have a complex flavor. You can find them jarred in oil in Italian markets or the condiment section of fine grocery stores. If they are not available, substitute jarred cherry peppers.

PAPAS ARRUGADAS (SPANISH WRINKLED POTATOES) WITH PARSLEY VINAIGRETTE SERVES 4 TO 6

2 pounds small potatoes, preferably
Peewee, marble, or baby
new, scrubbed
1 cup kosher salt
Parsley Vinaigrette (recipe follows)

Papas arrugadas are a Spanish tapas bar staple. I learned this authentic recipe for the wrinkled potatoes from renowned Basque gourmand, educator, and journalist Mikel Ceberio. He and I met a few years ago through a mutual friend, restaurateur Frank Leon. Frank and I visited Mikel in Bilbao, a wonderful city in the Basque country north of Barcelona that is home to scores of *txokos* (pronounced "cho-kos")—gentlemen's gastronomic social clubs of sorts—where distinguished members gather to talk food and politics, cook, play cards, and drink copious amounts of regional wine. When Mikel revealed to the other chefs, farmers, and vintners that I was *vegano*—no *pesce*, no *pollo*, no *carne*, no *jamón*, no *queso*—they looked baffled. On the final morning of our excursion, Mikel took Frank and me to his private *txoko*, which he opened just for us, and taught us how to prepare perfect papas arrugadas.

The recipe requires only the most basic ingredients—small potatoes, salt, and water. Simply, you boil the potatoes in their skins with an ample amount of salt until all of the water evaporates. Amazingly, they're not overly salty; the salt in the water draws out the starch in the potatoes, rather than being absorbed. The result is tender potatoes coated in a layer of salt that gives them a dusty look, with moist, perfectly cooked interiors and soft, salted skins.

Put the potatoes in a wide shallow pot, or a paella pan if you have one; it's key that the pan hold the potatoes in a single layer so the salt can penetrate them evenly. Sprinkle the salt over the potatoes and add just enough filtered water to cover. Bring to a boil over medium-high heat, then reduce the heat and simmer, uncovered, until the potatoes are fork-tender and most or all of the water has evaporated, about 45 minutes.

Tip out any remaining water and keep the potatoes over low heat for a few minutes, turning them over in the pan, until they're completely dry, wrinkled with brown spots, and covered with a fine coating of salt.

Using a pastry brush or clean dish towel, brush off the excess salt. Pile the potatoes on a serving platter, crack them open using a fork, and pour the vinaigrette over the top. Serve hot or warm.

PARSLEY VINAIGRETTE

MAKES 1 CUP

2 cups packed coarsely chopped
   fresh flat-leaf parsley

Juice of 1 lemon

1 tablespoon sherry vinegar

1 garlic clove, crushed

½ shallot, coarsely chopped

½ teaspoon agave nectar

½ teaspoon smoked paprika

½ cup extra-virgin olive oil

Kosher salt and freshly ground
   black pepper

Similar to green Spanish mojo sauce, this light citrusy parsley sauce gets its smoky heat from Spanish paprika. It is also good over sliced fresh tomatoes or grilled corn on the cob.

Put the parsley, lemon juice, and vinegar in the bowl of a food processor and pulse until the parsley is bright green and coarsely chopped, scraping down the sides of the bowl as needed. Add the garlic, shallot, agave, and paprika and pulse again to combine. With the motor running, pour in the oil in a steady stream, making sure it directly hits the blade (this is the best way to distribute the oil and emulsify it evenly and quickly), and process until the mixture is thick and well combined but not completely smooth; you want a little texture. Season with salt and pepper. The vinaigrette can be made ahead and kept covered in the refrigerator for up to 5 days; stir before serving.

SWEET POTATO LATKES
WITH SPIKED APPLESAUCE

SERVES 4; MAKES TWELVE 4-INCH PANCAKES

1 tablespoon Ener-G powdered egg
   replacer (see Note, page 143)

1 cup filtered water

½ cup ground chia seeds

1 onion

2 sweet potatoes
   (about 1½ pounds), peeled

1 russet (baking) potato
   (about \½ pound), peeled

Kosher salt and freshly ground
   black pepper

2 tablespoons rice flour

10 fresh chives, finely chopped,
   plus more for garnish

Expeller-pressed canola oil,
   for frying

Spiked Applesauce (recipe follows)

Latkes are found on every Hanukkah holiday table. These irresistible potato pancakes are made the same way my mother makes them, but without the eggs. I added sweet potatoes for color and a touch of sweetness. If you want lacy latkes with rough, crispy edges, you need to shred the potatoes into long strands. A food processor with a large shredding blade will make this go faster, but an old-fashioned box grater will perform the job just as well. Serve with the spiked applesauce or with Almond Greek Yogurt (page 263), or with Cavi-art black seaweed caviar (see Note, page 132) for a more elegant dish.

Preheat the oven to 250°F. Put a wire rack on a baking sheet and place in the oven.

Whisk the egg replacer, water, and ground chia seeds in a bowl until they have the consistency of beaten eggs. Set aside.

Using the large shredding blade of a food processor, shred the onion into long, thin ribbons. Transfer to a mixing bowl. Shred the sweet potatoes and russet potato in the food processor and add to the bowl. Toss the potatoes with the onions as you go to keep them from discoloring. (If you do not have a food processor with a large shredding blade, use the large holes of a box grater, grating down the length of the onion and potatoes to get long strands.)

Wrap the shredded potatoes and onion in a large square of cheese-cloth or a dish towel and twist it tightly to wring out the excess liquid. Put the potatoes and onion in a clean bowl and season generously with salt and pepper. Fold in the egg replacement mixture, along with the flour and chives, to bind the mixture together, making sure the ingredients are thoroughly combined.

Put a large cast-iron or nonstick skillet over medium heat, add ¼ inch of oil, and heat until hot. Working in batches, spoon about ¼ cup of the potato mixture into the hot oil for each latke, pressing lightly with a spatula to form 4-inch pancakes that are about ¼ inch thick. Take care not to overcrowd the pan.

CONTINUED

Fry, turning once, until crispy and golden, 3 to 4 minutes on each side. Transfer the fried latkes to the rack on the pan in the oven to keep warm while you cook the remaining batter, adding more oil as needed.

Season the latkes with salt and serve immediately with the applesauce, garnished with chopped chives.

ENER-G EGG REPLACER

Omitting the almighty egg in recipes can lead to serious cooking disasters. Vegan egg replacer powder is a great stand-in for eggs in most recipes where heat is involved. This binding powder consists of a blend of potato and tapioca starch, vegetable gum, and a leavener. It is also wheat-, dairy-, and cholesterol-free.

SPIKED APPLESAUCE

MAKES 2 CUPS

3 Gala or Fuji apples, peeled, cored, and coarsely chopped

3 Granny Smith apples, peeled, cored, and coarsely chopped

Juice of 1 lemon

2 tablespoons light brown sugar, or to taste

2 cinnamon sticks

$\frac{1}{8}$ teaspoon kosher salt

2 tablespoons brandy or unfiltered apple juice

Cooking sweet and tart apples, cinnamon, a touch of sugar, and a nip of brandy embodies the perfect smell of fall. You can spoon this applesauce over vanilla or caramel ice cream too. Any leftovers will keep covered in the refrigerator for up to 1 week.

Put the apples in a Dutch oven or other large pot set over medium heat and add the lemon juice, sugar, cinnamon, and salt. Cover the pot and simmer, stirring occasionally to mash up the apples, until the apples release their juices and completely break down, 20 to 25 minutes. If the apples seem dry, add a few tablespoons of filtered water and continue to cook until tender. Taste the applesauce for sweetness; it should be tart-sweet, but if you want it sweeter, add more sugar.

Stir in the brandy (or apple juice) and simmer for a few more minutes to cook off the alcohol. Remove from the heat and discard the cinnamon sticks.

Mash the apples with a potato masher or puree with an immersion blender until smooth. Serve warm, at room temperature, or cold.

SPAGHETTI SQUASH NOCE MOSCATA SERVES 4

1 spaghetti squash (about
2½ pounds), halved
lengthwise and seeds and
membranes removed
2 tablespoons extra-virgin olive oil
Kosher salt and freshly ground
black pepper
4 tablespoons (½ stick) Earth
Balance butter stick
1 shallot, minced
4 garlic cloves, minced
¼ teaspoon freshly grated nutmeg
6 tablespoons dry sherry
2 cups Scoty's Marinara Sauce
(page 275) or store-bought sauce
Chopped fresh flat-leaf parsley,
for garnish
¼ cup Walnut Parmesan (page 267)

If Scot could be reborn, he'd surely come back as Italian; his passion for the cuisine pumps through his veins. When he was the chef at Johnny's, a trattoria in Ohio, he turned out plate after plate of fettuccine Alfredo. The rich white sauce starts with butter, shallots, garlic, and freshly grated nutmeg, but one day, instead of adding cream to the pan, he accidentally grabbed marinara sauce, which changed the sauce entirely. A signature dish was born, and Scot named it Noce Moscato, which means "nutmeg" in English.

Preheat the oven to 425°F.

Drizzle the flesh of the squash with the oil and season generously with salt and pepper. Place the squash halves cut side down in a 9-by-13-inch baking dish. Roast until the squash is golden and tender when pierced with a knife, about 45 minutes. Remove from the oven.

When the squash is cool enough to handle, use a fork to scrape the flesh toward the center to create long strands. Put the strands into a mixing bowl and set aside. (The squash can be prepared a couple of hours in advance, covered, and held at room temperature.)

Put a saucepan over medium heat and add 2 tablespoons of the butter substitute. When it has melted, add half of the shallot, half of the garlic, and the nutmeg and cook, stirring, until the butter substitute starts to brown, about 1 minute; keep a close eye so it doesn't burn. Pour in half of the sherry and let the alcohol burn off for about 1 minute. Add the marinara sauce, season with salt and pepper, and simmer for 3 to 5 minutes. Cover the sauce to keep warm.

Put a large sauté pan over medium heat and add the remaining 2 tablespoons butter substitute. When it has melted, add the remaining shallot, garlic, and sherry and cook, stirring, for 1 minute to soften. Add the spaghetti squash and sauté until well coated and heated through, 3 to 4 minutes. Season with salt and pepper.

Pool a ladleful of the sauce in the center of each of four individual plates. Using a pair of tongs, twirl one-quarter of the spaghetti squash tightly into a nest and mound on top of the sauce, like a pile of noodles. Repeat with the remaining squash. Top the squash with the remaining sauce and sprinkle with parsley and the Walnut Parmesan.

ROASTED FENNEL WITH CLEMENTINE BEURRE BLANC AND TOASTED BUCKWHEAT SERVES 4

1 pound cipollini onions (see Note, page 44) or 16 shallots

12 baby fennel bulbs (about 2½ pounds), tops removed and fronds reserved, bulbs halved lengthwise, leaving the cores intact

4 clementines or tangerines, sliced ½ inch thick, any seeds removed

Kosher salt and freshly ground black pepper

½ teaspoon red pepper flakes

3 tablespoons expeller-pressed coconut oil (see Note, page 148)

1 bunch fresh thyme

6 fresh oregano sprigs

1 cup buckwheat groats (see headnote)

Clementine Beurre Blanc (recipe follows)

The Italian pairing of fennel and orange is classic, and when the two are roasted together with onions, their natural sugars caramelize. Roasting transforms the fennel so that it becomes soft, mellow, and sweet, with just a hint of anise flavor. The clementines are sliced whole, so you're eating the fruit rind, pith and all, but roasting removes the bitterness from the skins, making them tender and marmalade-like.

Despite its name, buckwheat is not related to wheat at all, so it is gluten-free. Toasting the buckwheat gives it a nutty flavor and texture that adds a firm crunch to this sweet-savory dish.

Preheat the oven to 400°F.

To prepare the onions: Bring a large pot of lightly salted water to a boil over high heat. Prepare an ice bath by filling a large bowl halfway with water and adding a tray of ice cubes.

Blanch the onions in the boiling water for about 1 minute, then drain them and plunge into the ice bath to cool them quickly. Drain the onions again and peel them. Halve the onions crosswise.

Arrange the onions, fennel, and clementines in a baking pan, stacking and alternating them so they intermingle. Season with salt, black pepper, and the red pepper flakes. Drizzle the coconut oil over all. Scatter the thyme and oregano on top.

Cover the pan with aluminum foil and roast for 15 minutes, or until the fennel is fork-tender. Remove the foil and roast uncovered for 20 minutes, or until the onions, fennel, and clementines are charred in spots. (The onions, fennel, and clementines can be prepared a couple of hours in advance, covered, and held at room temperature.)

To prepare the buckwheat: Bring a pot of lightly salted water to a boil over high heat. Add the buckwheat, give it a couple of good stirs with a wooden spoon, and reduce the heat to medium.

CONTINUED

Simmer, uncovered, until the buckwheat is tender, about 10 minutes. Drain well.

Put a large sauté pan over medium-high heat. Add the buckwheat and toast, stirring constantly to keep the grains moving, until it is browned and smells nutty, 4 to 5 minutes.

To serve: Spread the toasted buckwheat on a serving platter. Arrange the roasted onions, fennel, and clementines on top. Drizzle with the beurre blanc and scatter the reserved fennel fronds on top.

COCONUT OIL

Coconut oil has gained popularity in recent years, showing up on many supermarket shelves. Unlike most other oils from plant sources, coconut oil solidifies at room temperature, with a thick, buttery texture. It is perfect for roasting vegetables, and it prevents the fennel and clementines in this recipe from drying out. Look for expeller-pressed refined coconut oil, such as Spectrum; it lacks the distinctive tropical odor and flavor of the unrefined, or virgin, variety and is essentially tasteless, so it won't overpower the flavors of whatever you're cooking.

CLEMENTINE BEURRE BLANC

MAKES 1 CUP

Juice of 2 clementines or tangerines
   (about ¼ cup)
¼ cup dry white wine
½ large shallot, minced
1 tablespoon white wine vinegar or
   champagne vinegar
8 tablespoons (1 stick) cold
   Earth Balance butter stick, cut
   into chunks
Kosher salt and freshly ground
   black pepper

Beurre blanc is a silky French butter sauce that works well with citrus. Try this sauce over roasted root vegetables.

Combine the clementine juice, wine, shallot, and vinegar in a small saucepan and bring to a boil, then reduce the heat to medium and simmer until the liquid is reduced to 2 tablespoons, about 8 minutes.

Turn down the heat to very low. Whisk in the butter substitute one chunk at a time, adding a new piece only as the previous one melts. Don't allow the sauce to become too hot, or it will separate; move the pan on and off the heat if necessary. If the sauce starts to break, remove from the heat, add an ice cube, and whisk until it cools down and comes back together. Continue whisking in the butter substitute until the sauce is fully emulsified and thick. Season with salt and pepper. Serve immediately.

CAULIFLOWER WITH OLIVES AND SUN-DRIED TOMATOES SERVES 4

2 heads cauliflower (1½ pounds
   each), stems and cores
   removed, florets chopped into
   1-inch pieces
4 tablespoons extra-virgin olive oil
Kosher salt and freshly ground
   black pepper
½ red onion, finely diced
2 celery stalks, thinly sliced on
   a diagonal
1 cup mixed Niçoise and
   Castelvetrano olives, pitted and
   coarsely chopped
8 sun-dried tomatoes in oil,
   drained and coarsely chopped
   (about ½ cup)
3 jarred Calabrese peppers packed
   in oil (see Note, page 137), such
   as Frutto d'Italia, stemmed,
   halved lengthwise, seeded,
   and chopped
3 garlic cloves, minced
3 tablespoons white
   balsamic vinegar
½ cup fresh flat-leaf parsley leaves,
   coarsely chopped
¼ cup pine nuts, toasted
Zest of 1 lemon, removed with
   a zester

This is one of those recipes that is all about chopping time but takes very little cooking time, so it's critical to have all of the ingredients properly prepped before the cooking process begins. The mix of olives, vinegar, peppers, sun-dried tomatoes, and lemon zest will transform the cauliflower, and finely chopping each of the supporting ingredients will ensure you get a taste of each one with every bite.

Preheat the oven to 450°F.

Put the cauliflower in a large mixing bowl. Drizzle with 3 tablespoons of the oil, season with salt and pepper, and toss to coat evenly. Spread the cauliflower out in a single layer on a large baking sheet and roast for 30 to 35 minutes, shaking the pan from time to time, until tender and slightly charred. Set aside. (The roasted cauliflower can be prepared a couple of hours in advance, covered, and held at room temperature.)

Put a large sauté pan over medium heat and coat with the remaining tablespoon oil. When the oil is hot, add the onion and celery and cook, stirring, until soft, about 2 minutes. Add the olives, sun-dried tomatoes, peppers, and garlic and cook, stirring, until tender, about 2 minutes. Add the roasted cauliflower, along with the vinegar, tossing to combine, and heat through, about 1 minute. Season with salt and pepper.

Transfer the cauliflower to a serving bowl or individual plates and scatter the parsley, pine nuts, and lemon zest on top. Serve warm.

OVEN-ROASTED ROMANESCO ^{WITH} ONION AGRODOLCE ^{AND} GRAPPA-SOAKED RAISINS SERVES 4 TO 6

½ cup grappa (see Note, page 155)

⅓ cup golden raisins

2 heads romanesco (about
   2 pounds), stems and
   cores removed, florets
   halved lengthwise

2 tablespoons extra-virgin olive oil

Kosher salt and freshly ground
   black pepper

1 pound cipollini onions (see Note,
   page 44) or 16 shallots

1 tablespoon Earth Balance
   butter stick

⅓ cup unrefined cane sugar

⅓ cup white balsamic vinegar

2 tablespoons pine nuts, toasted

1 jarred Calabrese pepper packed in
   oil (see Note, page 137) such as
   Frutto d'Italia, stemmed, halved
   lengthwise, seeded, and chopped

Romanesco is an Italian crossbreed of cauliflower and broccoli, readily identified by its striking appearance. Its spiral crown of psychedelic lime-green spheres is like a work of art. And every head forms slightly differently, so no two are alike. The unique shape of romanesco means it keeps its texture after cooking, making it far more crunchy than cauliflower or broccoli, although either can be substituted in this recipe. The cipollini onions are glazed with agrodolce, an Italian sweet-and-sour sauce made with balsamic vinegar and sugar. Substitute shallots if you can't find cipollini.

To prepare the raisins: Heat the grappa in a small saucepan over low heat until warm to the touch. Put the raisins in a small bowl and pour the grappa over them. Cover and let steep for 1 hour. The grappa will soak into the raisins and plump them.

Meanwhile, prepare the romanesco: Preheat the oven to 400°F.

Put the romanesco in a large mixing bowl. Drizzle with 1 tablespoon of the oil, season with salt and pepper, and toss to coat evenly. Spread the romanesco out in a single layer on a large baking sheet and roast for 30 to 35 minutes, shaking the pan from time to time, until tender and slightly charred. Set aside. (The roasted romanesco can be prepared a couple of hours in advance, covered, and held at room temperature.)

To prepare the onion agrodolce: Bring a large pot of lightly salted water to a boil over high heat. Prepare an ice bath by filling a large bowl halfway with water and adding a tray of ice cubes.

Blanch the onions in the boiling water for about 1 minute, then drain them and plunge into the ice bath to cool them quickly. Drain the onions again and peel them. Coarsely chop the onions and set aside.

Put a large sauté pan over medium-high heat and add the remaining 1 tablespoon oil and the butter substitute. When the butter substitute has melted, add the onions and cook, stirring occasionally, until starting to brown, about 5 minutes. Add the sugar and vinegar;

continue to sauté until the onions are caramelized, about 5 minutes. Pour in ½ cup filtered water and reduce the heat to medium-low. Cover and simmer until the onions are tender, thick, and jam-like, about 20 minutes.

Add the raisins to the onions, along with any remaining grappa, the pine nuts, and the red pepper, and toss to combine. Cook for another 2 to 3 minutes to cook off any remaining alcohol. Remove from the heat.

To serve: Arrange the roasted romanesco on a platter or individual plates. Spoon the onion agrodolce on top, being sure to divide the raisins and other goodies equally.

GRAPPA

Grappa is an Italian brandy, distilled from the seeds and skins left over after pressing grapes for wine making. With its high alcohol content, about 40 percent, the kick is intense and the flavor is potent. Like wine, grappa comes in many varieties and qualities. Grappa Moscato, made from Muscat grapes, is preferred for this recipe for its floral flavor. Grappa is available at premium wine and spirits retailers, generally ranging from $20 to $50 per bottle, or more. It is best stored in a cool, dark place, where it can keep for several years, although it will lose some fragrance as it stands.

ITALIAN BUTTER BEANS
WITH PAN-ROASTED KALE, SHERRY AGLIO OLIO, AND TOASTED PUMPKIN SEEDS SERVES 4

BEANS

1½ cups dried Italian butter beans
   or gigante, borlotti, or lupini
   beans (about ¾ pound), soaked
   in water overnight, drained,
   and rinsed
2 fresh thyme sprigs
1 bay leaf
1 garlic clove, smashed
½ teaspoon whole
   black peppercorns
¼ teaspoon baking soda
1 teaspoon kosher salt

3 tablespoons grapeseed oil
2 garlic cloves, minced
6 ounces baby kale or spinach
   (about 6 cups)
Kosher salt and freshly ground
   black pepper
¼ teaspoon red pepper flakes
¼ cup dry sherry
1 tablespoon nutritional yeast flakes
   (see Note, page 6)
¼ cup Vegetable Stock (page 268)
   or store-bought stock
¼ cup toasted pumpkin
   seeds (pepitas)
Chopped fresh flat-leaf parsley,
   for garnish

A rich source of protein, dried beans have played a vital role in the nutritional health of many cultures from ancient times to the present, and I'm always striving to create dishes that feature unique varieties. Italian butter beans are big and meaty with a creamy, buttery texture and flavor. You'll need to soak the beans overnight, so plan accordingly. Adding baking soda to the cooking water helps tenderize the beans and allows them to absorb the water more evenly. If you can't find butter beans, substitute any large white beans, such as gigante, borlotti, or lupini.

To prepare the beans: Put the beans in a medium pot, add the thyme, bay leaf, garlic, peppercorns, and baking soda, and pour in filtered water to cover by 1 inch. Bring to a boil, then reduce the heat to medium-low and simmer until the beans are nearly tender, about 1 hour. Stirring the beans during cooking can cause them to break apart; stir gently and only as needed.

Add the salt and continue to simmer until the beans are tender but still hold their shape, 30 to 40 minutes longer; add more water as needed to keep the beans submerged. Drain and rinse the beans. Pinch off the skins. (The beans can be prepared a day ahead and refrigerated, covered.)

Put a large sauté pan over medium heat and add the oil. When the oil is hot, add the garlic and cooked beans, tossing to combine. Add the kale, turning the leaves over with a spoon to incorporate. Season with salt, black pepper, and the red pepper flakes. When the kale begins to wilt, pour in the sherry and cook for 1 minute to evaporate some of the alcohol. Sprinkle in the nutritional yeast flakes and stir in the stock to loosen the sauce.

Transfer to a serving platter or individual plates and top with the pumpkin seeds and parsley.

ROASTED BABY PARSNIPS WITH SHERRY-MAPLE GLAZE AND CHANTERELLES SERVES 4

24 baby parsnips, trimmed, or
8 regular parsnips, root ends
trimmed and peeled

3 tablespoons extra-virgin olive oil

Kosher salt and freshly ground
black pepper

¼ cup pure maple syrup

2 tablespoons sherry vinegar

½ teaspoon red pepper flakes

2 tablespoons Earth Balance
butter stick

1 shallot, minced

2 garlic cloves, minced

½ pound chanterelles, wiped clean,
quartered if large

Finely chopped fresh flat-leaf
parsley, for garnish

Flaked sea salt, such as Maldon

Baby parsnips are so tender that you don't even need to peel them. (And if you did, there wouldn't be much vegetable left!) Parsnips have a sharp flavor reminiscent of parsley's and become incredibly sweet when roasted. Here they are drizzled with a glaze of maple syrup, a pinch of red pepper flakes for heat, and a splash of vinegar. Chanterelle mushrooms don't come cheap, but they add a woodsy flavor to this winter dish.

To prepare the parsnips: Preheat the oven to 400°F.

If using larger parsnips, peel and quarter them lengthwise so the pieces will be uniform in size and cook more evenly. Put the parsnips in a large mixing bowl, drizzle with 2 tablespoons of the oil, season with kosher salt and black pepper, and toss to coat evenly. Spread the parsnips out in a single layer on a large baking sheet and roast for about 20 minutes, shaking the pan from time to time, until tender and slightly charred. Set aside. (The roasted parsnips can be prepared a couple of hours in advance, covered, and held at room temperature. Reheat before serving.)

Meanwhile, prepare the glaze: Combine the maple syrup, vinegar, and red pepper flakes in a small saucepan and cook over medium-low heat, swirling the pan around occasionally, until the mixture is reduced and syrupy, about 10 minutes. Cover and hold warm.

To prepare the mushrooms: Put a large sauté pan over medium heat and add the remaining 1 tablespoon oil and the butter substitute. When the butter substitute has melted, add the shallot and sauté until soft but not browned, about 1 minute. Add the garlic, tossing to combine. Add the mushrooms and sauté, stirring frequently, until they lose their moisture, soften, and begin to brown, about 5 minutes. Remove from the heat.

To serve: Crisscross the parsnips on a platter, overlapping them just slightly. Drizzle with the maple glaze and top with the mushrooms. Scatter chopped parsley on top and season with flaked sea salt.

CREAMY POLENTA
WITH ROASTED CORN AND PORCINI MUSHROOM–BORDELAISE SAUCE SERVES 4

2 ears of corn

4 cups filtered water

2 teaspoons kosher salt

1½ cups finely ground yellow cornmeal or polenta (not quick-cooking)

2 tablespoons Earth Balance butter stick

½ cup unsweetened plain almond milk

2 tablespoons nutritional yeast flakes (see Note, page 6)

½ teaspoon freshly ground black pepper

Porcini Mushroom–Bordelaise Sauce (recipe follows)

Somewhere down the line, polenta picked up a reputation for being laborious to make. This is simply not true. Polenta doesn't take an hour to cook—25 to 30 minutes is plenty—and contrary to recipes that insist it must be stirred constantly, stirring it once every couple of minutes will do the job just fine. While stirring, though, be sure to run the spoon along the bottom and sides of the pot so the polenta doesn't stick and scorch. The individual grains should be tender yet retain a bit of texture, and the final consistency should be that of a thick soup.

To prepare the corn: Shuck the corn and pull off the corn silk strands; leave the stems on if you have them—they make great handles. Put the corn directly on a gas burner over high heat and char, turning often, until well blackened in spots but not completely burnt; the corn tends to pop like popcorn. (If you don't have a gas stove, roast the corn on a baking sheet in a preheated 400°F oven for 30 minutes, turning occasionally.) Remove the corn from the heat.

When the corn is cool enough to handle, using a sharp knife, cut off the stems and then cut off the kernels from the cobs. You should have about 2 cups kernels. Set aside.

To prepare the polenta: Bring the water and salt to a simmer in a large saucepan over medium heat. Gradually whisk in the cornmeal in a slow, steady stream, then reduce the heat to medium-low, switch to a wooden spoon, and cook, stirring often, until the polenta is very thick and pulls away from the sides of the pan, about 25 minutes.

Fold in the charred corn, reserving a handful for garnish, and cook and stir for 5 minutes to heat through. Remove from the heat and stir in the butter substitute, almond milk, and nutritional yeast flakes until incorporated. Season with the pepper.

To serve: Divide the polenta among shallow bowls, spoon the mushroom sauce over the top, and garnish with the reserved corn.

PORCINI MUSHROOM–BORDELAISE SAUCE MAKES 1½ CUPS

1 cup dry red wine, such as
    Cabernet Sauvignon or Syrah,
    plus a splash if needed

3 shallots, coarsely chopped

2 fresh thyme sprigs

1 bay leaf

1 tablespoon grapeseed oil

1 tablespoon Earth Balance
    butter stick

½ pound fresh porcini mushrooms,
    wiped of grit and sliced,
    or 1 ounce dried porcini,
    reconstituted (see Note)

Kosher salt and freshly ground
    black pepper

1 cup Demi-Glace (page 270) or
    store-bought demi-glace, such as
    More Than Gourmet

1 tablespoon finely chopped fresh
    flat-leaf parsley

1 teaspoon finely chopped
    fresh rosemary

¼ teaspoon unrefined cane sugar

A few years ago, Le Cordon Bleu, the French culinary school, invited me to teach master classes on vegetarian cooking as a guest instructor at all of their U.S. campuses. It was a thrill to get the students interested in cooking things that they never had before. I developed plant-based versions of many classic dishes, among them vegan renditions of the five French mother sauces, including espagnole sauce and demi-glace. Try this bordelaise on grilled portobello mushrooms or mashed potatoes.

Combine the wine, shallots, thyme, and bay leaf in a small saucepan, bring to a simmer over medium heat, and gently simmer until the wine is reduced by half, to about ½ cup, 8 to 10 minutes.

Meanwhile, put a large sauté pan over medium heat and add the oil and butter substitute. When the butter substitute has melted, add the mushrooms, season with salt and pepper, and sauté until the mushrooms lose their moisture, soften, and begin to brown, about 8 minutes.

Strain the wine mixture into a medium saucepan; discard the solids. Put over low heat and stir in the demi-glace.

Fold the mushrooms, along with any liquid in the pan, into the sauce. Stir in the parsley, rosemary, and sugar and cook, stirring, for 2 minutes. Add a splash of red wine to brighten up the flavor of the sauce, if desired.

The sauce can be made up to 1 day in advance, covered, and refrigerated; reheat before serving.

PORCINI MUSHROOMS

Porcini mushrooms are a hallmark of Italian cuisine. With their meaty texture and earthy, somewhat nutty flavor, they are unequaled among mushrooms and lend themselves to countless dishes. If you can't get your hands on fresh porcini (which are quite expensive), dried porcini are very good and will add a chestnut-like flavor to this sauce.

To reconstitute dried porcini mushrooms: Put the dried mushrooms in a bowl and pour hot water over them to cover (here, about 2 cups). Soak for 30 minutes, or until the mushrooms soften. Carefully lift the mushrooms out of the soaking liquid with a fork, so as not to disturb the sediment settled at the bottom of the bowl. When reconstituted, 1 ounce dried porcini will equal about ½ cup.

SWEET CORN RISOTTO WITH BUTTERED LEEKS, CHERRY TOMATOES, AND TOMATO-SHERRY CREAM SAUCE SERVES 4

4 cups Vegetable Stock (page 268)
or store-bought stock

2 large leeks, white and pale green
parts only

2 tablespoons grapeseed oil

3 tablespoons Earth Balance
butter stick

1 shallot, thinly sliced

2 garlic cloves, minced

1 cup Arborio rice

¼ teaspoon kosher salt

⅛ teaspoon freshly ground
black pepper

1 cup dry sherry

2 ears of corn, shucked and kernels
cut from the cob, or 2 cups
thawed frozen corn kernels

8 cherry tomatoes, halved

½ cup Cashew Cream (page 264)

½ cup Scoty's Marinara Sauce
(page 275) or store-bought sauce

1 tablespoon nutritional yeast flakes
(see Note, page 6)

Chopped fresh flat-leaf parsley,
for garnish

¼ cup Walnut Parmesan (page 267)

Good risotto gets its creaminess from the starch in the rice, so the water or stock needs to be added slowly over time, and the rice is stirred constantly at each stage in the cooking process until all the water is absorbed and a velvety texture emerges. The cream—in this case, cashew cream—is added at the end.

Pour the stock into a medium saucepan and bring to a gentle simmer over low heat. Cover and keep warm.

Meanwhile, halve the leeks lengthwise and then cut crosswise into ½-inch slices. You should have about 2 cups sliced leeks. Put the sliced leeks in a colander and rinse really well under cool water, checking for dirt between the layers. Drain well.

Put a large deep sauté pan over medium heat and add the oil and 2 tablespoons of the butter substitute. When the butter substitute has melted, add the leeks, shallot, and garlic and cook, stirring with a wooden spoon, until the leeks are soft, about 3 minutes. Add the rice and stir for 1 to 2 minutes, until the grains are well coated and opaque. Season with the salt and pepper, add the sherry, and cook, stirring, for 2 minutes to evaporate some of the alcohol.

Pour in 1 cup of the warm stock and cook, stirring, until the rice has absorbed all of the liquid. Keep stirring while adding the stock little by little, allowing the rice to drink it in each time before adding more. This whole process should take about 20 minutes. You may not need all of the stock.

Fold in the corn and tomatoes and stir for 2 minutes to heat through. Stir in the cashew cream and marinara sauce and cook, stirring, until incorporated, about 2 minutes. Remove the risotto from the heat and stir in the remaining tablespoon of butter substitute and the nutritional yeast flakes.

Serve it immediately. Divide it among four plates and top with chopped parsley and the walnut Parmesan.

FIG CAPONATA WITH POLENTA FRIES

SERVES 4 TO 6 (MAKES 6 CUPS CAPONATA)

½ cup extra-virgin olive oil, plus
    more as needed
1 teaspoon red pepper flakes
1 celery stalk, cut into medium dice
1 onion, cut into medium dice
3 garlic cloves, minced
1 large Italian eggplant (about
    1 pound), cut into ½-inch cubes
2 cups Scoty's Marinara Sauce
    (page 275) or store-bought sauce
2 jarred roasted red peppers,
    drained, rinsed, and chopped
    (about ¾ cup)
8 dried figs, finely chopped (about
    ½ cup)
¼ cup pine nuts, toasted
3 tablespoons capers, drained
    and rinsed
2 tablespoons balsamic vinegar
1 tablespoon unrefined cane sugar
½ bunch fresh basil, leaves
    stripped from the stems and
    hand-torn
Kosher salt and freshly ground
    black pepper
Polenta Fries (recipe follows)
Fresh flat-leaf parsley, for garnish

Few dishes capture the soul of Sicily like caponata. With its blend of capers and balsamic vinegar, this chunky eggplant stew is a flavor explosion of sweet, salty, and tangy. It's traditionally made with raisins, but Scot adds figs. Serve it hot or at room temperature. This caponata will keep for several days in the fridge; also try it as a quick pasta sauce or spread on a sandwich.

Put a large saucepan over medium heat and add the oil and red pepper flakes. When the oil is hot, add the celery, onion, and garlic and cook, stirring, until softened, about 3 minutes. Add the eggplant and cook, tossing or stirring occasionally, until it softens and browns, 10 to 15 minutes.

Stir in the marinara sauce, then add the roasted red peppers, figs, pine nuts, capers, vinegar, sugar, and basil. Season with salt and black pepper and stir well. Lower the heat and slowly simmer until the sauce thickens slightly, about 15 minutes.

Crisscross the polenta fries on a serving platter or individual plates. Serve hot or at room temperature, with the fig caponata on the side or spooned on top. Garnish with parsley leaves.

POLENTA FRIES

SERVES 4 TO 6

4 cups filtered water

Kosher salt

2½ cups finely ground yellow
   cornmeal or polenta
   (not quick-cooking)

6 scallions, white and light green
   parts only, finely chopped

1 ear corn, shucked and kernels cut
   from the cob, or 1 cup thawed
   frozen corn kernels

2 tablespoons Earth Balance
   butter stick

½ cup unsweetened plain
   almond milk

2 tablespoons nutritional yeast
   flakes (see Note, page 6)

Freshly ground black pepper

1 cup rice flour

Expeller-pressed canola oil,
   for frying

This recipe takes polenta in a different direction from the soft, creamy pool of cornmeal most folks are familiar with. This is an ideal make-ahead recipe: prepare the polenta in the morning, chill it, and cut into sticks just before frying. Crisp on the outside and creamy inside, the polenta sticks, a twist on French fries, make a satisfying snack or finger food. Serve with the fig caponata or with Scoty's Marinara Sauce (page 275) for dipping.

Line an 8-by-11-inch baking dish with plastic wrap, leaving an overhang on the two long sides. Set aside.

Bring the water and 2 teaspoons salt to a simmer in a large saucepan over medium heat. Gradually whisk in 1½ cups of the cornmeal in a slow, steady stream, then reduce the heat to medium-low, switch to a wooden spoon, and cook, stirring often, until the polenta is very thick and pulls away from the sides of the pan, about 25 minutes.

Fold the scallions and corn into the polenta and cook, stirring, until slightly softened, about 5 minutes. Remove from the heat and stir in the butter substitute, almond milk, nutritional yeast flakes, and salt and pepper to taste until incorporated.

Pour the polenta into the prepared baking dish, spreading it evenly with a rubber spatula; it will be about ½ inch thick. Refrigerate, covered, until completely cool and firm, at least 1 hour, or, even better, overnight. It's important that the polenta sets up completely and gets quite dense so it's easy to cut into pieces that won't fall apart when you fry them. (The polenta can be made up to 2 days in advance and kept covered in the refrigerator.)

Grab the ends of the plastic wrap, lift the polenta out of the baking dish, and flip it onto a cutting board. Remove the plastic wrap. Cut the polenta crosswise into 4 strips, about 2½ inches wide, then cut the strips into 8 pieces each, about ¾ inch wide, so you end up with 32 fries.

Combine the remaining 1 cup cornmeal with the flour in a large mixing bowl, season with salt and pepper to taste, and toss to distribute the ingredients evenly. Dredge the fries in the cornmeal and rice flour mixture, turning to coat completely.

Heat 3 inches of oil to 350°F in a deep fryer or deep pot. (If you don't have a deep-fry thermometer, a good way to test the oil is to stick the end of a wooden spoon or chopstick in it. If bubbles circle around the end, you're good to go.)

Working in batches to avoid overcrowding and to keep the oil temperature constant, put the polenta fries in the fryer basket or a spider or other strainer, carefully lower into the hot oil, fry until golden brown and crispy, 3 to 5 minutes, then remove to a paper towel–lined platter to drain. Season lightly with salt while the fries are still hot.

Serve hot or at room temperature.

PASTA

PASTA DOUGH   174

CHIVE FETTUCCINE WITH ASPARAGUS,
MORELS, AND PROSECCO SAUCE   181

PAPPARDELLE BOLOGNESE   185

LINGUINE WITH BALSAMIC-ROASTED
MUSHROOMS AND TOMATO-BASIL
BUTTER SAUCE   189

ACORN SQUASH RAVIOLI WITH KALE
AND BLACK GARLIC BUTTER SAUCE   191

TORTELLINI WITH SUN-DRIED-TOMATO
RICOTTA AND SWEET PEAS   195

CAPPELLACCI WITH SPINACH
CREAM SAUCE   197

GRILLED GARDEN VEGETABLE
LASAGNA WITH PUTTANESCA SAUCE   201

FAVA BEAN AGNOLOTTI WITH PARSLEY
AND AGLIO OLIO SAUCE   205

GNOCCHI   209

If I had to choose one food to eat every day for the rest of my life, it would definitely be pasta. We make pasta fresh daily at Crossroads. We always have Pappardelle Bolognese (page 185) on the menu and a featured stuffed pasta of the night, like Acorn Squash Ravioli with Kale and Black Garlic Butter Sauce (page 191) or Fava Bean Agnolotti (page 205).

There is no rule that says fresh pasta must contain eggs. In fact, in southern Italy, most pasta dough is prepared without them. Eggless pastas are softer than those containing eggs and have a more supple, toothsome bite.

The idea of making fresh pasta may seem intimidating, but the process is pretty straightforward and I enjoy every step of it, from kneading the dough to rolling out the pasta sheets to filling and shaping stuffed pastas. Working with your hands is a rewarding experience; you fall into a rhythm whether working by yourself or with someone else.

No matter how good store-bought pasta can be, nothing compares to the pasta you prepare yourself and it makes a world of difference when it comes to turning out a top-notch dish. Our handmade pasta is full of character, with a silky-chewy texture, lots of flavor, and a bright-yellow color (from red palm oil). The dough can be rolled out and cooked right away or tightly sealed in plastic wrap and refrigerated or frozen.

To make the pastas in this chapter, you need only a few simple tools—a pasta machine and, for the stuffed pastas, ring cutters and a wheeled pasta cutter.

PASTA DOUGH MAKES 1 POUND

Half of a 14-ounce package firm tofu
  (see headnote), drained

1½ cups "00" pasta flour, plus more
  as needed

1½ cups semolina flour, plus more
  as needed

3 tablespoons red palm oil
  (see Note)

2 tablespoons filtered water, plus
  more if needed

½ teaspoon fine sea salt

Although these directions are quite detailed, making fresh pasta dough is not at all difficult. I actually find the process therapeutic, and using a food processor makes quick work of mixing the dough. Good pasta dough is firm, elastic, and easy to work with. Often the dough includes eggs as a binder; I use firm silken tofu, which has the custardy texture of flan and gives the dough structure while also adding some protein. It's virtually impossible to detect a difference between this and classic egg pasta dough. Do note that silken tofu is not packaged in tubs of water and sold in the refrigerator section like regular tofu; it's shelf stable and sold in boxes.

You will need a pasta maker to cut the pasta—either the manual kind or an attachment to your stand mixer. The dough can be cut and rolled out after its 1-hour rest in the refrigerator and cooked right away or tightly wrapped and stored in the refrigerator for up to 1 day or frozen for up to 1 month. Allow the dough to come to room temperature before you roll it out. Fresh-made pasta takes only a few minutes to cook; test for doneness by taking a bite.

Add the tofu, flours, oil, water, and salt to the bowl of a food processor and process until the flour is evenly moistened and crumbly; this will take about 10 seconds. Then continue to process until the dough comes together to form a loose ball and feels moist but not sticky, about 2 minutes. Pinch the dough to test its consistency: If the dough seems excessively sticky, add more "00" flour 1 tablespoon at a time, processing until just incorporated. If the dough is too dry, add a teaspoon or so of water. Dough is all about feel.

Remove the ball of dough from the food processor and wrap tightly in plastic wrap. (The buzz of the processor blades heats up the dough and makes it too soft to work with right away.) Let the dough rest in the refrigerator for at least 1 hour to firm it up and make it easier to roll out. (The dough can be refrigerated for up to 1 day or frozen for up to 1 month.)

Flour the work surface and your hands. Cut the chilled dough into 4 equal pieces. Working with one piece at a time (cover the others to prevent them from drying out), roll or press the pasta out on a lightly floured surface into a rough rectangle. Feed the dough through the widest setting of a pasta machine; pull and stretch the sheet of dough with the palm of your hand as it emerges from the rollers. Lightly dust both sides of the pasta with a little flour if needed. Run the dough through the machine 2 more times, and fold it into thirds when it is long enough. You'll feel the dough starting to become silky smooth. Then reduce the setting by one and crank the dough through again 2 or 3 times. Continue reducing the dial setting and rolling the dough through until the machine is at the second-to-narrowest setting (number 2 on most machines); the sheet should be about $1/16$ inch thick. Cut the long sheet into 2 workable pieces, put them on a baking sheet dusted with flour and semolina, and cover with a damp towel. Repeat with the remaining pieces of dough.

The dough should be cut or shaped shortly after being rolled out so it won't dry out. Or, to store the sheets of pasta, stack between pieces of wax paper, tightly wrap in plastic wrap, and freeze for up to 1 month.

VARIATION

CHIVE PASTA DOUGH

Add 1 bunch coarsely chopped chives (about $1/2$ cup) to the food processor once the dough has come together and process just to incorporate. Do not overmix; you should see green flecks through-out the dough.

RED PALM OIL

Not to be confused with palm kernel oil, natural red palm oil is pressed from the fruit of the oil palm tree. Extremely high in antioxidants, it is regarded as one of the most nutritious oils in the world. It has a deep, rich orange-red color that gives this pasta dough an egg-yolk-yellow color. Palm oil originated in tropical West Africa, but it is now harvested in South America and Asia as well. Unfortunately, many of the palm trees grown commercially in other countries are extremely destructive to the environment and are threatening the rainforests. Be sure to purchase *only* unprocessed palm oil that comes from West Africa.

Tips for Making Fresh Pasta

Here are some guidelines for successful homemade pasta-making.

Keep the Dough Covered

Pasta dough dries out quickly if left uncovered, which makes it difficult to work with and prone to tearing. Work with one piece of dough at a time, keeping the dough you are not working with covered tightly with plastic wrap.

Don't Overstuff the Pasta

It's tempting to overstuff pastas like tortellini and ravioli, because what we like about them is the tasty filling. But overstuffing makes the pasta tricky to seal and can result in dumplings that explode in the boiling water. Practice restraint, and stick to the amount of filling specified in the recipe.

Use Ample Flour

Pasta loves to stick to the baking sheet and to itself. Be sure to dust the baking sheet with a good amount of flour and semolina and lightly dust the dough too. And don't let filled pasta shapes touch each other once you've formed them.

Give Yourself Enough Time and Space

Making fresh pasta is not difficult, but it does take time. Give yourself at least a couple of hours to make an entire batch—and rope a few friends or family members into helping if you can! Start with a clean countertop, and clear plenty of space to spread out as you work.

Pasta 101

There are a few simple rules for cooking pasta perfectly every time.

Use Lots of Well-Salted Boiling Water

Bring a pot of heavily salted water to a rolling boil. A generous amount of salt in the water seasons the pasta internally as it absorbs liquid and swells. As a result, your pasta dish may require less salt overall.

Return the Water to a Boil Quickly

After you add the pasta, keep the heat on high to bring the water back to the boil as quickly as possible (put a lid on the pot if necessary). Then cook the pasta, uncovered, at a fast boil.

Stir During the First Minute or Two of Cooking to Prevent Sticking

This is the crucial time, when the surface of the pasta is still coated with sticky, glue-like starch. If you don't stir, the pieces of pasta can stick together. Frequent stirring with a wooden spoon will ensure the pieces move freely and help the pasta cook evenly.

Do Not Add Oil to the Cooking Water

Oil added to the cooking water will coat the pasta and keep the sauce from adhering to it. The sauce won't be absorbed and, as a result, the pasta will be flavorless.

Do Not Rinse

Rinsing the pasta after cooking cools the pasta and prevents it from absorbing the sauce; the starch remaining on cooked pasta helps the sauce cling. Just drain the pasta in a large colander standing in the sink and then shake it well to remove excess water.

Use the Cooking Water

It's always a good idea to reserve a bit of the cooking water when you drain the pasta to stir into the sauce. The small amount of starch left in the cooking water can thicken your sauce slightly while loosening it at the same time.

Do Not Oversauce

Toss pasta with just enough sauce to coat it to avoid a big puddle on the bottom of the plate. It's always best to add the pasta to the sauce, not the other way around.

CHIVE FETTUCCINE ^{WITH} ASPARAGUS, MORELS, ^{AND} PROSECCO SAUCE

SERVES 4 (MAKES 1 CUP SAUCE)

FETTUCCINE

"00" pasta flour, for dusting

1 pound Chive Pasta Dough
   (page 175) or store-bought dry
   eggless fettuccine

Semolina flour, for dusting

SAUCE

1 tablespoon extra-virgin olive oil

2 tablespoons Earth Balance
   butter stick

1 shallot, minced

3 garlic cloves, minced

1 small bunch asparagus (about
   ½ pound), tough ends trimmed
   and cut on the diagonal into
   ½-inch pieces

½ pound fresh morel mushrooms,
   cleaned and sliced, or 1 ounce
   dried morels, reconstituted
   (see Note, page 184)

Kosher salt and freshly ground
   black pepper

½ cup Prosecco or other
   sparkling wine

6 fresh chives, minced

4 fresh flat-leaf parsley
   sprigs, chopped

2 tablespoons nutritional yeast
   flakes (see Note, page 6) or
   Walnut Parmesan (page 267)

There's an old saying that "if it grows together, it goes together," and this springtime pasta is a perfect combination of seasonal ingredients. The flavorful morel mushrooms pair nicely with the nuanced, grassy asparagus. The Prosecco sauce, which is a snap to make, brings the whole dish together. If you somehow drink all of the bubbly before dinner, you can make the sauce with any dry white wine.

If using fresh pasta dough, make the fettuccine: Dust your work surface with flour, lay a sheet of pasta dough on it, and sprinkle with flour. Keep the remaining sheets covered. Using a rolling pin, roll the dough out slightly to make it more pliable. Trim the edges so they are straight.

Lightly dust a baking sheet with flour and semolina. Run the pasta sheet through the fettuccine-cutter on your pasta machine. Lightly dust the strands with flour and semolina. Coil the fettuccine into a nest and set on the baking sheet. Repeat with the remaining sheets of pasta, making sure to keep the pasta nests separated so they don't stick together. Allow the fettuccine to dry until a little firmer and less sticky, about 10 minutes. This will help prevent the pasta from clumping and sticking together when cooked. (The fettuccine can be stored in an airtight container or resealable plastic bags in the refrigerator for up to 1 day or in the freezer for up to 1 month. You do not need to thaw the fettuccine before cooking.)

Bring a large pot of salted water to a boil.

Meanwhile, prepare the sauce: Put a large sauté pan over medium heat and add the oil and butter substitute. When the butter substitute has melted, toss in the shallot and garlic and cook, stirring, until softened, about 1 minute. Add the asparagus and morels, season with salt and pepper, and toss until the asparagus and mushrooms are well coated, 1 to 2 minutes. Pour in the Prosecco, allowing it to bubble up, sprinkle in the chives and parsley, and cook the sauce down until reduced by half, about 2 minutes.

CONTINUED

When the water comes to a boil, add the pasta, give it a couple of good stirs with a wooden spoon, and cook until tender yet firm, 1½ to 2 minutes. Drain the pasta well, reserving ¼ cup of the starchy cooking water to use in the sauce if necessary.

Add the fettuccine to the sauce, tossing with tongs to coat. Season again with salt and pepper and toss to distribute evenly. If the sauce gets too thick, thin it with enough of the reserved pasta water so the fettuccine is thoroughly coated.

Divide the fettuccine among four plates or transfer to a pasta bowl and sprinkle with the nutritional yeast flakes. Serve immediately.

MOREL MUSHROOMS

Morel mushrooms are a springtime delicacy. Their earthy perfume marries well with other spring ingredients, especially asparagus and chives. When buying morels, look for ones that have a deep mushroom smell and feel firm; turn down any that have signs of mold or look shriveled or mushy. Morels have sponge-like crevices where dirt—and critters—tend to get trapped, making them the only mushrooms you really need to wash.

To clean, flush the centers of the morels with a steady stream of cold water, then put the morels in a large bowl of lightly salted cold water; the salt will help to draw out any impurities. Quickly swish the mushrooms around in the water, then lift them out, leaving behind any grit or insects in the bottom of the bowl, and lay them on a clean kitchen towel or layers of paper towels. Pat the mushrooms dry before slicing them, and check for dirt or other matter in the center and crevices as you work. Clean morels just before using, as they will absorb a bit of water in the cleaning process, making them more susceptible to mold if stored.

To reconstitute dried morel mushrooms: Put the dried mushrooms in a bowl and pour hot water over them to cover (here, about 2 cups). Soak for 30 minutes, or until the mushrooms soften. Carefully lift the mushrooms out of the soaking liquid with a fork, so as not to disturb the sediment settled at the bottom of the bowl. Coarsely chop the mushrooms. When reconstituted, 1 ounce dried morels will equal about ½ cup.

PAPPARDELLE BOLOGNESE

SERVES 4 TO 6 (MAKES 4 CUPS SAUCE)

PAPPARDELLE

"00" pasta flour, for dusting

1 pound Pasta Dough (page 174)
 or store-bought dry
 eggless pappardelle

Semolina flour, for dusting

SAUCE

One 13-ounce package Field Roast
 Italian-style vegan sausage

½ cup extra-virgin olive oil

2 tablespoons Earth Balance
 butter stick

2 carrots, finely chopped

2 celery stalks, finely chopped

1 red onion, finely chopped

2 garlic cloves, minced

⅛ teaspoon freshly grated nutmeg

Kosher salt and freshly ground
 black pepper

½ cup dry white wine

4 cups Scoty's Marinara Sauce
 (page 275) or store-bought sauce

1 cup Cashew Cream (page 264)

This recipe is 100 percent Scot's baby. When he was fresh out of culinary school, he landed a job at Johnny's, a red-checked-tablecloth Italian restaurant in Cleveland, owned by the Santosuosso family. Grandma Santosuosso was famous for her staff Sunday suppers, the platters piled high with freshly made pasta, meatballs, and Bolognese sauce. Scot begged her to give him her recipe, until finally one day, she dragged him by his ear over to the pot and told him to watch and learn.

When Scot joined me at Crossroads, we adapted the sauce into a plant-based version using all the ingredients that Grandma Santosuosso did with the exception of the meat. We don't feature a lot of meat substitutes in our food, but when we do, they're only the best. Field Roast Italian sausage is an artisan vegan sausage made by hand in Seattle. The fennel seeds in the sausage add a complexity to the sauce. Serve it over ribbons of pappardelle, and you have a hearty meal.

The recipe below makes twice as much sauce as you need. Refrigerate or freeze the extra for another meal. And the cashew cream needs to be prepared a day in advance, so plan accordingly.

If using fresh pasta dough, make the pappardelle: Dust your work surface with flour, lay a sheet of pasta dough on it, and sprinkle with flour. Keep the remaining sheets covered. Using a rolling pin, roll the dough out slightly to make it more pliable. Trim the edges so they are straight.

Lightly dust a baking sheet with flour and semolina. Starting at one of the short ends of the pasta sheet, fold the sheet over on itself in thirds, creating a small rectangle of 3 layers of pasta. With a sharp knife, cut folded dough cleanly into 1-inch-wide strips. Separate and unfold the strips, shaking them into long noodles, and sprinkle lightly with flour and semolina so they don't stick together. Coil the pappardelle into a nest and set on the baking sheet. Repeat with the remaining sheets of pasta, making sure to keep the pasta nests separated so they don't stick together. Allow the pappardelle to dry while you make the sauce. This will help prevent the pasta from clumping and sticking together when cooked. (The pappardelle can be stored in an airtight container or resealable plastic bags in the refrigerator for up to 1 day or in the freezer for up to 1 month. You do not need to thaw the pappardelle before cooking.)

To prepare the sauce: Cut the vegan sausage links into chunks, put in a food processor, and pulse to form crumbles.

Put a medium pot over medium-high heat. When it is hot, add the sausage crumbles and cook, stirring, until crispy, about 5 minutes. Add the oil and butter substitute. When the butter substitute has melted, add the carrots, celery, and onion and sauté for 1 minute to combine, then add the garlic and nutmeg, season with salt and pepper, and cook, stirring, until the vegetables are translucent, about 5 minutes. Pour in the wine and stir for 2 minutes to evaporate some of the alcohol.

Add the marinara sauce, stirring to combine. Bring to a boil, then reduce the heat and gently simmer, stirring occasionally, until thick, about 30 minutes.

Remove from the heat and stir in the cashew cream until fully incorporated. Season again with salt and pepper. Transfer half of the sauce to a covered container and reserve for another dish. (The sauce can be refrigerated for up to 3 days or frozen for up to 1 month.) Keep the remaining sauce warm over very low heat.

To cook the pasta: Bring a large pot of salted water to a boil.

When the water comes to a boil, add the pasta, give it a couple of good stirs with a wooden spoon, and cook until tender yet firm, 1½ to 2 minutes. Drain the pasta well, reserving ¼ cup of the starchy cooking water to use in the sauce if necessary.

Add the pappardelle to the warm sauce, tossing with tongs to coat. If the sauce gets too thick, thin it with enough of the reserved pasta water so the pappardelle is thoroughly coated.

Divide the pappardelle among shallow bowls or transfer to a pasta bowl. Serve immediately.

LINGUINE ^{WITH} BALSAMIC-ROASTED MUSHROOMS ^{AND} TOMATO-BASIL BUTTER SAUCE

SERVES 4 TO 6 (MAKES 4 CUPS SAUCE)

LINGUINE

"00" pasta flour, for dusting

1 pound Pasta Dough (page 174) or
    store-bought dry eggless linguine

Semolina flour, for dusting

SAUCE

2 pounds mixed mushrooms,
    such as cremini and shiitake,
    stemmed, wiped of grit,
    and quartered

4 large shallots, halved lengthwise
    and cut crosswise into large
    slices, plus 1 shallot, minced

2 tablespoons extra-virgin olive oil

¼ cup Balsamic Reduction
    (page 271)

Kosher salt and freshly ground
    black pepper

½ teaspoon red pepper flakes

Nonstick cooking spray

4 tablespoons (½ stick) Earth
    Balance butter stick, cut
    into chunks

3 garlic cloves, minced

¼ cup dry sherry

4 cups Scoty's Marinara Sauce
    (page 275) or store-bought sauce

8 large fresh basil leaves, cut
    into chiffonade

This dish was created on the fly for a special guest who came into Crossroads one night when the restaurant was closed. The humble ingredients are staples in our kitchen—mushrooms, onions, balsamic, and tomatoes. They may be basic, but when you put them together in a sauce and ladle it over fresh linguine, you get something wonderful.

If using fresh pasta dough, make the linguine: Dust your work surface with flour, lay a sheet of pasta dough on it, and sprinkle with flour. Keep the remaining sheets covered. Using a rolling pin, roll the dough out slightly to make it more pliable. Trim the edges so they are straight.

Lightly dust a baking sheet with flour and semolina. Run the pasta sheet through the linguine-cutter on your pasta machine. Lightly dust the strands with flour and semolina. Coil the linguine into a nest and set on the baking sheet. Repeat with the remaining sheets of pasta, making sure to keep the pasta nests separated so they don't stick together. Allow the linguine to dry while you make the sauce. This will help prevent the pasta from clumping and sticking together when cooked. (The linguine can be stored in an airtight container or resealable plastic bags in the refrigerator for up to 1 day or in the freezer for up to 1 month. You do not need to thaw the linguine before cooking.)

To prepare the balsamic mushrooms and shallots for the sauce: Preheat the oven to 400°F.

Put the mushrooms and sliced shallots in a mixing bowl and drizzle with the oil. Pour in the balsamic reduction, season with salt, black pepper, and ¼ teaspoon of the red pepper flakes, and turn the mushrooms and shallots over so they are well coated. Spread the vegetables out in a single layer on a baking sheet that has been coated with nonstick cooking spray and roast for 20 to 25 minutes, until tender and deep brown. Set aside. (The roasted mushrooms and shallots can be prepared a couple of hours in advance, covered, and held at room temperature.)

CONTINUED

Bring a large pot of salted water to a boil.

Meanwhile, prepare the sauce: Put a large sauté pan over medium heat and add 3 tablespoons of the butter substitute. When it has melted, toss in the minced shallot and garlic and cook, stirring, until softened, about 1 minute. Season with salt, black pepper, and the remaining $\frac{1}{4}$ teaspoon red pepper flakes, add the roasted balsamic mushrooms and shallots, and toss until well coated. Pour in the sherry and cook for 30 seconds to evaporate some of the alcohol. Stir in the marinara sauce and simmer until heated through, about 5 minutes.

When the water comes to a boil, add the pasta, give it a couple of good stirs with a wooden spoon, and cook until tender yet firm, $1\frac{1}{2}$ to 2 minutes. Drain the pasta well, reserving $\frac{1}{4}$ cup of the starchy cooking water to use in the sauce if necessary.

Add the linguine to the sauce, tossing with tongs to coat. Add the remaining 1 tablespoon butter substitute and the basil, season with salt and black pepper, and toss to distribute evenly. If the sauce gets too thick, thin it with enough of the reserved pasta water so the linguine is thoroughly coated.

Divide the linguine among plates or transfer to a bowl. Serve immediately.

ACORN SQUASH RAVIOLI ^{WITH} KALE ^{AND} BLACK GARLIC BUTTER SAUCE SERVES 4 (MAKES 2 CUPS SAUCE)

FILLING

1 medium acorn squash
    (about 1 pound), halved
    lengthwise and seeds and
    membranes removed
8 tablespoons (1 stick) Earth
    Balance butter stick
3 garlic cloves, coarsely chopped
1 shallot, coarsely chopped
¼ cup sweet Marsala
¼ cup sweet Madeira
1 tablespoon sherry vinegar
½ teaspoon red pepper flakes
½ teaspoon cayenne
Kosher salt and freshly ground
    black pepper

RAVIOLI

"00" pasta flour, for dusting
½ pound Pasta Dough (page 174)
Semolina flour, for dusting

SAUCE

2 tablespoons extra-virgin olive oil
2 tablespoons Earth Balance
    butter stick
4 black garlic cloves (see Note,
    page 54), sliced
1 shallot, minced
4 cups baby kale or spinach
    (about 4 ounces)
Kosher salt and freshly ground
    black pepper
½ cup Vegetable Stock (page 268)
    or store-bought stock
¼ cup dry sherry
1 tablespoon nutritional yeast flakes
    (see Note, page 6)

Ravioli is the easiest stuffed pasta to pull off, and these flavorful giant pillows of pasta are everything a great Italian dish should be. Three of these ravioli per person is plenty, especially if you serve a crisp green salad alongside.

To prepare the filling: Preheat the oven to 425°F.

Place the squash cut side down in a 9-by-13-inch baking dish. Roast for 45 minutes, until the squash is golden and is tender when pierced with a knife. Set aside to cool. (The squash can be prepared a couple of hours in advance, covered, and held at room temperature.)

In the meantime, put a small saucepan over medium heat and add the butter substitute. When it has melted, add the garlic and shallot and sauté until soft, about 3 minutes. Pour in the Marsala, Madeira, and vinegar and simmer until the liquid is reduced by three-quarters, 10 to 12 minutes. Season with the red pepper flakes and cayenne. Remove from the heat.

When the squash is cool enough to handle, scoop the flesh out with a spoon and put in the bowl of a food processor. With the motor running, carefully pour in the butter substitute–wine mixture a little at a time and puree until smooth and thick. Season with salt and black pepper. Transfer to a bowl and let cool. (The filling can be prepared up to 2 hours in advance, covered, and refrigerated.)

To make the ravioli: Dust your work surface with flour, lay a sheet of pasta dough lengthwise on it, and sprinkle with flour. Keep the remaining 3 sheets covered. Using a rolling pin, roll the dough out slightly to make it more pliable. Trim the edges so they are straight.

Lightly dust a baking sheet with flour and semolina. Drop 3 heaping tablespoons of the filling side by side, about 2 inches apart and about ½ inch from the bottom edge of the pasta sheet, so you have 3 mounds of filling in a row. Dip a pastry brush or your finger in water and brush around the filling and the edges of the dough (this will act as the glue that holds the ravioli together). Fold the top half of the dough over the filling like a blanket to cover. Using an upside-down 2-inch ring cutter or the mouth of an espresso cup, gently press around each mound of filling to push out air pockets and fill in any gaps. Take care that you do not cut through the pasta. Use your fingers to smooth the indentation left by the mold and then gently pat the tops down so the filling is even and not mounded in the center. Use a 3-inch ring cutter or the mouth of a glass (the cutter should be bigger than the mound so you have a border of pasta all around the filling) to cut out the ravioli. Press the edges to ensure that you have a tight seal.

Lightly dust the ravioli with flour and semolina and arrange them faceup on the baking sheet, keeping them separated so they won't stick together. Cover with plastic wrap and repeat with the remaining 3 sheets of dough and filling. (The ravioli can be stored in an airtight container in the freezer for up to 1 month. You do not need to thaw the ravioli before cooking.)

To prepare the sauce: Put a large sauté pan over medium-high heat and add the oil and butter substitute. When the butter substitute has melted, add the black garlic and shallot and sauté until fragrant and very soft, about 2 minutes. Add the kale in handfuls, turning the leaves over with a spoon as you add them and allowing each batch to wilt before adding more. Season with salt and pepper. Pour in the stock and sherry, stirring to incorporate. Reduce the heat to medium-low, sprinkle in the nutritional yeast flakes, and simmer until the sauce has thickened slightly, about 5 minutes. Season again with salt and pepper, cover, and keep warm.

Meanwhile, bring a large pot of salted water to a boil. Add the ravioli in batches and cook until they float to the surface, about 4 minutes; be careful not to overcrowd the pot. Lift the ravioli from the water with a large strainer or slotted spoon, draining well, put in the pan of sauce, and gently toss to coat.

To serve: Divide the ravioli among four plates, spooning the kale on top, and drizzle with a bit more of the sauce remaining in the pan.

TORTELLINI WITH SUN-DRIED-TOMATO RICOTTA AND SWEET PEAS

SERVES 4 (MAKES 1 CUP SAUCE)

FILLING

½ cup Herb Ricotta (recipe follows)

4 sun-dried tomatoes packed in oil, drained and finely chopped (about ¼ cup)

TORTELLINI

"00" pasta flour, for dusting

½ pound Pasta Dough (page 174)

Semolina flour, for dusting

SAUCE

2 tablespoons extra-virgin olive oil

2 tablespoons Earth Balance butter stick

3 garlic cloves, minced

1 shallot, minced

½ cup fresh or frozen peas, run under cool water to thaw if frozen

2 sun-dried tomatoes packed in oil, drained and chopped (about 2 tablespoons)

Kosher salt and freshly ground black pepper

½ cup Vegetable Stock (page 268) or store-bought stock

¼ cup dry white wine

1 tablespoon nutritional yeast flakes (see Note, page 6)

¼ cup Walnut Parmesan (page 267)

Tortellini are stuffed pasta rings typically filled with a mixture of cheese and meat and simmered in broth or coated with a rich sauce. While the hole in the center of the tortellini is traditional, why have an empty ring of air when you can have more delicious filling? When forming them, fill the pasta and connect the two ends together instead of wrapping the tortellini around your finger. This will get rid of the hole in the center and make the tortellini more plump.

Made with sun-dried tomatoes, the sauce is concentrated and intense, so a little goes a long way. Serve with a green salad or sliced heirloom tomatoes drizzled with good olive oil.

To prepare the filling: Put the ricotta in a bowl. Add the sun-dried tomatoes and mix well. (The filling can be prepared up to 1 day in advance, covered, and refrigerated.)

To make the tortellini: Dust your work surface with flour, lay a sheet of pasta dough lengthwise on it, and sprinkle with flour. Keep the remaining 3 sheets covered. Using a rolling pin, roll the dough out slightly to make it more pliable. Trim the edges so they are straight.

Lightly dust a baking sheet with flour and semolina. Use a 2½-inch round cutter or the mouth of a glass to cut 8 circles from the dough. Drop ½ teaspoon of the ricotta filling in the center of each circle; take care not to overfill. Dip a pastry brush or your finger in water and run it around the edges of one round of dough (this will act as the glue that holds the tortellini together). Fold the dough over to form a half-moon and gently press out any air, then press the edges with your fingers to seal. Pick up the half-moon and gently press one finger into the center of the filling to create an indentation, then push up the rounded edge in the back. Simultaneously, bring the two ends together and pinch to seal.

Lightly dust the tortellini with flour and semolina and stand it upright on the baking sheet. Repeat with the remaining dough circles, making sure to keep the tortellini separated so they won't stick together.

CONTINUED

Then repeat with the remaining 3 sheets of dough and filling, so you end up with 32 tortellini. (The tortellini can be stored in an airtight container in the freezer for up to 1 month. You do not need to thaw the tortellini before cooking.)

To prepare the sauce: Put a large sauté pan over medium-high heat and add the oil and butter substitute. When the butter substitute has melted, add the garlic and shallot and sauté until fragrant and softened, about 2 minutes. Add the peas and sun-dried tomatoes, tossing to combine, and season with salt and pepper. Pour in the stock and wine, stirring to incorporate, and reduce the heat to medium-low. Sprinkle in the nutritional yeast flakes and simmer until the sauce has thickened slightly, about 5 minutes. Season again with salt and pepper. Cover and keep warm.

Meanwhile, bring a large pot of salted water to a boil. Add the tortellini in batches and cook until they float to the surface, 3 to 4 minutes; be careful not to overcrowd the pot. Lift the tortellini from the water with a large strainer or slotted spoon, draining well, put in the pan of sauce, and gently toss to coat.

To serve: Divide the tortellini among four plates, spooning the peas and sun-dried tomatoes on top, and drizzle with a bit more of the sauce remaining in the pan. Finish with a sprinkle of the walnut Parmesan.

HERB RICOTTA
MAKES ABOUT 4 CUPS

4 cups Kite Hill almond ricotta

6 fresh basil leaves, finely chopped

4 fresh flat-leaf parsley leaves, finely chopped

3 garlic cloves, minced

1 shallot, minced

Kosher salt and freshly ground black pepper

We add fresh herbs to the almond ricotta to bring a little something extra to the pasta filling. We also use the herb ricotta filling for cappellacci (opposite) and lasagna (page 201).

Mash together the almond ricotta, basil, parsley, garlic, and shallot in a bowl. Season with salt and pepper. The ricotta can be prepared in advance, covered, and refrigerated for up to 5 days before using it as a pasta filling; leftovers keep in the refrigerator for up to 5 days.

CAPPELLACCI WITH SPINACH CREAM SAUCE SERVES 4 (MAKES 2 CUPS SAUCE)

CAPPELLACCI

"00" pasta flour, for dusting
½ pound Pasta Dough (page 174)
Semolina flour, for dusting

FILLING

¾ cup Herb Ricotta (opposite)

ROASTED TOMATOES

16 cherry tomatoes
Extra-virgin olive oil
Kosher salt and freshly ground
  black pepper

SAUCE

8 tablespoons (1 stick) Earth
  Balance butter stick
3 garlic cloves, minced
1 shallot, minced
¼ cup dry white wine
2 cups Cashew Cream (page 264)
1 tablespoon nutritional yeast flakes
  (see Note, page 6)
Juice of ½ lemon
Kosher salt and freshly ground
  black pepper
3 cups baby spinach leaves
  (about 3 ounces)

1 tablespoon Earth Balance
  butter stick
Kosher salt and freshly ground
  black pepper
Frisée leaves
Fresh flat-leaf parsley leaves

Cappellacci, tortellini's cousin, are oversized pillows of stuffed pasta so huge you only need to serve three per person.

Charlie Trotter was famous for adding pureed fresh spinach to soups and sauces to intensify the color and flavor. I created this vibrant sauce in honor of one of the greatest chefs who ever lived. The cashew cream needs to be prepared a day in advance, so plan accordingly.

To make the cappellacci: Dust your work surface with flour, lay a sheet of pasta dough lengthwise on it, and sprinkle with flour. Keep the remaining 3 sheets covered. Using a rolling pin, roll the dough out slightly to make it more pliable. Trim the sheet of pasta to 4 inches wide.

Lightly dust a baking sheet with flour and semolina. Cut the sheet of pasta into three 4-inch squares. Drop 1 tablespoon of the ricotta filling in the center of each square; take care not to overfill. Dip a pastry brush or your finger in water and run it around the edges of one square of dough (this will act as the glue that holds the cappellacci together). Fold the dough over corner to corner to form a triangle and gently press out any air, then press the edges with your fingers to seal. Pick up the triangle and gently press your finger into the center of the filling to create an indentation, bring the two ends together, and push the pointed end up to form the cappellacci. Pinch the ends together to seal.

Lightly dust the cappellacci with flour and semolina and stand it upright on the baking sheet. Repeat with the remaining dough squares, making sure to keep the cappellacci separated so they won't stick together. Then repeat with the remaining 3 sheets of dough and filling, so you end up with 12 cappellacci. (The cappellacci can be stored in an airtight container in the freezer for up to 1 month. You do not need to thaw the cappellacci before cooking.)

To prepare the roasted tomatoes: Preheat the oven to 400°F.

CONTINUED

Put the cherry tomatoes on a large baking sheet. Drizzle with oil, season generously with salt and pepper, toss to coat, and spread out in a single layer. Roast, shaking the pan from time to time, for 15 to 20 minutes, until the tomatoes are lightly charred and collapsed. Set aside to cool. (The roasted tomatoes can be prepared a couple of hours in advance, covered, and held at room temperature.)

Meanwhile, prepare the sauce: Put a large sauté pan over medium-high heat and add the butter substitute. When it has melted, add the garlic and shallot and sauté until fragrant and softened, about 2 minutes. Pour in the wine and cook for 30 seconds to evaporate some of the alcohol. Reduce the heat to medium-low and add the cashew cream, nutritional yeast flakes, and lemon juice. Season with salt and pepper and simmer, stirring constantly, until the sauce has thickened slightly, about 5 minutes.

Working in batches, ladle the sauce into a blender, filling it no more than halfway each time and adding a handful of the spinach to each batch. (If you have an immersion blender, use it.) Puree the sauce, until completely smooth and emerald green (be sure to hold down the lid with a kitchen towel for safety), then pour through a fine-mesh strainer into a saucepan. Season again with salt and pepper. Cover and keep warm.

Meanwhile, bring a large pot of salted water to a boil. Add the cappellacci in batches and cook until they float to the surface, 3 to 4 minutes; be careful not to overcrowd the pot. Lift the cappellacci from the water with a large strainer or slotted spoon, draining well, and put in a mixing bowl. Add the 1 tablespoon butter substitute, season with salt and pepper, and gently toss the cappellacci to coat.

To serve: Spread a ladleful of sauce over the base of each plate. Set 3 cappellacci in a row on top. Garnish with the roasted cherry tomatoes, frisée, and parsley leaves.

GRILLED GARDEN VEGETABLE LASAGNA WITH PUTTANESCA SAUCE

SERVES 8 TO 12

4 red or yellow bell peppers (about ¾ pound)

4 large zucchini (1½ pounds), sliced on a diagonal about ¼ inch thick

1 large Italian eggplant (about 1 pound), sliced into ¼-inch-thick rounds

1 large onion (about ½ pound), sliced into ¼-inch-thick rounds

¼ cup extra-virgin olive oil, plus more for coating the grill pan

6 large fresh basil leaves, chopped

3 fresh thyme sprigs, leaves stripped from the stems and chopped

2 garlic cloves, minced

1 shallot, minced

Kosher salt and freshly ground black pepper

Herb Ricotta (page 196)

2 cups Basil Pesto (page 272)

Puttanesca Sauce (recipe follows)

1 pound lasagna noodles, cooked in boiling salted water just until al dente, drained, and rinsed

10 ounces soy mozzarella, preferably Follow Your Heart Vegan Gourmet, shredded (4 cups)

Zucchini can be watery and lacking in flavor or texture, so when Scot proposed putting a vegetable lasagna that featured zucchini on the menu, I was skeptical. But the flavors he builds into this lasagna are extraordinary. It's an Italian flag on a plate—green pesto, white almond ricotta, and rich red puttanesca sauce. The grilled eggplant, roasted red bell peppers, and zucchini that intermingle with the pasta layers cut down on carbs and calories and add nutrition.

Put each pepper directly on a gas burner over high heat and char, turning periodically with tongs, until the skin is wrinkled and blistered on all sides, about 10 minutes. Alternatively, you can roast the peppers using a broiler, turning them occasionally. Put the peppers into a bowl, cover with plastic wrap, and let them steam for about 10 minutes to loosen the skins.

Pull out the cores of the peppers and remove the seeds. Pull off and discard the blackened skin. Dip your fingers in water as you work to keep the charred bits from sticking. Cut the roasted peppers into ½-inch-wide strips and put in a large mixing bowl, along with any juices that have collected. Add the sliced zucchini, eggplant, and onion, tossing to combine.

Combine the oil, basil, thyme, garlic, and shallot in a small bowl or measuring cup, season with salt and pepper, and whisk to blend. Pour the marinade over the vegetables, tossing to coat evenly. Set aside for 10 minutes so the vegetables can soak up the flavor.

Preheat an outdoor grill and coat with oil, or coat a grill pan with oil and put over medium-high heat. Alternatively, preheat the broiler.

Arrange the peppers, zucchini, eggplant, and onion on the grill or grill pan (if using a grill pan, you will have to do this in batches) and grill, turning the vegetables once, until they are tender and lightly browned and have released most of their moisture, about 5 minutes per side. Or, if using the broiler, arrange the vegetables in a single layer on two nonstick baking sheets and broil in 2 batches. Set the vegetables aside.

Mix together the herb ricotta and 1 cup of the basil pesto in a large bowl. Season with salt and pepper.

CONTINUED

Once you have the sauce ready, the vegetables grilled, and the filling made, you can start assembling the lasagna. Preheat the oven to 375°F.

Ladle about 1 cup of the sauce into a 9-by-13-inch baking dish, to just cover the bottom. Slightly overlap 6 lasagna noodles crosswise so they completely cover the bottom of the dish, with no gaps. Top the noodles with one-third of the ricotta-pesto mixture, spreading it evenly with a rubber spatula. Sprinkle 1 cup of the soy mozzarella over the ricotta. Shingle one-third of the roasted peppers, zucchini, eggplant, and onion in an even layer on top. Repeat the process, layering sauce, lasagna noodles, ricotta-pesto, soy mozzarella, and vegetables 2 more times. Finally, top with the remaining 6 lasagna noodles and sauce.

Cover the lasagna with aluminum foil and bake for 45 minutes to 1 hour, until bubbly. Remove the foil and top the lasagna with the remaining 1 cup soy mozzarella. Bake for another 5 minutes, or until the cheese has melted. Allow the lasagna to cool for 10 minutes before cutting into 8 squares.

To serve: Divide the remaining 1 cup pesto among eight to twelve plates, spreading it out with the back of a spoon. Set a lasagna square on top.

PUTTANESCA SAUCE
MAKES 8 CUPS

¼ cup extra-virgin olive oil

6 garlic cloves, minced

2 shallots, finely chopped

1 teaspoon red pepper flakes

¼ cup dry white wine

2 tablespoons tomato paste

6 cups Scoty's Marinara Sauce
   (page 275) or store-bought sauce

1 cup pitted Kalamata olives, halved
   lengthwise

⅓ cup capers, drained

8 fresh basil leaves, cut
   into chiffonade

Kosher salt and freshly ground
   black pepper

Puttanesca is a robust old-school Italian red sauce made from pantry staples—olives, capers, and red pepper flakes. Serve it with any of the pastas in this chapter. It can be made up to 3 days in advance and stored in an airtight container in the refrigerator.

Put a medium pot over medium heat and add the oil. When the oil is hot, add the garlic, shallots, and red pepper flakes and cook, stirring, until the shallots are translucent, 2 to 3 minutes.

Pour in the wine and cook, stirring, for 1 to 2 minutes to evaporate some of the alcohol. Stir in the tomato paste and marinara sauce and bring to a simmer. Reduce the heat to medium-low, add the olives, capers, and basil, and season with salt and black pepper. Gently simmer, stirring occasionally, until the sauce has thickened slightly, about 30 minutes.

FAVA BEAN AGNOLOTTI
WITH PARSLEY AND AGLIO OLIO SAUCE SERVES 4 TO 6 (MAKES 1 CUP SAUCE)

FILLING

2 tablespoons Earth Balance
    butter stick

2 tablespoons extra-virgin olive oil

1 shallot, minced

4 garlic cloves, minced

5 pounds whole fresh fava beans,
    shelled and peeled (3 cups; see
    Note, page 23), or one 15-ounce
    can fava beans, drained
    and rinsed

Kosher salt and freshly ground
    black pepper

½ cup dry sherry

4 fresh flat-leaf parsley sprigs,
    leaves stripped from the stems
    and chopped

4 fresh mint sprigs, leaves stripped
    from the stems and chopped

2 fresh thyme sprigs, leaves
    stripped from the stems
    and chopped

1 fresh rosemary sprig, leaves
    stripped from the stem
    and chopped

½ teaspoon red pepper flakes

AGNOLOTTI

"00" pasta flour, for dusting

½ pound Pasta Dough (page 174)

Semolina flour, for dusting

SAUCE

4 tablespoons extra-virgin olive oil

4 tablespoons Earth Balance
    butter stick

3 garlic cloves, minced

1 small shallot, minced

Agnolotti are stuffed pasta bites, plump with a creamy filling. They're my favorite pasta to make, because with a pastry bag, you can bang out a bunch at a time rather than have to cut and fill pasta squares individually. Once you get the hang of it, agnolotti are easy and quick to make.

Fava beans have a dense structure, so you don't need to add any cheese to this filling. You could also fill the agnolotti with pureed pumpkin, cooked artichoke hearts, or sun-dried tomatoes, but keep in mind the filling must be smooth enough to pipe.

To prepare the filling: Put a large sauté pan over medium heat and add the butter substitute and oil. When the butter substitute has melted, add the shallot, garlic, and fava beans and cook, stirring, until the shallots and garlic begin to soften and get some color, about 3 minutes. Season with salt and black pepper. Pour in the sherry, stirring to deglaze the pan, and cook for 1 minute to evaporate some of the alcohol. Add the herbs and red pepper flakes and stir to combine.

Carefully transfer the fava bean mixture to the bowl of a food processor and puree for 1 minute, or until completely smooth and emerald green; add water 1 tablespoon at a time if necessary. It is important that the filling is smooth enough to pipe with a pastry bag. Transfer the filling to a pastry bag fitted with a ½-inch plain tip and set aside, covered, in the refrigerator. (The filling can be made up to 1 day in advance and kept refrigerated.)

To make the agnolotti: Dust your work surface with flour, lay a sheet of pasta dough on it, and sprinkle with flour. Keep the remaining 3 sheets covered. Using a rolling pin, roll the dough out slightly to make it more pliable. Trim the edges so they are straight.

Lightly dust a baking sheet with flour and semolina. Working from left to right, pipe a straight line of filling across the bottom of the pasta sheet, leaving a 1-inch border below it. Dip a pastry brush or your finger in water and brush a line above the filling (this will act as the glue that holds the agnolotti together). Fold the bottom

1 teaspoon red pepper flakes

Kosher salt and freshly ground
    black pepper

¼ cup dry sherry

1 cup Vegetable Stock (page 268) or
    store-bought stock

2 tablespoons nutritional yeast
    flakes (see Note, page 6)

4 fresh flat-leaf parsley sprigs,
    finely chopped

edge of the dough up over the filling to make a tube, gently press-ing your thumbs or a bench scraper back against the filling to push out air pockets and fill in any gaps. Roll the dough over the seam by ¼ inch. Once the agnolotti are pinched and cut into individual pieces, this seam creates a little pocket that will catch the sauce.

Starting at one end, use your thumb and forefinger to pinch around the filling at 1-inch increments, sealing off one agnolotti from another. Make sure you have a thumb-size space between them with no filling, or the agnolotti may come unsealed when cut. Cover the dough you just cut to keep it from drying out. Use a wheeled pasta cutter or a sharp knife to cut off the top part of the sheet of dough above the tubes. Then, cut between the agnolotti, separating them into individual pillows. You should end up with 6 agnolotti. Repeat with the remaining dough from the sheet. You should get a dozen agnolotti per sheet of dough.

Lightly dust the agnolotti with flour and semolina and stand them up on the baking sheet, keeping them separated so they won't stick together. Repeat with the remaining 3 sheets of dough and filling. (The agnolotti can be stored in an airtight container in the freezer for up to 1 month. You don't need to thaw the agnolotti before cooking.)

To prepare the sauce: Put a large sauté pan over medium-high heat and add the oil and butter substitute. When the butter substitute has melted, add the garlic and shallot and sauté until fragrant and soft-ened, about 2 minutes. Season with the red pepper flakes, salt, and black pepper. Pour in the sherry and cook until nearly evaporated, 30 seconds. Add the stock, stirring to incorporate, and simmer for 4 minutes. Reduce the heat to medium-low, sprinkle in the nutritional yeast flakes and parsley, and simmer until the sauce has thickened slightly, about 5 minutes. Season again with salt and black pepper. Cover and keep warm.

Meanwhile, bring a large pot of salted water to a boil. Add the agnolotti in batches and cook until they float to the surface, about 4 minutes; be careful not to overcrowd the pot. Lift the agnolotti from the water with a large strainer or slotted spoon, draining well, put in the pan of sauce, and gently toss to coat. Add the parsley and toss to combine.

To serve: Divide the agnolotti among four to six plates and spoon any remaining sauce over the top.

GNOCCHI SERVES 6

4 large russet (baking) potatoes
(about 2 pounds)

1 tablespoon extra-virgin olive oil

1½ teaspoons kosher salt

1½ cups "00" pasta flour, plus more
for dusting

1½ cups sauce of your choice, such
as Basil Pesto Cream Sauce
(page 272), Puttanesca Sauce
(page 202), or Spinach Cream
Sauce (page 197)

Gnocchi is prepared by mixing cooked potatoes with flour. You knead the mixture into a dough and shape it into delicate little dumplings. Although it's easy to make, with no pasta machine needed, gnocchi can become a belly bomb if you overwork the dough, so treat it gently. This recipe doesn't include eggs, of course, and we bake the potatoes instead of boiling them, to ensure that the moisture is kept at a minimum.

Dress the cooked gnocchi with any sauce. It makes a substantial starter on its own, or serve it with a salad as a main course.

Once you form the gnocchi, they must be cooked immediately or frozen (for up to 2 months). Freeze the gnocchi on the baking sheet, covered with the plastic wrap, then transfer to an airtight container. You do not need to thaw the gnocchi before cooking.

Preheat the oven to 400°F.

Put the potatoes on a baking sheet and pierce each one several times so that moisture can escape during baking. Bake the potatoes for 45 minutes to 1 hour, until they are easily pierced with a fork.

Carefully halve the potatoes lengthwise while they are still hot. Scoop out the flesh and press through a potato ricer into a large bowl. Add the oil and salt. Sprinkle in the flour a little at a time, mixing with your hands until a rough dough forms; take care not to overwork the dough, or it will become tough. Transfer the dough to a lightly floured surface and gently knead it for 1 to 2 minutes, until smooth, adding a little more flour if necessary to keep it from sticking.

Break off a piece of the dough and roll it back and forth into a snake about the thickness of your index finger. Cut the rope into 1-inch pieces. Gently roll each piece down the back of the prongs of a fork while pressing on it with your finger to make a small dimple. The gnocchi should be slightly curved and marked with ridges; this will allow them to hold sauce when served. Place them in a single layer on a baking sheet dusted with flour, and cover with plastic wrap. Repeat with the remaining dough.

To cook the gnocchi: Bring a large pot of salted water to a boil. Add the gnocchi in batches and cook until they float to the surface, 1 to 2 minutes. Remove the gnocchi with a slotted spoon and toss with the sauce of your choice.

DESSERTS

CANNOLI WITH CANDIED
KALAMATA OLIVES   215

DARK CHOCOLATE RICE PUDDING WITH
SUGARED PINE NUTS AND RASPBERRIES   223

GRILLED MARINATED NECTARINES
WITH VANILLA-BASIL ICE CREAM   225

SUMMER BERRY GALETTE   229

OAT FLORENTINE COOKIES WITH
MOCHA SIPPING CHOCOLATE   232

BANANA BREAD   236

PUMPKIN PARFAITS   238

DECADENT DARK CHOCOLATE CAKE
WITH FIGS AND HAZELNUTS   243

I met Serafina Magnussen several years ago, when she was a student at Pasadena's Le Cordon Bleu California School of Culinary Arts, and we've been working together ever since. Serafina has the gift of baking desserts that appeal to what people crave in sweets, whether vegan or not, and she can adapt traditional desserts into plant-based renditions that are indistinguishable from the originals. Baking without eggs, butter, and cream is challenging, and often plant-based sweets can lack the indulgent "wow" factor. Not so with Serafina's desserts. Her versions of homey, familiar sweets, like banana bread (see page 236), rice pudding (see page 223), and chocolate cake (see page 243), taste even better than those you remember.

Serafina has a "mad scientist" perspective too, eagerly experimenting with different ingredients and techniques and deciphering how everything works together. She realized, for example, that flaxseeds, when ground and combined with water, work remarkably well in place of eggs, as a binder in cake and muffin batters. Flaxseeds also contribute a slightly earthy, nutty taste and a wealth of health benefits. Solid fats like Earth Balance butter sticks and Spectrum shortening have a smooth consistency and incorporate into cookie and pastry dough the same way butter does. Both products are gluten-free, non-GMO, and, unlike most margarines, do not contain hydrogenated oils. Earth Balance butter sticks, not the spread sold in tubs, work best in baking. Almond milk, canned coconut milk, and Cashew Cream (page 264) are rich alternatives to dairy. And using seasonal produce is just as important in sweet recipes as it is in savory ones. If the fruit you use, whether nectarines, berries, or figs, is sweet and ripe, you don't need to add much sugar.

CANNOLI WITH CANDIED KALAMATA OLIVES

SERVES 8 TO 12; MAKES 24 CANNOLI

SHELLS

4 teaspoons Ener-G egg replacer
  (see Note, page 143)

2 tablespoons filtered water

2 cups unbleached all-purpose flour,
  plus more for dusting

½ cup unrefined cane sugar

½ teaspoon ground cinnamon

¼ teaspoon kosher salt

¼ cup orange liqueur, such as
  Combier or Grand Marnier, or
  1 teaspoon grated orange zest

1 tablespoon unsweetened plain
  almond milk, or as needed

1 tablespoon unfiltered apple
  cider vinegar

2 tablespoons cold Earth Balance
  butter stick

Nonstick cooking spray

3 tablespoons Ener-G egg replacer

¼ cup filtered water

Expeller-pressed canola oil,
  for deep-frying

Whipped Sweet Lemon Ricotta
  Cream (recipe follows)

Candied Kalamata Olives
  (recipe follows)

Confectioners' sugar, for dusting
  (optional)

Nothing says classic Italian dessert like cannoli. While they are traditionally spiked with Marsala, we give these little tubes of pastry a French twist by using orange liqueur, with a pinch of cinnamon, in the shells and lemon in the almond ricotta filling. And rather than dip the ends of the cannoli in chopped chocolate and nuts, we use sugared Kalamata olive bits for a surprisingly delicious sweet-briny crunch. The dough can be made ahead and refrigerated or frozen; defrost the dough before shaping and frying.

Cannoli tubes and round ring cutters can be purchased online or in kitchen supply shops. (Ring cutters are great to have on hand; they're versatile tools that will serve you well for all sorts of recipes.) The tubes, which are 5½ inches long and 1 inch in diameter, come in packs of four and are relatively inexpensive; if you are a cannoli lover, you may want to purchase a dozen of them to make the rolling and frying process easier. If you have multiple tubes, you can preroll the cannoli, arrange them on a sprayed parchment-lined baking sheet, wrap tightly in plastic wrap, and refrigerate for up to 1 day before frying.

For a quick treat, cut the dough scraps into strips, fry them, and sprinkle with cinnamon sugar for a nibble to eat with your coffee.

To prepare the cannoli dough: Combine the egg replacer and water in a small bowl and whisk until frothy. Set aside for 2 minutes to thicken.

Meanwhile, combine the flour, cane sugar, cinnamon, and salt in a large mixing bowl, stirring to distribute evenly.

Stir together the orange liqueur, almond milk, and vinegar in a small bowl.

Using a pastry blender, cut the butter substitute into the dry ingredients until well incorporated. Add the liqueur mixture and egg replacer mixture, using your hands to incorporate them.

CONTINUED

Turn the dough out onto a lightly floured countertop and knead for a few minutes, until smooth. It will start out a bit crumbly but will come together when kneaded. Add a few sprinkles of almond milk if it seems too dry.

Shape the dough into a disk and wrap tightly in plastic wrap. Put it in the refrigerator to chill for at least 30 minutes to relax the gluten. (The dough can be refrigerated for up to 2 days or frozen for up to 2 months.)

To prepare the cannoli shells: Line a baking sheet with parchment paper and coat it with nonstick spray. Set aside.

Dust your work surface and rolling pin with flour. Divide the dough into quarters; keep the pieces you are not working with covered in the refrigerator. Gently knead one piece of dough with lightly floured hands and press into a disk. Roll the dough out, rotating it frequently and dusting the work surface and dough lightly with flour as necessary, as thin as possible, about $1/16$ inch thick, into either a circle or a rectangle. Let the dough rest for a minute or two if it seems tight and the gluten needs to relax, then continue to roll it out.

Dust the dough lightly with flour. Use a $3\frac{1}{2}$-inch round ring cutter to cut out the shells. Put the dough rounds on the lined baking sheet, about 2 inches apart, and put another sheet of sprayed parchment paper, oiled side down, on top, to prevent the dough from drying out. Spray the top of the sheet with nonstick spray. Repeat the process until all of the dough is rolled and cut out, with each layer of parchment paper sprayed on both sides. The dough scraps can be folded gently together and rerolled if necessary to make a total of 24 shells.

To shape and fry the cannoli shells: Line another baking sheet with parchment paper and coat with nonstick spray. Line a third baking sheet with several layers of paper towels. Set both aside.

Combine the egg replacer and $\frac{1}{4}$ cup water in a small bowl and whisk until smooth and frothy. Set aside for 2 minutes to thicken. This will be your "glue" to seal the edges of the cannoli dough.

Spray as many cannoli tubes as you have (see headnote) very well with cooking spray, taking care to coat on all sides. Wrap a cannoli shell around one tube toward one end of the tube and use the egg replacer mixture to seal the seam, using your fingertip to brush it onto the edge of the dough, then pressing the seam together firmly to seal. Wipe off any excess egg replacer wash with your finger. To tighten the seal, gently roll the cannoli back and forth, seam side down, on the work surface. Place on the prepared parchment-lined pan and repeat with the remaining tubes.

Heat 3 inches of oil to 350°F in a deep fryer or deep pot. (If you don't have a deep-fry thermometer, a good way to test if the oil is hot enough is to stick the end of a wooden spoon or chopstick in it; if bubbles circle around the end, you're good to go.) Working in batches, put a few of the cannoli in a fryer basket or spider or other strainer, carefully lower into the hot oil, and fry for 5 to 6 minutes, until golden brown and crispy, carefully rotating them with tongs to avoid scorch marks on the shells. Carefully remove the cannoli shells with the strainer or tongs, allowing the excess oil to drain off and being very careful to drain all of the hot oil off the tubes. Set the cannoli shells on the paper towel–lined pan to drain. Make sure the oil is at the proper temperature before adding the next batch.

The cannoli shells must be removed from the tubes while still hot, or they will crack—they shrink as they cool. Wrap a couple of folded paper towels around the end of each tube, then wrap another folded one around the shell and gently slide it off the tube. Be extremely careful, as they will be hot. Cool on the paper towel–lined pan. Once the tubes have cooled, spray them again and continue shaping and frying the shells. It's a good idea to have a few extra in case of breakage.

Once the shells are cool, transfer to an airtight container. (They will hold for 2 days at room temperature, but they are best served the day they are fried.)

To fill the cannoli: Put the ricotta cream in a pastry bag fitted with an open star tip. Fill the cannoli shells from both ends so the cream comes all the way out to the ends of the shells.

Put the candied olive bits in a small bowl and gently dip both ends of each cannoli into them. If you like, dust the tops with confectioners' sugar. Serve immediately.

WHIPPED SWEET LEMON RICOTTA CREAM

MAKES 4 CUPS

3½ cups (about 28 ounces) Kite Hill
   almond ricotta
¾ cup confectioners' sugar
Finely grated zest of 1 lemon

This lightly sweetened ricotta cream with fresh lemon is delicious on just about anything, not just as a filling for the cannoli. Garnish sliced summer stone fruit or figs with a dollop or two. Or use it as a dip for cookies or a topping for coffee cake or the Summer Berry Galette (page 229).

Drain the almond ricotta in a fine-mesh sieve placed over a bowl for 20 minutes. Put in a food processor, add the sugar, and puree until silky smooth, about 1 minute.

Turn out into a bowl and fold in the lemon zest. Cover and chill for at least 1 hour, or up to 1 day. The ricotta cream needs to firm up before you pipe it.

CANDIED KALAMATA OLIVES

MAKES 2 CUPS

2 cups Kalamata olives, pitted

2 cups unrefined cane sugar

1 cup filtered water

DESICCANT PACKS

Silica desiccant packs absorb excess moisture when storing food. The packs are food-safe (though they aren't meant to be ingested). You can buy them online.

Salty and sweet, these candied olives go well with the citrusy flavors in the cannoli. Be sure to save the sugar syrup for the Sophia cocktail (page 258), which is made with the syrup and garnished with whole candied olives.

Rinse the olives very well in a strainer or colander and let drain for a few minutes. You want to wash away most of the brine.

Gently pat the olives dry with paper towels. If using the olives for the cannoli, put them in the bowl of a food processor and pulse to make small pieces, about the size of mini chocolate chips; take care not to overdo it and puree them. Leave the olives whole if using for the Sophia cocktail (see headnote).

Combine the sugar and water in a medium saucepan, set over medium-high heat, and stir to dissolve the sugar. Add the olives and bring to a simmer, stirring occasionally. Reduce the heat to medium-low and simmer, stirring periodically and tasting frequently, until the syrup has reduced by half and the olives taste sweet, 40 to 45 minutes.

Preheat the oven to 250°F. Line a baking sheet with parchment paper or a silicone baking mat and set aside.

Drain the olives in a strainer set over a bowl. Let the syrup cool (you should have 1 cup), then cover and refrigerate to use in the Sophia cocktail. Spread the olives out in an even layer on the prepared pan. Bake for approximately 3 hours, stirring occasionally to break up any chunks of sugar and to make sure the olives are drying evenly. To test the olives, remove a tablespoon or two and let them cool to room temperature; they should be crunchy. If they are still sticky and chewy, continue to bake, checking every 15 minutes, until crunchy. With gloved hands, crumble the warm olives with your fingers to prevent them from hardening into large clumps, like brittle. You want tiny pieces for the cannoli. Set the olives aside to cool and crisp for 2 hours.

The olives can be stored in an airtight container for up to 2 weeks. Silica desiccant packs (see Note) can help to prolong their shelf life. These absorb the moisture that can make the olives soft and sticky. If the olives start to soften, you can recrisp them in a 300°F oven for 5 to 10 minutes.

DARK CHOCOLATE RICE PUDDING WITH SUGARED PINE NUTS AND RASPBERRIES SERVES 4

2 cups Cashew Cream (page 264)

¼ cup canned coconut milk

¼ cup packed dark brown sugar

⅓ cup unrefined cane sugar

⅓ cup unsweetened cocoa powder, such as Valrhona

2 cinnamon sticks

1 vanilla bean, split and scraped, or 2 teaspoons Bourbon vanilla extract, such as Nielsen-Massey

¼ teaspoon kosher salt

1 cup Arborio or Carnaroli rice

3 cups filtered water, plus more if needed

4 ounces 70% dark chocolate, such as Valrhona, Guittard, or Cordillera, coarsely chopped (1 cup)

3 tablespoons cold Earth Balance butter stick, cut into chunks

1 cup Sugared Pine Nuts (recipe follows)

Rice pudding is a beloved childhood favorite, and this version made with dark chocolate is the ultimate grown-up comfort dessert. It's very chocolatey and has a rich creamy texture. If you prefer a sweeter version, use a chocolate that is in the 50% to 60% cacao range. Serve the pudding warm or chilled. The cashew cream needs to be prepared a day in advance, so plan accordingly.

Combine the cashew cream, coconut milk, sugars, cocoa powder, cinnamon, vanilla seeds and pod, and salt in a medium pot, set over medium heat, and whisk to combine well. Stir in the rice and bring to a simmer, stirring constantly to prevent sticking or scorching, then reduce the heat to medium-low. Gradually add the water 1 cup at a time, stirring constantly. (Adding the water slowly and stirring constantly allows the rice to absorb the water and activate the starch, adding a creaminess to the pudding.) Continue to gently simmer, stirring constantly, until the rice is tender and the mixture is creamy and has started to thicken, about 25 minutes. Taste the rice; it should be tender and cooked through. If it is still firm and has a bite, add more water, a little at a time, and cook until tender. The pudding will firm up as it cools.

Once the rice is cooked, remove from the heat and discard the cinnamon sticks and vanilla bean. Add in the chocolate and butter substitute, stirring well to melt them and incorporate into the pudding.

Serve immediately, or portion into serving dishes and chill until cold, then cover with plastic wrap and keep refrigerated for up to 2 days.

To serve, top each pudding with a couple of tablespoons of sugared pine nuts.

SUGARED PINE NUTS

MAKES 2 CUPS

¼ cup filtered water

½ cup unrefined cane sugar

2 large strips orange peel,
    without any white pith

2 cups raw pine nuts

1 teaspoon ground cinnamon

Pinch of fine sea salt

Any variety of nut, or a combination, can be substituted in this recipe, but if using bigger nuts like walnuts and pecans, it's best to chop them into smaller pieces so they are uniform in size. This recipe makes more than you will need for the Dark Chocolate Rice Pudding, which is a good thing. They are an addictive snack on their own, but you can also scatter them on salads or even popcorn.

Position a rack in the center of the oven and preheat the oven to 325°F. Line a baking sheet with parchment paper or a silicone baking mat. Set aside.

Combine the water, ¼ cup of the sugar, and the orange peel in a small saucepan, set over medium heat, and bring to a boil, stirring occasionally to dissolve the sugar. Once the mixture thickens into a syrup, about 2 minutes, remove from the heat. Cover and set aside for about 10 minutes to infuse the orange flavor.

Combine the nuts, the remaining ¼ cup sugar, the cinnamon, and salt in a bowl and toss to mix.

Remove the orange peel from the sugar syrup and pour the syrup over the nuts. Using a silicone spatula, fold the nuts over to coat them evenly. Spread the nuts out on the lined baking pan.

Bake for about 10 minutes, until the nuts are lightly golden brown. Stir the nuts occasionally and rotate the pan halfway through baking for even coloring and to prevent burning. Cool to room temperature.

The nuts can be stored in an airtight container for up to 1 week.

GRILLED MARINATED NECTARINES WITH VANILLA-BASIL ICE CREAM SERVES 8

2 cups filtered water

2 cups balsamic vinegar

1 cup unrefined cane sugar

Finely grated zest and juice of
2 limes

2 cinnamon sticks

1 vanilla bean, split and scraped, or
1 tablespoon vanilla bean paste,
such as Nielsen-Massey

¼ teaspoon freshly ground
black pepper

Pinch of cayenne

2 cups lightly packed fresh
basil leaves

4 slightly unripe nectarines, halved
and pitted

Expeller-pressed canola oil,
for the grill

Vanilla-Basil Ice Cream
(recipe follows)

Nothing says summer like ripe, juicy stone fruit: peaches, plums, pluots, apricots, and, especially, nectarines. Marinating and grilling the fruit is a simple way to amplify the flavor of summer's bounty. Infused fresh basil in the fruit marinade, as well as in the ice cream base, imparts an herbaceous essence to the dessert.

You can use peaches, plums, or other fruit in place of the nectarines; be sure they're slightly unripe and give a little when squeezed.

Combine the water, vinegar, sugar, lime zest and juice, cinnamon, vanilla seeds and pod, black pepper, and cayenne in a large saucepan and bring to a boil over high heat, stirring to dissolve the sugar. Remove from the heat and stir in the basil. Steep the basil in the liquid until cool, about 1 hour.

Arrange the nectarines cut side down in a shallow baking dish. Strain the marinade through a fine-mesh sieve (discard the solids) and pour over the nectarines. Set aside at room temperature for 1 hour for the flavor to infuse into the fruit.

Using a slotted spoon, remove the nectarines from the marinade and set them aside. Pour the marinade into a small pot, bring to a simmer over medium-high heat, and simmer until reduced, thick, and syrupy, about 50 minutes. You should have about 1 cup syrup. Remove the syrup from the heat and set aside.

Preheat an outdoor grill or grill pan to medium-high.

Rub the grill grates with oil to prevent sticking. Grill the nectarines, cut side down, for 3 minutes, or until you see grill marks. Don't move the nectarines around, or you'll tear the flesh. Turn the nectarines over with tongs and grill the other side until the skin begins to caramelize and char, about 4 minutes. The juices from the fruit should start to bubble in the centers. Remove the nectarines from the grill.

Arrange the nectarines cut side up on individual serving plates. Put a scoop of ice cream in the center of each one, drizzle with the balsamic syrup, and serve.

VANILLA-BASIL ICE CREAM

MAKES 1 QUART

4 teaspoons arrowroot powder

Pinch of guar gum (see Note)

1 cup unsweetened plain
    almond milk

1½ cups thick Cashew Cream (see
    variation, page 264)

One 15-ounce can coconut milk

1 cup unrefined cane sugar

1 teaspoon expeller-pressed
    coconut oil

1 vanilla bean, split and scraped, or
    1 tablespoon vanilla bean paste,
    such as Nielsen-Massey

Pinch of fine sea salt

2 cups packed fresh basil leaves

GUAR GUM

Guar gum is a natural thickening agent derived from guar beans. Often used in gluten-free baking to aid in structure and binding, it also keeps ice cream smooth by preventing ice crystals from forming. Bob's Red Mill is a popular brand that can be found at Whole Foods and many other grocery stores.

Dissatisfied with the flavor and texture of almost all commercial brands of dairy-free ice cream, Serafina makes this recipe, with cashew cream and coconut milk, for vegan ice cream lovers everywhere. This is a versatile base recipe; the flavor possibilities are endless. Omit the basil, for example, add another vanilla bean, and you'll have classic vanilla ice cream. It's best to make the custard base 24 hours before churning to allow the flavors to develop and intensify.

Combine the arrowroot and guar gum in a small mixing bowl. Pour in the almond milk to make a slurry, whisking vigorously to ensure that it is smooth with no lumps. Set aside.

Combine the cashew cream, coconut milk, sugar, coconut oil, vanilla seeds and pod, and salt in a medium pot over medium-high heat and whisk constantly until the mixture comes to a gentle boil. Reduce the heat to medium and simmer gently, stirring, until the sugar is dissolved, about 5 minutes. Ideally, the temperature should be 175°F (just scalding). Reduce the heat to medium-low and simmer gently for 2 more minutes.

Slowly pour the arrowroot slurry into the pot, whisking vigorously to prevent any lumps from forming. Simmer for about 5 minutes, whisking often, until the mixture is thickened and the raw starch taste is cooked out; taste to be sure there is no starchy flavor. Strain through a fine-mesh sieve into a large bowl.

Crush the basil leaves gently with your hands to help release the oils, add to the ice cream base, and stir gently. Let the mixture stand at room temperature for 1 hour to infuse the basil flavor into the base.

Pour the ice cream base through a fine-mesh strainer into a bowl or other container, pressing gently on the basil leaves to extract the flavor; discard the basil. Cover the ice cream base with plastic wrap, pressing the plastic wrap directly against the surface to prevent a skin from forming. Refrigerate for at least 4 hours, preferably 24—the longer the base sits, the better the flavor.

Churn the ice cream base in an ice cream maker according to the manufacturer's directions. When it's done, the ice cream will be the consistency of soft-serve. To harden the ice cream fully, freeze it in a covered plastic container. The ice cream keeps for up to 3 weeks.

SUMMER BERRY GALETTE

SERVES 4; MAKES 4 INDIVIDUAL GALETTES OR 1 LARGE GALETTE (MAKES 2 POUNDS DOUGH)

DOUGH

½ cup filtered water

3 ice cubes

¾ teaspoon kosher salt

½ teaspoon unfiltered apple cider vinegar

2¾ cups unbleached all-purpose flour, plus more for dusting

2½ sticks Earth Balance butter sticks, cut into ½-inch chunks and frozen

¾ cup Spectrum butter-flavored shortening, refrigerated for at least 30 minutes

GALETTE

2 tablespoons whole white chia seeds or 1 tablespoon ground chia seeds

½ cup filtered water, at room temperature, plus more if needed

5 cups mixed fresh berries, such as raspberries, blackberries, blueberries, and strawberries (strawberries halved if large), rinsed, well drained, and patted dry

Freshly squeezed lemon juice to taste

Unrefined cane sugar to taste

Coarse natural sugar, such as Demerara or turbinado

A galette is a free-form tart. The dough has a rich, buttery flavor, and while the instructions may seem fussy, it is actually quite easy to make. The technique for incorporating the fats into the flour distributes long, thin layers of fat throughout the dough, which makes the crust light and flaky. When making this dough, keep in mind that the butter substitute can melt very quickly, more so than regular butter. You don't want to prepare the dough next to a hot oven or on a very hot day.

If berries aren't in season, use sliced stone fruit like peaches and cherries, or try pears and apples in the fall. Be sure to use fresh fruit; frozen has too much moisture and will make the galette soggy. Adding lemon juice and sugar to the fruit draws out its natural juices, so if making individual galettes, it's important to add them to each portion of fruit just before filling the crust, to prevent the berry juices from seeping out and making the dough soggy.

To prepare the dough: Combine the water, ice, salt, and vinegar in a small mixing bowl. Set aside to allow the ice to chill the water and melt.

On a large work surface, spread the flour out into a rectangle about 8 inches by 12 inches. Scatter the chunks of frozen butter substitute and the shortening on top of the flour and toss a little of the flour on top so that your rolling pin won't stick. Starting at one end, pat the rolling pin down onto the fats to start flattening them out. Scrape off any fat that has stuck to the rolling pin and start rolling the dough out and incorporating the fat into the flour. Scrape off the rolling pin and dust with a little more flour as needed. You want the butter substitute and shortening to flatten out into long, thin strands. Blending the dough in this way will create long alternating layers of fat and dough. Then, as the crust bakes, the fat between the layers creates steam and makes it flaky. Using a bench scraper, scoop up the ends of the dough and fold them over toward the center, keeping the dough rectangle about 12 inches long. Repeat the rolling and scraping process 3 times; the dough should be crumbly.

CONTINUED

Make a well in the center of the dough, running lengthwise like a trough, and pour the ice water into it. With the bench scraper, scoop up the sides of the dough toward the center, folding the water mixture into it. Continue to scrape, scoop, and fold until the dough comes together. It will be sticky and shaggy.

Form the dough into a large rectangle. Generously dust with flour and roll out about ½ inch thick. Fold the dough crosswise in half and then in half again, dust with flour, and repeat the process 2 to 3 times, until the dough is smooth. To check the consistency of the dough, squeeze a small amount together between your fingers: there should be just enough moisture to bind the dough together without it being wet or sticky.

Shape into a disk and wrap tightly in plastic wrap. Put it in the refrigerator and chill for at least 1 hour until firm. (The dough can be refrigerated for up to 1 day or frozen for up to 2 months. Thaw in the refrigerator or at room temperature.)

To prepare the galettes: Line a baking sheet with parchment paper or a silicone baking mat. If you're making individual galettes, line two sheet pans. Set aside. Dust your work surface and rolling pin with flour.

If making individual galettes, roll the dough out into a large square about ¼ inch thick. Using the lid from the shortening container or a 6-inch plate, cut out 4 dough rounds. Dust the tops lightly with flour, then roll the dough rounds out to about 8 inches in diameter. (This will give you a border of dough to fold over and encase the berry filling.)

Put two dough rounds on the parchment-lined baking sheets, about 2 inches apart, and chill in the refrigerator. (It's very important that the dough remain cold, or the fats will melt, making the crust heavy and flat.)

If making one large galette, simply roll out the dough into a 12-inch circle, put on the baking sheet, and refrigerate.

If using whole chia seeds, put them in a clean coffee or spice grinder and buzz until finely ground. Transfer to a bowl. With a small whisk (a battery-powered milk frother is a terrific tool for this task), whip the ground chia seeds with the water to make a wash. It should be the consistency of beaten eggs. Set aside. The chia wash will get thicker as it sits; add water a little at a time if needed to thin it.

Combine all the berries with lemon juice and cane sugar to taste. (The amount of lemon and sugar depends on the ripeness of the fruit and your personal preference.)

If making individual galettes, spoon the berry mixture into the center of one dough circle, leaving about a 1-inch border around the edges.

Brush the edges of the dough with the chia wash. Carefully bring the edges of the dough up over the filling, leaving the fruit exposed in the center, gently folding the dough and pinching it to seal any cracks if needed. (Any tears will allow the juices from the fruit to seep out.) Gently brush the chia wash over the edges of the dough and sprinkle the dough generously with coarse sugar.

Carefully transfer the galette to the prepared baking sheet and repeat with the remaining fruit, lemon juice, cane sugar, dough, chia wash, and coarse sugar, spacing the galettes about 2 inches apart.

For one large galette, spoon the berry mixture into the center of the dough circle, leaving a 1-inch border around the edges, and proceed as for the individual galettes.

Refrigerate the galette(s) for 15 to 30 minutes, so the fats in the dough can firm up; this will ensure that the pastry puffs when baked.

Meanwhile, 30 minutes before baking, preheat the oven to 375°F.

Bake the galette(s) for 30 to 35 minutes, or until the crust is puffy and golden brown and the fruit is bubbling.

Slide a knife or large spatula under the galettes (or galette) to loosen them from the parchment paper. Serve warm or at room temperature.

OAT FLORENTINE COOKIES ^{WITH} MOCHA SIPPING CHOCOLATE MAKES 36 COOKIES

12 tablespoons (1½ sticks) Earth
    Balance butter sticks

2 cups Bob's Red Mill gluten-free or
    regular quick-cooking oats

1 cup gluten-free flour mix
    (see Note, page 234), such as
    Pamela's Artisan Flour Mix or
    Authentic Foods Multi-Blend
    Flour, or unbleached
    all-purpose flour

1 cup unrefined cane sugar

1 teaspoon ground cinnamon

Finely grated zest of 1 small orange

¼ teaspoon kosher salt

¼ cup unsweetened plain
    almond milk

3 tablespoons agave nectar

2 teaspoons pure vanilla extract,
    such as Nielsen-Massey

Mocha Sipping Chocolate
    (recipe follows)

Because Serafina is gluten-intolerant, she loves making delicious gluten-free treats to satisfy her sweet tooth. If you are serving these cookies to those with wheat issues, especially celiac disease, it is very important that the oats be certified gluten-free. While oats themselves don't contain gluten, they are often cross-contaminated with gluten during growing, processing, and/or packaging. If gluten is not a concern, you can use regular all-purpose flour and regular quick-cooking oats. The cookie dough freezes well, so if you don't want to bake all the cookies at once, you can freeze the remaining dough for another time. The recipe also halves or doubles easily.

These cookies are the best for dunking; snack on them with a mug of Mocha Sipping Chocolate (page 235).

Melt the butter substitute in a small saucepan over low heat. Remove from the heat.

Combine the oats, flour mix, sugar, cinnamon, orange zest, and salt in a mixing bowl and stir well.

Combine the almond milk, agave, and vanilla in a measuring cup. Pour the almond milk mixture and melted butter into the dry mixture and stir well with a spoon or rubber spatula to combine. The dough will be thick and sticky. Set aside to cool.

Form the dough into a ball and wrap in plastic wrap. Chill in the refrigerator for at least 2 hours, or overnight. This chilling time allows the dough to absorb flavor and moisture. (The cookie dough can also be frozen for up to 2 months.)

When ready to bake, remove the dough from the refrigerator; the dough should be at room temperature before you put the cookies into the oven so they spread out when baked and get really crispy. Position a rack in the middle of the oven and preheat the oven to 350°F. Line three baking sheets with parchment paper or silicone baking mats. Set aside.

CONTINUED

Using a tablespoon, scoop out portions of dough and roll them in your palms into 1-inch balls (about the size of a Ping-Pong ball). Alternatively, use a ½-ounce ice cream scoop. Put the balls of dough on one of the prepared baking sheets, about 4 inches apart, and press them with your fingers into thin 3-inch rounds; you should be able to fit 12 cookies on the pan. (You can also preportion balls of dough and freeze them for up to 1 week in a tightly sealed container, if desired. Defrost before flattening out and baking.)

Bake for 10 to 12 minutes, rotating the pan halfway through baking, until the cookies are set and golden brown on the edges. Watch the cookies closely so they don't burn. Cool on the pan for 5 minutes, then transfer to a wire rack to cool completely. Shape and bake the remaining cookies. (The cookies will stay crisp in an airtight container at room temperature for 2 to 3 days.)

Serve the cookies with the sipping chocolate for dunking.

GLUTEN-FREE FLOUR

You can buy gluten-free flour mixes or buy the ingredients to make your own mix. The mixes are usually a blend of white or brown rice flour, tapioca starch or flour, and potato starch. Also available are whole-grain flours such as sorghum, quinoa, and amaranth; bean flours like garbanzo and fava; and nut flours such as almond and coconut. As with cake flour, whole wheat flour, and regular all-purpose, they all have different functions in baking, depending on their carbohydrate and protein contents. Gluten-free flour mixes almost always include a binder such as xanthan or guar gum to provide structure and some elasticity in the absence of the gluten found in wheat flours. You have to experiment to get to know each flour or blend and discover the variance in flavor and texture.

We use several types of flour mixes in these dessert recipes. Pamela's Artisan Flour Mix and Authentic Foods Multi-Blend Flour both contain sweet rice flour (which is different from regular rice flour). The rice flour results in a very chewy texture that is terrific for cookies like these Oat Florentine Cookies but not ideal for baked goods such as cakes. For the pumpkin spice cake in the Pumpkin Parfaits (page 238), we use Arrowhead Mills All-Purpose Baking Mix, a blend of sorghum, tapioca, and organic rice flour; sorghum is very good for you, so there is some nutritional value, and the flour results in a light texture that is perfect in cakes.

MOCHA SIPPING CHOCOLATE

SERVES 8; MAKES 4 CUPS

2 cups unsweetened plain
  almond milk

1 cup canned coconut milk

½ cup unrefined cane sugar

4 tablespoons (½ stick) Earth
  Balance butter stick

¼ cup instant espresso powder,
  such as Medaglia d'Oro

2 tablespoons unsweetened
  cocoa powder

2 teaspoons pure vanilla extract,
  such as Nielsen-Massey

½ teaspoon kosher salt

4 ounces 63% dark chocolate,
  such as Valrhona, Guittard, or
  Cordillera, chopped into chunks

Coconut Whipped Cream (see
  page 238), for serving (optional)

This thick hot chocolate is great for drinking (or dunking), and it can also be used as a sauce: drizzle over slices of cake or Banana Bread (page 236). Curiously, many people are under the assumption that all chocolate contains dairy. Thankfully, that's not the case; except for milk chocolate, chocolate is completely vegan, so there's no need to resort to carob.

Combine the almond milk, coconut milk, sugar, butter substitute, espresso powder, cocoa, vanilla, and salt in a large saucepan over medium heat, whisk to blend, and bring to a gentle simmer, whisking until the sugar is dissolved and the ingredients are well incorporated. Add the chocolate chunks and whisk constantly to melt and incorporate them. Be careful not to allow the hot chocolate to boil or scorch. Serve warm in espresso cups, topped with a dollop of Coconut Whipped Cream if you like.

The hot chocolate can be made up to 3 days ahead. Pour the hot chocolate into a heatproof container and store covered in the refrigerator. When ready to serve, gently reheat the hot chocolate in a saucepan over low heat, stirring constantly.

BANANA BREAD

MAKES 1 LARGE LOAF OR 8 MINI LOAVES

Earth Balance butter stick,
    for buttering the pan(s)
2½ cups unbleached all-purpose
    flour, plus more for dusting
    the pan(s)
1 teaspoon ground cinnamon
1½ teaspoons baking powder
½ teaspoon baking soda
½ teaspoon kosher salt
1 tablespoon finely
    ground flaxseeds
3 tablespoons filtered water
⅔ cup grapeseed oil
½ cup packed light brown sugar
½ cup unrefined cane sugar
1 tablespoon pure vanilla extract,
    such as Nielsen-Massey
4 large extra-ripe bananas

This recipe from Serafina's mother is one of the first that she ever "veganized." She replaced the eggs with ground flaxseeds, which have a mucilaginous coating that binds the batter while also adding moisture and healthy omega-3 fatty acids. The bread is quick and easy to make and a great use for overripe bananas. You can save peeled brown or black ripe bananas in your freezer and make a loaf whenever the desire strikes you. (Let them defrost at room temperature before baking.) Eat this bread for breakfast or an afternoon snack, or toast slices and serve for dessert.

Preheat the oven to 350°F. Butter and lightly flour a 9-by-5-inch loaf pan or eight 4-by-2½-inch mini loaf pans. Set aside.

Whisk the flour, cinnamon, baking powder, baking soda, and salt in a mixing bowl to combine.

Stir the flaxseed and water together in a large mixing bowl. Let sit for a few minutes to thicken.

Add the oil, sugars, and vanilla to the flaxseed slurry and whisk well to combine. Add the bananas, smashing them with the whisk, then whisk to blend. Using a rubber spatula, fold in the flour mixture until just combined.

Pour the batter into the loaf pan or mini loaf pans, to just over two-thirds full. Let the batter rest for 10 minutes—you get a better rise with vegan baked goods after resting to activate the leavening.

Bake until the top of the loaf springs back when gently pressed, 55 to 60 minutes for a large loaf, or 20 to 25 minutes for mini loaves. You should see cracks on the top of the bread. Cool completely in the pan(s) before cutting or serving.

PUMPKIN PARFAITS ^{SERVES 8}

CAKE

Nonstick cooking spray

1½ tablespoons flaxseeds,
    preferably golden, finely ground

⅔ cup filtered water

2 cups gluten-free flour mix, such
    as Arrowhead Mills All-Purpose
    Baking Mix (see Note, page 234)

2 teaspoons baking powder

2 teaspoons ground cinnamon

1 teaspoon kosher salt

½ teaspoon ground ginger

½ teaspoon baking soda

⅔ cup unsweetened plain
    almond milk

½ cup organic
    unsweetened applesauce

1 tablespoon pure vanilla extract,
    such as Nielsen-Massey

1½ teaspoons unfiltered apple
    cider vinegar

8 tablespoons (1 stick) cold Earth
    Balance butter stick

1⅓ cups packed light brown sugar

COCONUT WHIPPED CREAM

Two 15-ounce cans coconut milk,
    chilled for at least 24 hours in the
    refrigerator (see headnote)

½ cup confectioners' sugar, sifted

1 vanilla bean, split and scraped, or
    1 tablespoon vanilla bean paste,
    such as Nielsen-Massey

ROASTED PUMPKIN MOUSSE

One 15-ounce can organic
    pumpkin puree

2 tablespoons unrefined cane sugar

⅔ cup packed light brown sugar

1 tablespoon arrowroot powder

1 teaspoon ground cinnamon

Spice cake, ginger syrup, and pumpkin mousse make up the layers of these petite parfaits. Although the dessert requires a handful of components, don't be intimidated. The cake, mousse, ginger syrup, and crunchy topping can all be made ahead of time and held until you're ready to assemble the parfaits.

For the coconut whipped cream, be sure to chill the cans of coconut milk for at least 24 hours to separate the water from the coconut cream.

To prepare the cake: Position a rack in the center of the oven and preheat the oven to 350°F. Generously spray the bottom and sides of a 9-by-13-inch baking pan with nonstick spray.

Whisk the ground flaxseed and water in a bowl until well combined.

Meanwhile, combine the flour mix, baking powder, cinnamon, salt, ginger, and baking soda in a large bowl and mix well.

Stir the almond milk, applesauce, vanilla, and apple cider vinegar together in a mixing bowl until blended. Set aside.

Put the butter substitute and brown sugar in the bowl of a stand mixer fitted with the paddle attachment and cream together on low to medium speed until light and fluffy, about 4 minutes. With the mixer on low, gradually add the flaxseed mixture and mix until smooth, about 1 minute. Be sure to scrape down the sides and the bottom of the bowl to fully incorporate the ingredients.

Gradually add the dry ingredients, mixing until fully incorporated. Mixing on low, pour in the almond milk/applesauce mixture. Scrape down the sides of the bowl. Increase to medium speed and mix until the batter is smooth, about 1 minute.

Pour the batter into the prepared pan and smooth the surface with an offset spatula. The batter is thick; wet your spatula a bit to help smooth the surface if necessary. Let rest, away from heat, for 10 minutes. This rest helps the gluten-free starches absorb some moisture and results in a better rise when baked.

Bake for 20 to 25 minutes, or until the cake is lightly golden at the edges and springs back when touched. A toothpick inserted into the center should come out clean.

CONTINUED

½ teaspoon agar-agar powder or
   1½ teaspoons agar-agar flakes
   (see Note, page 241)
⅛ teaspoon ground ginger
⅛ teaspoon kosher salt
⅛ teaspoon finely ground
   black pepper
¼ teaspoon finely grated lemon zest
Pinch of freshly grated nutmeg
Pinch of ground cloves
Pinch of ground cardamom
One 15-ounce can coconut milk
½ teaspoon pure vanilla extract,
   such as Nielsen-Massey
1½ cups Coconut Whipped
   Cream (below)

SPICED PUMPKIN AND ALMOND
   CRUNCH TOPPING
½ cup raw pumpkin seeds (pepitas)
½ cup sliced blanched almonds
¼ cup gluten-free flour mix, such
   as Arrowhead Mills All-Purpose
   Baking Mix (see Note, page 234)
2 tablespoons light brown sugar
2 tablespoons dark
   muscovado sugar
2 tablespoons unrefined cane sugar
¼ teaspoon ground ginger
¼ teaspoon ground cinnamon
¼ teaspoon finely ground
   black pepper
Pinch of freshly grated nutmeg
Pinch of guar gum (see Note,
   page 227)
Pinch of kosher salt
3 tablespoons Earth Balance butter
   stick, melted

GINGER SYRUP
¼ cup unrefined cane sugar
¼ cup filtered water
2 tablespoons Canton ginger liqueur
   or one 1-inch piece fresh ginger,
   peeled and chopped

Remove from the oven and let cool for 30 minutes, then invert the cake onto a rack, lift off the pan, and cool completely. (In the meantime, prepare the whipped cream, mousse, topping, and syrup.)

To prepare the coconut whipped cream: Put the bowl and whisk attachment of a stand mixer (or a metal bowl and the beaters of a hand mixer) in the freezer for at least 30 minutes.

Carefully turn over the cans of chilled coconut milk and puncture the bottoms with 2 holes; drain off and discard the clear coconut water. Then open the cans from the bottom and scrape the thick coconut cream into the chilled mixer (or mixing) bowl. Add the confectioners' sugar and vanilla bean seeds (or paste). Fit the stand mixer with the cold whisk attachment (or attach the cold beaters to the hand mixer) and start the mixer on low, then gradually increase and whip for a few minutes, until the cream is light and fluffy. Cover and refrigerate until ready to use, up to 2 days. (You will use 1½ cups of the whipped cream for the pumpkin mousse and the remaining 1 cup for the topping.)

To prepare the mousse: Preheat the oven to 325°F. Line a baking sheet with parchment or wax paper.

Spread the pumpkin puree out evenly onto the pan and sprinkle the cane sugar evenly over the top.

Put the pan on the middle rack of the oven and bake for 15 to 20 minutes, or until the pumpkin looks dry and has cracked on the surface; it may be a bit toasty at the edges. Let cool to room temperature.

Spoon the roasted pumpkin into the bowl of a food processor and puree until smooth.

Combine the brown sugar, arrowroot, cinnamon, agar-agar, ginger, salt, pepper, lemon zest, nutmeg, cloves, and cardamom in a medium saucepan and whisk to combine. Stir in the coconut milk and vanilla. (If using agar flakes, let the mixture sit for 10 minutes.) Set the pan over medium heat and bring to a gentle boil, whisking constantly. Cook to thicken, until the mixture is thick and gel-like, 2 to 3 minutes. Or, if using agar flakes, cook for 6 to 7 minutes. Be careful not to scorch the bottom of the pan.

Remove from the heat and transfer the mixture to the bowl of a food processor with the roasted pumpkin and puree. Scoop the mixture into a large bowl and let cool to room temperature.

Agar-agar is a gelling agent derived from a type of red algae. Gelatin is made from animal collagen; agar is a vegetarian substitute used to stabilize and thicken a variety of dishes. Like ordinary gelatin, agar is flavorless and becomes gelatinous when dissolved in water. Agar-agar is sold in powder or flakes and can be found at health food stores, Asian markets, and Whole Foods.

Using a large whisk, whip the 1½ cups coconut whipped cream into the pumpkin mixture until well blended and fluffy. Cover and chill in the refrigerator for at least 30 minutes to firm up. (The mousse can be refrigerated for up to 3 days.)

To prepare the crunch topping: Preheat the oven to 350°F. Line a baking sheet with parchment paper or a silicone baking mat.

Combine the pumpkin seeds, almonds, flour mix, sugars, ginger, cinnamon, pepper, nutmeg, guar gum, and salt in a mixing bowl and toss well. Pour in the melted butter substitute and, using your hands or a wooden spoon, gently fold it into the dry ingredients. You want to keep some crumbs and texture in the mixture.

Spread the pumpkin seed mixture out in an even layer on the prepared pan. Bake for 8 to 10 minutes, until the almonds look golden and the pepitas start to puff and pop. Cool to room temperature, then transfer to an airtight container. (The topping can be stored at room temperature for up to 3 days.)

To prepare the ginger syrup: Bring the cane sugar and water to a boil in a small saucepan, whisking to dissolve the sugar. Remove from the heat and add the ginger liqueur (or fresh ginger). Set aside at room temperature to cool and to infuse the ginger flavor.

If using fresh ginger, strain the syrup to remove it. Refrigerate the syrup until ready to assemble the parfaits. (The syrup can be refrigerated for up to 5 days.)

To assemble the parfaits: Transfer the cake to a cutting board. Using a 2-inch round cutter, cut the cake into 16 rounds. (Eat the scraps.) Using a pastry brush, brush the top of each cake with the ginger syrup.

Put the pumpkin mousse in a pastry bag fitted with an open star tip. Pipe a ½-inch-thick layer of mousse into the bottom of a 6-ounce juice glass. Carefully set a round of cake on top, gently pressing it into the glass. Sprinkle on a tablespoon of the crunch topping.

Pipe another ½-inch-thick layer of mousse on top. Add a second round of cake.

Put the remaining 1 cup coconut whipped cream in a pastry bag fitted with an open star tip. Finish the parfait with a generous swirl of coconut whipped cream and another generous tablespoon of the crunch topping. Repeat to make 7 more parfaits. Serve at once.

DECADENT DARK CHOCOLATE CAKE ^{WITH} FIGS ^{AND} HAZELNUTS

SERVES 10 TO 12

CAKE

Nonstick cooking spray

5 ounces 60% to 70% dark chocolate, such as Valrhona, Guittard, or Cordillera, coarsely chopped

3 cups unbleached all-purpose flour (see headnote)

2 cups unrefined cane sugar

1 cup unsweetened cocoa powder, such as Valrhona

2 teaspoons baking soda

1 teaspoon kosher salt

2 cups filtered water

⅔ cup grapeseed oil

2 teaspoons pure vanilla extract, such as Nielsen-Massey

2 teaspoons pure coffee extract, such as Trablit

2 teaspoons unfiltered apple cider vinegar

FIG-HAZELNUT JAM

½ pound (1 pint) ripe Black Mission or Brown Turkey figs, rinsed, dried, stemmed, and quartered (see Note, page 245)

¼ cup packed light brown sugar

¼ cup Frangelico or other hazelnut liqueur

½ teaspoon freshly squeezed lemon juice, plus more if needed

⅛ teaspoon kosher salt

1 to 2 tablespoons unrefined cane sugar if needed

This is the only chocolate cake recipe you will ever need—vegan or not. The rich, moist chocolate layers are brushed with a hazelnut syrup and spread with fresh fig jam, then coated with figgy fudge frosting. Serafina makes this decadent celebration cake for birthdays, anniversaries, and special occasions. Be sure to use good-quality dark chocolate and cocoa powder for the cake.

If you want to make the cake gluten-free, use Arrowhead Mills All-Purpose Baking Mix (see Note, page 234) in place of the all-purpose flour. If doing so, you'll need to add an additional ½ cup water (2½ cups total) to the batter.

To prepare the cake: Position a rack in the center of the oven and preheat the oven to 350°F. Coat the bottom and sides of two 9-inch round cake pans with cooking spray. Line the pans with parchment or wax paper and coat them lightly with cooking spray. Set aside.

Put the chocolate in the bowl of a food processor and pulse into pieces about the size of mini chocolate chips. (Take care that the chocolate does not begin to melt from the heat of the processor blades.) You should have 1 cup of chocolate bits. Set aside.

Sift together the flour, cane sugar, cocoa, baking soda, and salt into a large mixing bowl and whisk to combine. Make a well in the center of the dry ingredients.

Whisk together the water, oil, vanilla and coffee extracts, and vinegar in a mixing bowl. Pour into the well in the dry ingredients and, with a rubber spatula, fold in until combined and smooth. Be sure to scrape down the sides and bottom of the bowl. Gently fold in the chocolate bits until evenly distributed.

Divide the batter between the prepared pans (the pans should be half full) and smooth the surface with a spatula. Bake for 35 to 40 minutes, or until a toothpick inserted in the center comes out clean and the cake springs back when touched. (Take care not to

6 cups confectioners' sugar

2 cups Dutch-processed cocoa
powder, such as Valrhona

¾ pound (3 sticks), Earth Balance
butter stick, well chilled

½ cup fig-hazelnut jam (above)

½ cup plain unsweetened
almond milk

HAZELNUT SYRUP

¼ cup unrefined cane sugar

¼ cup filtered water

¼ cup Frangelico hazelnut liqueur

GARNISH

½ cup hazelnuts, toasted and
crushed (see Note, page 44)

½ pound (1 pint) ripe Black Mission
or Brown Turkey figs, rinsed,
dried, stemmed, and quartered
(see Note)

stick the toothpick into a chocolate chunk, or it will come out gooey.) Cool the cakes completely in the pans on a wire rack. (In the meantime, prepare the jam, frosting, and syrup.)

To prepare the fig jam: Combine the figs, brown sugar, hazelnut liqueur, lemon juice, and salt in a medium saucepan set over medium heat. Mix well, bring to a simmer, stirring occasionally, and cook until the figs are soft and the sugar is syrupy, 6 to 8 minutes.

Carefully pour the fig mixture into the bowl of a food processor and puree until smooth, about 1 minute. Taste and adjust the sweet-and-sour balance by adding cane sugar or more lemon juice if needed. (The balance will depend on the ripeness and sweetness of the figs.) Chill ½ cup of the jam for the frosting and the remainder for the filling. (The jam can be stored covered in the refrigerator for up to 3 days.)

To prepare the frosting: Sift the confectioners' sugar and cocoa together into a bowl or onto a piece of parchment paper. Set aside.

Put the butter substitute and the fig-hazelnut jam in the bowl of a stand mixer fitted with the paddle attachment and cream together on low speed until light and fluffy, about 5 minutes. With the mixer on low, gradually add the sugar-cocoa mixture in increments, mixing until smooth. Add the almond milk 1 tablespoon at a time, mixing well after each addition, until smooth and creamy. Be careful not to add the liquid too quickly; you want the frosting smooth and creamy but not too soft, and you may not use all of the almond milk. Cover the frosting with plastic wrap to prevent it from drying out. (The frosting can be refrigerated for up to 1 day or frozen for up to 1 month. Bring to room temperature before using and rewhip to make it fluffy. See "Storing Frosting for Later Use," opposite.)

To prepare the hazelnut syrup: Combine the cane sugar, water, and hazelnut liqueur in a small saucepan over medium heat and bring to a simmer, stirring to dissolve the sugar. Remove from the heat and set aside to cool to room temperature. (The syrup can be made up to 1 week in advance; store it covered in the refrigerator.)

To assemble: When the cake layers are completely cool, run a thin-bladed knife around the sides of each pan to release the cake and invert the layers onto a wire rack. Remove the parchment paper and carefully turn each layer right side up. If they are domed in the middle, level the tops of the layers with a serrated knife. Carefully invert one of the cake rounds onto a cake stand, platter, or cake board. Now carefully flip the cake back over. Using a pastry brush, lightly brush the top of the cake with ¼ cup of the hazelnut syrup.

If fresh figs are not available, substitute ½ pound dried. Soak them overnight at room temperature in the hazelnut liqueur and 1 cup hot water, covered. Simmer as directed in the recipe; be sure to include any soaking liquid left over in the bowl. You can also substitute 1 cup high-quality fig jam. Garnish the cake with just the hazelnuts.

Scoop about 1½ cups of the frosting into a pastry bag fitted with an open star tip or a ½-inch plain round tip. Pipe a ring of frosting around the outside edge of the cake. This is your barrier so the filling won't seep out of the cake. Reserve the frosting left in the bag to decorate the cake.

Put the remaining fig jam in the center of the cake, and spread it out with an offset spatula to cover the cake evenly. Carefully place the second cake round upside down on top (this gives you a nice flat surface to finish the cake). Lightly brush the top of the cake with the remaining ¼ cup hazelnut syrup until absorbed.

Using a large offset spatula, cover the entire cake with a thin layer of frosting. This is your crumb coat, which creates a seal before the final frosting. Refrigerate for 30 minutes to firm up.

Frost the sides and the top of the cake with the remaining frosting, then use the reserved frosting in the pastry bag to decorate the cake if desired. (The cake can be assembled up to 1 day in advance and stored, covered with a cake dome, in the refrigerator.)

One hour before serving, remove the cake from the refrigerator and let come to room temperature. Just before serving, garnish the top of the cake with the toasted hazelnuts and arrange the fresh figs decoratively around the top. (This prevents the hazelnuts from getting soft in the refrigerator and the figs from seeping and/or drying out; if using dried figs, just decorate with hazelnuts.)

To serve: Slice the cake with a thin, nonserrated knife, dipping it in very hot water and wiping it dry before each cut.

Storing Frosting for Later Use

Here's a trick for storing frosting in the refrigerator or freezer for later use: Cut two large pieces of plastic wrap and place them on the counter or work surface. Divide the frosting evenly into 2 portions and place in the center of each of the pieces of plastic wrap. Fold the wrap around the frosting to make 2 small parcels. Wrap each in another layer of plastic wrap, label with the date, and refrigerate or freeze. To use after refrigeration, bring to room temperature and mix in a stand mixer for a couple of minutes to smooth and fluff up the frosting. Thaw frozen frosting overnight in the refrigerator, then bring to room temperature and mix as above.

COCKTAILS

RESPECTABLE   250

HARD TIMES   253

PARISIAN STANDARD   254

HAPPY HARLEQUIN   257

SOPHIA   258

One of the things that sets Crossroads apart from more casual vegan restaurants is our bar program. Reflecting the same sensibilities as the kitchen, we use only fresh juices and plant-based spirits to create quality craft cocktails.

Chances are that if you love good food, you appreciate a well-balanced drink made with fresh ingredients and care. Living a plant-based lifestyle doesn't mean you can't imbibe. But I do have a few requirements for my cocktails: they shouldn't need more than a few ingredients to make, they should be all natural, and they should be totally delicious. You don't need a dcgrcc in chemistry to make the cocktails in this chapter—none of them calls for elaborate syrups, lengthy infusions, or hard-to-find ingredients—and they pair perfectly with our Mediterranean dishes. Invest in a few simple tools like a cocktail shaker, a fine-mesh strainer, and a couple of jiggers, and you'll be on your way to mixing up cocktails complex in flavor but free of hassle.

Honey, egg whites, and dairy products are obviously not part of our cocktails, but the vast majority of hard alcohol is innately vegan, since most spirits are derived from grains, vegetables, and fruits. However, some types of wine, beer, or liquor do use animal products during processing and filtration. If you're unsure, check out websites like Barnivore.com and VeganProducts.org; they have thorough databases listing the vegan status of most alcohol. For gin, Beefeater and Hendrick's are my favorite plant-based brands; for vodka, it's American Star and Fair Trade Quinoa Vodka.

These clever cocktails were created by our friend mixologist Jeremy Lake. Be adventurous—any of the cocktails in this chapter are guaranteed to get your evening hopping.

RESPECTABLE SERVES 2

3 ounces (6 tablespoons) vodka

1½ ounces (3 tablespoons)
coffee liqueur

1½ ounces (3 tablespoons)
Coconut Cream (recipe follows)

½ ounce (1 tablespoon)
Simple Syrup (recipe follows)

2 orange twists

Ground cloves for dusting

A riff on a White Russian, this cocktail got its name from my restaurant partner, Steve Bing, who calls it "a respectable mixed drink." Coconut cream is the nondairy substitute for the usual cream, and the result is not as heavy. Enjoy it in the autumn or winter as an after-dinner drink.

Combine the vodka, liqueur, coconut cream, and simple syrup in a shaker with ice, cover, and shake really well to break up the ice into shards. Strain into two stemmed cocktail or martini glasses. Twist the orange peel over the surface of each cocktail; discard the peel. Sprinkle a dusting of ground cloves over the top.

COCONUT CREAM
MAKES ABOUT 2 CUPS

One 15-ounce can full-fat
coconut milk

Pour the coconut milk into a chilled mixing bowl. Whip with an electric hand mixer until thick. The cream keeps covered in the refrigerator for up to 1 week.

SIMPLE SYRUP
MAKES 1 CUP

1 cup unrefined cane sugar

1 cup filtered water

Simple syrup has a multitude of uses. It is an essential ingredient in many mixed drinks, and it's great for sweetening cold beverages such as iced tea, in which regular sugar won't dissolve easily.

Combine the sugar and water in a small saucepan over medium heat, bring to a simmer, and gently simmer, swirling the pan now and then, until the sugar is dissolved and the liquid becomes clear, about 2 minutes. Do not allow the syrup to boil. Let cool completely.

The syrup keeps nearly indefinitely in a jar or other covered container in the refrigerator.

HARD TIMES SERVES 2

2 ounces (¼ cup) 90-proof bourbon

2 ounces (¼ cup) 80-proof
apple brandy

1½ ounces (3 tablespoons) freshly
squeezed lemon juice

1½ ounces (3 tablespoons) pure
maple syrup

2 lemon twists

Ras el Hanout (recipe follows) or
store-bought ras el hanout,
for dusting

Named for a song by my friend John Joseph's legendary New York hard-core punk band the Cro-Mags, this bold-flavored cocktail definitely will take the edge off. Incorporating the flavors of autumn, Hard Times is a combination of bourbon, apple brandy, and maple syrup, with the exotic spice blend ras el hanout.

Combine the bourbon, brandy, lemon juice, and maple syrup in a shaker with ice, cover, and shake really well to break up the ice into shards. Strain the cocktail into two old-fashioned glasses filled with ice. Twist a lemon peel over the surface of each cocktail and drop it into the glass or place it on the rim. Put the ras el hanout in a tea strainer or an empty sugar shaker and sprinkle a fine dusting over the top of the cocktails.

RAS EL HANOUT
MAKES 2 TABLESPOONS

2 cardamom pods

1 whole clove

½ cinnamon stick

1½ teaspoons coriander seeds

½ teaspoon cumin seeds

½ teaspoon fennel seeds

¼ teaspoon red pepper flakes

Ras el hanout is a Moroccan spice blend with a flavor that is warm and pungent. Making it fresh is ideal, but you can also purchase it in many grocery stores and gourmet markets.

Combine the cardamom, clove, cinnamon, coriander, cumin, fennel, and red pepper flakes in a small dry skillet over low heat and toast for just a minute or two to release the fragrant oils, shaking the pan so the spices don't burn.

Grind the toasted spices into a fine powder in a spice mill or clean coffee grinder. Store in a small covered jar or container.

PARISIAN STANDARD SERVES 2

1 large Bartlett pear

4 ounces (½ cup) gin or vodka

1½ ounces (3 tablespoons) freshly
    squeezed lemon juice

1 ounce (2 tablespoons) elderflower
    liqueur, such as St-Germain

½ ounce (1 tablespoon)
    agave nectar

2 ounces (¼ cup) brut sparkling
    rosé wine

2 grapefruit twists

Made with a dry sparkling rosé, this bubbly cocktail is zesty and floral from the addition of elderflower liqueur. Diced pear goes into the drink and a few pretty pear slices garnish the glass.

Remove the stem, cut the pear lengthwise in half, and scoop out the core. Cut one half of the pear into thin slices and set aside for garnish. Dice the remaining half and put in a cocktail shaker.

Using a muddler or the handle of a wooden spoon, smash and crush the diced pear to release the juice. Add the gin (or vodka), lemon juice, elderflower liqueur, agave, and ice, cover, and shake really well to break up the ice into shards. Add the sparkling wine. Strain the cocktail into two old-fashioned glasses filled with ice. Twist a grapefruit peel over the surface of each cocktail and drop it into the glass. Garnish each cocktail with the reserved pear slices.

HAPPY HARLEQUIN SERVES 2

1½ ounces (3 tablespoons) freshly
squeezed lemon juice

1½ ounces (3 tablespoons) Mamma
Chia Blackberry Hibiscus chia
seed drink

1½ ounces (3 tablespoons) Simple
Syrup (page 250)

15 fresh mint leaves (¼ cup),
plus (optional) 2 mint sprigs
for garnish

6 thin slices cucumber (optional)

3 ounces (6 tablespoons)
seltzer water

Chia seeds, for garnish

Light and refreshing, this nonalcoholic cocktail is named for a beautiful variety of camellia. Chia seeds are a great way to incorporate superfoods into your diet. As it turns out, they have benefits beyond growing botanical garden pets.

Combine the lemon juice, chia seed drink, simple syrup, mint leaves, and 4 of the cucumber slices in a shaker with ice, cover, and shake really well to break up the ice into shards. Add the seltzer. Strain the cocktail into two Collins glasses filled with ice; be sure to allow the chia seeds to strain into the glasses. If you like, skewer the remaining 2 cucumber slices on the sprigs of mint and drop one into each cocktail. Sprinkle each cocktail with a pinch of chia seeds.

SOPHIA

3 ounces (6 tablespoons) mezcal

1 ounce (2 tablespoons)
blanco tequila

2 ounces (¼ cup) freshly squeezed
lime juice

1 ounce (2 tablespoons) freshly
squeezed grapefruit juice

1½ ounces (3 tablespoons) syrup
from Candied Kalamata Olives
(page 221)

Splash of seltzer

¼ lemon

Kosher salt

6 whole Candied Kalamata Olives
(page 221)

This riff on the classic Paloma cocktail includes smoky mezcal as well as tequila and the briny syrup from the candied Kalamata olives; it's garnished with whole candied olives as well.

Combine the mezcal, tequila, lime juice, grapefruit juice, and Kalamata syrup in a shaker with ice, cover, and shake really well to break up the ice into shards. Add the seltzer.

Rim the edges of two Collins glasses with the lemon and dip in salt. Fill the glasses with ice and pour in the cocktail. Place 3 candied olives in each cocktail.

BASICS

ALMOND GREEK YOGURT 263

CASHEW CREAM 264

WALNUT PARMESAN 267

VEGETABLE STOCK 268

ROASTED VEGETABLE STOCK 269

DEMI-GLACE 270

BALSAMIC REDUCTION 271

BASIL PESTO 272

BASIL PESTO CREAM SAUCE 272

SCOTY'S MARINARA SAUCE 275

ALMOND GREEK YOGURT <corner>MAKES 1 CUP</corner>

1 cup Kite Hill almond ricotta

Juice of ½ lemon

While this is not really yogurt, Kite Hill almond ricotta has sweet and cultured overtones and a thick texture similar to that of Greek-style yogurt. A quick spin in a food processor with a squeeze of lemon juice makes the ricotta completely smooth and gives it extra tang. Spoon it onto Tomato and Watermelon Gazpacho (page 97) or Cream of Fava Bean and Pea Soup (page 98), or whip into a fruit smoothie.

Combine the almond ricotta and lemon juice in a food processor and puree until smooth. The yogurt can be kept covered in the refrigerator for up to 1 week.

CASHEW CREAM MAKES 3 CUPS

2 cups whole raw cashews, rinsed
Filtered water

Cashew cream, made from soaking raw cashews and blending them with water, is an indispensable part of my vegan cooking. It stands in for heavy cream in a variety of ways—in the batter for Hearts of Palm Calamari (page 117) and as a base for Spinach Cream Sauce (page 197) among others. The cream is at its best when used for cooking; it thickens up even faster than heavy cream and adds richness. You will never miss dairy if you use cashew cream.

It's essential to use raw cashews to make the cream; the raw nuts have little flavor of their own but provide a fatty creaminess. Roasted cashews taste too strong and won't blend as well.

Making cashew cream requires planning ahead, since you have to soak the cashews for at least 12 hours. Use only filtered water; the impurities in tap water will add a grayish tinge to the final product. The cream keeps for up to 4 days in the refrigerator and can be frozen for up to 3 months. Thaw it in the refrigerator, at room temperature, or in a large bowl of warm water. The cream will separate upon defrosting, so give it a whirl in a blender to re-emulsify.

Put the cashews in a bowl and pour in enough cold filtered water to cover. Cover with plastic wrap and refrigerate for at least 12 hours, or up to 1 day.

Drain the cashews in a colander and rinse with cold water. Transfer the cashews to a blender, preferably a Vitamix, and pour in enough cold filtered water to cover them by 1 inch, about 3 cups. Blend on high for 2 to 3 minutes, until very smooth and creamy without any trace of graininess. The cashew cream should be smooth on the palate; add more water if necessary. If you're not using a heavy-duty blender, you may need to strain the cashew cream through a fine-mesh sieve to get rid of any grittiness.

Cover and refrigerate until ready to use. It will thicken as it sits, so blend with ½ cup or so filtered water if needed to reach the desired consistency. It can also be frozen; see the headnote.

VARIATION

To make thick cashew cream, which is used in the Vanilla-Basil Ice Cream (page 227), reduce the amount of water in the blender so that it just covers the cashews, about 2 cups. (Makes 2 cups)

WALNUT PARMESAN ^{MAKES ABOUT 1 CUP}

½ cup raw walnut halves, frozen

Nonstick cooking spray

2 teaspoons nutritional yeast flakes
(see Note, page 6)

Kosher salt and freshly ground
black pepper

Many folks tell me that when adopting a plant-based lifestyle, their Achilles' heel is Parmesan cheese. Nutty, salty, and with a subtle umami flavor, Parmesan has the ability to elevate just about any dish. But this walnut Parmesan, made with shaved nuts tossed with nutritional yeast flakes, is a satisfying alternative that mimics the cheese's seductive flavor and texture.

You will need a razor-sharp truffle shaver or a Microplane to shave the nuts—watch your fingers—and be sure the walnuts are frozen solid, which will make them easier to work with. The walnut Parmesan's salty, cheesy flavor adds another dimension to many of our pasta dishes and risottos.

Using a truffle shaver, thinly shave the walnuts and put in a bowl. (Alternatively, use a Microplane to coarsely grate the nuts.) You should have about 1 cup. Coat with cooking spray and toss with the nutritional yeast flakes, salt, and pepper. The Parmesan keeps covered in the refrigerator for up to 1 month.

VEGETABLE STOCK
MAKES ABOUT 1 GALLON

2 celery stalks, quartered

2 fennel bulbs, coarsely chopped

2 leeks, trimmed, halved lengthwise,
   and washed

2 carrots, halved

1 onion, halved

4 garlic cloves, smashed

2 bay leaves

2 teaspoons whole
   black peppercorns

12 fresh flat-leaf parsley sprigs

6 fresh thyme sprigs

1 teaspoon kosher salt

About 1 gallon cold filtered water

A flavorful stock is one of the fundamentals of cooking. A good stock should enhance, rather than overwhelm, whatever sauce or dish you make with it. Every layer of flavor creates the sum of the parts, so the goal with making stock is versatility. This vegetable stock has a fairly neutral flavor that works in all kinds of preparations. The recipe couldn't be easier—chop up some vegetables, cover with water, and simmer—you're done.

The majority of commercial brands of vegetable stock are too dark in color and overly salty and/or sweet. If you're pressed for time and must use a prepared stock, More Than Gourmet is our favorite. It has no artificial anything and contains no MSG or excess sodium.

Combine the vegetables, bay leaves, peppercorns, herb sprigs, and salt in a large stockpot and add enough cold filtered water to cover. Slowly bring to a boil over medium heat, then reduce the heat to low and gently simmer, uncovered, for 45 minutes. Turn off the heat and let the stock steep and settle for 10 minutes.

Strain the stock through a fine-mesh sieve into another pot; discard the solids. Place the pot in a sink full of ice water and stir to cool the stock down quickly. The stock can be covered and refrigerated for up to 1 week or frozen for up to 1 month.

ROASTED VEGETABLE STOCK MAKES ABOUT 1 GALLON

1 bunch celery, cut into large chunks

8 large carrots, cut into
    large chunks

3 onions, quartered

2 large beefsteak
    tomatoes, quartered

Extra-virgin olive oil

Kosher salt and freshly ground
    black pepper

2 cups dry red wine, such as
    Cabernet Sauvignon or Syrah

1 gallon filtered water

One 15-ounce can cannellini beans,
    drained and rinsed

6 fresh thyme sprigs

4 fresh rosemary sprigs

2 bay leaves

1 ounce dried porcini (see Note,
    page 162) or shiitake mushrooms

1 teaspoon whole
    black peppercorns

Roasting the vegetables until they are caramelized is the essential first step in making this rich brown stock; the browning adds deep color and flavor to the stock that you won't get otherwise. Deglazing the roasting pan with wine ensures that you don't lose any of the concentrated brown bits on the bottom of the pan—those bits have intense flavor. Vegetables don't contain any gelatin (the stuff that makes meat stocks gel when chilled), so we use the natural starch in cannellini beans to add body and make the stock a little richer. This stock is the base of our Demi-Glace (page 270).

Preheat the oven to 450°F.

Spread the celery, carrots, onions, and tomatoes out in a large roasting pan. Drizzle generously with oil and season with salt and ground pepper. Roast for about 45 minutes, shaking the pan from time to time, until the vegetables are charred and completely soft.

Using a slotted spoon or tongs, transfer the roasted vegetables to a stockpot. Pour the wine into the hot roasting pan and scrape up the brown bits in the bottom with a wooden spoon. Pour the wine and drippings into the pot of vegetables. Add the water, beans, thyme, rosemary, bay leaves, dried mushrooms, and peppercorns and bring to a boil over high heat, then reduce the heat to low and simmer, uncovered, stirring occasionally, for 45 minutes to 1 hour.

Strain the stock through a fine-mesh sieve into another pot; discard the solids. Put the pot in a sink full of ice water and stir to cool the stock down quickly. The stock can be refrigerated covered for up to 4 days or frozen for up to 3 months.

DEMI-GLACE

¼ cup unbleached all-purpose flour
or rice flour

2 tablespoons Earth Balance butter
stick, cut into chunks

4 cups Roasted Vegetable Stock
(page 269), hot

Our demi-glace is essentially reduced roasted vegetable stock—and the key ingredient in velvety Porcini Mushroom–Bordelaise Sauce (page 162). Sophisticated but fairly simple to make, the demi-glace is shiny, rich, and almost meaty looking. At the restaurant, we simmer the vegetable stock for 8 hours or more so it reduces and thickens slowly into demi-glace. At home, you can thicken the sauce with roux, as in this recipe, and simmer it for just an hour or so. Note that while the ratio of fat to flour in a classic roux is one-to-one, Earth Balance doesn't absorb flour in the same way as butter and so you need twice as much flour to thicken the sauce.

Put a 3-quart saucepan over medium-low heat, add the flour, and toast, stirring constantly with a wooden spoon, until lightly golden, about 1 minute. Add the butter substitute, stirring constantly to prevent lumps—the roux may be slightly sticky at first, but it will loosen as you stir it over the heat. Continue to cook, stirring constantly, until the raw flour taste has been cooked out and the roux is walnut-colored and smells nutty, about 20 minutes.

Slowly pour in the stock, stirring constantly. Reduce the heat to medium-low and cook until the sauce is reduced and coats the back of a spoon, about 1 hour. The demi-glace can be stored covered in the refrigerator for up to 4 days or frozen for up to 3 months.

BALSAMIC
REDUCTION MAKES ½ CUP

½ cup agave nectar

1 cup balsamic vinegar

1 shallot, halved

Kosher salt and freshly ground
    black pepper

Made from the slow reduction of balsamic vinegar and agave nectar, this intensely flavored condiment is tart and thick. Be sure to keep an eye on the syrupy reduction as it simmers to prevent it from burning. Use it for Balsamic-Roasted Mushrooms with Shallots and Toasted Marcona Almonds (page 124), among other recipes, or drizzle over fresh strawberries.

Heat the agave in a small saucepan over medium-low heat until it thins out and is warmed, about 5 minutes. Add the vinegar and shallot and gently simmer, swirling the pan a few times, until the sauce has reduced and thickened to the consistency of maple syrup and coats the back of a spoon, about 50 minutes.

Remove the shallot and add a good pinch each of salt and pepper. The reduction can be stored covered at room temperature for up to 3 months.

BASIL PESTO MAKES 1 CUP

2 cups fresh basil leaves

½ cup fresh flat-leaf parsley leaves

¼ cup nutritional yeast flakes
(see Note, page 6)

¼ cup pine nuts, toasted

4 garlic cloves, smashed

½ teaspoon kosher salt

¼ teaspoon freshly ground
black pepper

¼ teaspoon red pepper flakes

½ cup extra-virgin olive oil

Pesto, among the best-known sauces to come out of Italy, is simple to make, requires no cooking, and has only a few ingredients. Yet it adds the most delicious pop of color and flavor to pastas, soups, and roasted vegetables; we also use it in Grilled Garden Vegetable Lasagna (page 201). When most of us think of pesto, we think of basil and pine nuts, but you can change it up and use other ingredients you have on hand, like arugula and walnuts, or sun-dried tomatoes and almonds. The pesto can be stored covered in the refrigerator for 1 day; freezing is not ideal, because it will change color and make the pesto very dark.

Combine the basil, parsley, nutritional yeast flakes, nuts, garlic, salt, black pepper, and red pepper flakes in a food processor and pulse until a paste forms, pushing down the basil and parsley as needed. With the motor running, pour in the oil in a steady stream, making sure it directly hits the blade (this is the best way to distribute the oil and emulsify it evenly and quickly). Transfer to a container. If you're not going to use the pesto immediately, press a piece of plastic wrap against the surface to keep it from oxidizing.

BASIL PESTO CREAM SAUCE MAKES ABOUT 1½ CUPS

2 tablespoons extra-virgin olive oil

1 small shallot, minced

1 garlic clove, minced

3 tablespoons Basil Pesto (above)

1½ cups Cashew Cream (page 264)

Fresh basil pesto transforms into a velvety sauce with the addition of cashew cream. The cashew cream needs to be prepared a day in advance. Serve with gnocchi (page 209).

Put a small saucepan over medium heat and add the oil. When the oil is hot, add the shallot and garlic and sauté until softened, about 1 minute. Stir in the pesto and cashew cream, bring to a simmer, and simmer, stirring often, until the sauce is reduced slightly and thick, about 3 minutes. Remove from the heat.

The sauce can be stored covered in the refrigerator for 1 day.

SCOTY'S MARINARA SAUCE MAKES 6 CUPS

Two 28-ounce cans whole tomatoes,
  preferably San Marzano

3 tablespoons extra-virgin olive oil

1 onion, finely chopped

4 garlic cloves, minced

1 carrot, finely grated (about ½ cup)

Kosher salt and freshly ground
  black pepper

½ teaspoon red pepper flakes

Pinch of baking soda

4 fresh basil leaves, chopped

1 tablespoon Earth Balance
  butter stick

If tomorrow was my last day on earth, I'd request a fresh piece of focaccia dunked in a vat of Scoty's marinara for my last meal. A well-made marinara should be thick enough to cling to pasta and vegetables yet light and fresh enough to balance whatever it's paired with. Cooked in under an hour, Scoty's sauce is thick but not heavy. Grated carrot is the secret weapon, lending both its natural sweetness and texture.

Be sure to seek out canned San Marzano tomatoes, which are now available at most grocery stores. This Italian tomato variety is coveted for its low acidity, bright flavor, and deep red color. This is the only marinara sauce you'll ever need. We use it in Fig Caponata (page 167), Spiced Chickpeas (page 128), and Puttanesca Sauce (page 203), among other dishes.

Working in batches, put the tomatoes, along with their juice, in a food processor or blender and puree just until semi-smooth; you want a little bit of chunky texture.

Put a medium pot over medium heat and add the oil. When the oil is hot, add the onion, garlic, and carrot, season with salt, black pepper, and the red pepper flakes, and sauté until the vegetables are soft, about 10 minutes.

Add the pureed tomatoes, stirring to combine, and bring to a boil. Reduce the heat to medium-low and simmer, uncovered, until the sauce thickens, about 45 minutes. Season the sauce with more salt and black pepper, to taste. Remove from the heat, stir in the baking soda, making sure it dissolves, and add the basil and butter substitute.

Once cooled, the sauce can be refrigerated covered for up to 3 days or frozen for up to 2 months.

ACKNOWLEDGMENTS

Thank you to everyone below who made Crossroads and this book possible. I am surrounded by such incredibly talented people, and I'm genuinely happy—and proud—to recognize them here.

The Crossroads staff, our family, both front and back of the house for everything you do day in and out to make the restaurant thrive.

Our general manager, Brian Moynan; assistant general manager, Jake Elliott; and chef, Duane Taguchi, for your commitment, hard work, and leadership.

My business partner and friend, Steve Bing. I've learned so much about life and work from you. I'm fortunate to have you in my life.

My investors, who made Crossroads a reality. I am forever grateful.

My family, especially my mother and sister Lia, for a lifetime of love and support.

JoAnn Cianciulli for capturing the Crossroads message, my voice, and the food we prepare, and for your leadership and hard work throughout the entire project.

Lisa Romerein for being the most solid, confident, and talented photographer I've ever met. This beautiful book came to life because of your exceptional photos and vision.

Judy Pray for your patience and guidance. And everyone at Artisan, including Lia Ronnen, Michelle Ishay-Cohen, Sibylle Kazeroid, Nancy Murray, and Allison McGeehon, for believing in this book.

LA Specialty for all of your amazing produce.

Serafina Magnussen for your delicious desserts and your loyalty and dedication.

Scoty for sharing this amazing journey with me, I couldn't imagine doing it without you.

Michael Voltaggio for your heartfelt foreword and your friendship.

Much appreciation to our regular guests and all of the folks who have shared a meal with us. You make me look forward to each day.

From Scot:
Thank you to my mother, Nancy Jones, and my father, John Jones, to Tal, and to Joe Iacomini, aka Papa Joe, who gave me my start in cooking.

From Serafina:
Thank you to my mom, dad, and big brother Brontosaurus, and to Jeffrey—my deepest gratitude for the love and support and for always challenging me to be more than I thought I could be. And to Tal, thank you for the incredible opportunities and adventures and for always having faith in me.

INDEX

Note: Page numbers in *italics* refer to illustrations.

Acorn Squash Ravioli with Kale and Black Garlic Butter Sauce, 191–92, *193*
agar-agar (note), 241
aïoli: Lemon-Caper Aïoli, 119
almond milk:
  Cannoli with Candied Kalamata Olives, *214*, 215–17
  Creamy Polenta with Roasted Corn and Porcini Mushroom–Bordelaise Sauce, *160*, 161–62
  Fudge-Fig Frosting, 244
  Lentil Skillet Bread, 14–15, *16–17*
  Mocha Sipping Chocolate, 235
  Oat Florentine Cookies with Mocha Sipping Chocolate, 232, *233*, 234–35
  Polenta Fries, 168–69
  Pumpkin Parfaits, 238, *239*, 240–41
  Vanilla-Basil Ice Cream, 227
almond ricotta:
  Almond Greek Yogurt, 263
  Baby Beet Salad with Apples, Candied Walnuts, and Balsamic Reduction, 32–33, *34–35*
  Bloomsdale Spinach Salad with Black Garlic Vinaigrette, 52, *53*, 55
  Butternut Squash–Puree Flatbread with Mustard Greens and Fried Brussels Sprout Leaves, 82, *83*, 84, 85
  Grilled Garden Vegetable Lasagna with Puttanesca Sauce, 201–2, *203*
  Herb Ricotta, 196
  Kale Spanakopita with Harissa Sauce and Mint Oil, 120–21, *122*, 123
  Kite Hill, 77
  Melon Salad with Watercress and Oroblanco Vinaigrette, 45, *46*, 47
  Watermelon Salad with Persian Cucumbers, Cherry Tomatoes, and Balsamic Reduction, *38*, 39
  Whipped Sweet Lemon Ricotta Cream, 220
almonds:
  Balsamic-Roasted Mushrooms with Shallots and Toasted Marcona Almonds, 124, *125*
  Israeli Couscous with Champagne Grapes, Haricots Verts, and Marcona Almonds, 56, *57*
  Marinated Mediterranean Olives with Rosemary-Fried Almonds, 7, *8*
  Oven-Roasted Okra with Calabrese Peppers and Pickled Scallions, *136*, 137
  Rosemary-Fried Almonds, *8*, 9
  Spiced Pumpkin and Almond Crunch Topping, 240, 241
  Spicy Moroccan Carrot Salad with Chili and Cumin, 36, *37*
apples:
  Baby Beet Salad with Apples, Candied Walnuts, and Balsamic Reduction, 32–33, *34–35*
  Pumpkin Parfaits, 238, *239*, 240–41
  Spiked Applesauce, 143
apricots: Tagine Sauce, 87
artichoke hearts, 24
  Vegetable Bouillabaisse with Rouille, 108, *109*, 110
  Warm Kale and Artichoke Dip, *24*, 25

Artichoke Oysters with Tomato Béarnaise and Kelp Caviar, *130*, 131–34, *135*
asparagus: Chive Fettuccine with Asparagus, Morels, and Prosecco Sauce, *180*, 181, 184

Baba Ganoush, 20
Balsamic Reduction, 271
  Baby Beet Salad with Apples, Candied Walnuts, and Balsamic Reduction, 32–33, *34–35*
  Watermelon Salad with Persian Cucumbers, Cherry Tomatoes, and Balsamic Reduction, *38*, 39
Balsamic-Roasted Mushrooms with Shallots and Toasted Marcona Almonds, 124, *125*
Banana Bread, 236, *237*
basics, 261–75
  Almond Greek Yogurt, 263
  Balsamic Reduction, 271
  Basil Pesto, 272, *273*
  Basil Pesto Cream Sauce, 272
  Cashew Cream, 264
  Demi-Glace, 270
  Roasted Vegetable Stock, 269
  Scoty's Marinara Sauce, *274*, 275
  Vegetable Stock, 268
  Walnut Parmesan, 267
basil:
  Basil Pesto, 272, *273*
  Basil Pesto Cream Sauce, 272
  Grilled Marinated Nectarines with Vanilla-Basil Ice Cream, 225, *226*, 227
  Israeli Couscous with Champagne Grapes, Haricots Verts, and Marcona Almonds, 56, *57*
  Linguine with Balsamic-Roasted Mushrooms and Tomato-Basil Butter Sauce, *188*, 189–90
  Spicy Tomato-Pepper Jam, *17*, 18
  Summer Minestrone with Basil Pesto, 94, *95*
beans:
  Cream of Fava Bean and Pea Soup, 98, *99*
  Egyptian Fava Bean Spread, *17*, 22–23
  fava (note), 23
  Fava Bean Agnolotti with Parsley and Aglio Olio Sauce, *204*, 205–6, *207*
  Israeli Couscous with Champagne Grapes, Haricots Verts, and Marcona Almonds, 56, *57*
  Italian Butter Beans with Pan-Roasted Kale, Sherry Aglio Olio, and Toasted Pumpkin Seeds, *156*, 157
  Roasted Vegetable Stock, 269
  Smoked White Bean Hummus, *5*, 6
  Summer Minestrone with Basil Pesto, 94, *95*
beets: Baby Beet Salad with Apples, Candied Walnuts, and Balsamic Reduction, 32–33, *34–35*
berries: Summer Berry Galette, *228*, 229–31
Black Garlic Vinaigrette, 55
Bloomsdale Spinach Salad with Black Garlic Vinaigrette, 52, *53*, 55
bouillabaisse: Vegetable Bouillabaisse with Rouille, 108, *109*, 110
Brussels sprouts:
  Butternut Squash–Puree Flatbread with Mustard Greens and Fried Brussels Sprout Leaves, 82, *83*, 84, 85

Shaved Brussels Sprouts with Za'atar, Lemon, and Pine Nuts, 48, *49*
Butternut Squash Farinata with Arugula Salad and Pomegranate Vinaigrette, *58*, 59–60, *61*
Butternut Squash–Puree Flatbread with Mustard Greens and Fried Brussels Sprout Leaves, 82, *83*, 84, 85

Candied Kalamata Olives, 221
Candied Walnuts, 33
Cannoli with Candied Kalamata Olives, *214*, 215–17
capers:
  Cauliflower Bisque with Fried Capers, 100–101, *103*
  Fig Caponata with Polenta Fries, *166*, 167–69
  Fried Capers, 101
  Lemon-Caper Aïoli, 119
  Puttanesca Sauce, 202
Cappellacci with Spinach Cream Sauce, 197, *199*, 200
carrots:
  Pappardelle Bolognese, 185–86, *187*
  Pickled Vegetables, 10, *11*, 12
  Roasted Spring Root Vegetable Flatbread with Leek Pâté and Crispy Shallots, 69, *70*, 71
  Roasted Vegetable Stock, 269
  Shaved Brussels Sprouts with Za'atar, Lemon, and Pine Nuts, 48, *49*
  Spicy Moroccan Carrot Salad with Chili and Cumin, 36, *37*
  Vegetable Stock, 268
Cashew Cream, 264
  Artichoke Oysters with Tomato Béarnaise and Kelp Caviar, *130*, 131–34, *135*
  Basil Pesto Cream Sauce, 272
  Cappellacci with Spinach Cream Sauce, 197, *199*, 200
  Cauliflower Bisque with Fried Capers, 100–101, *103*
  Cream of Fava Bean and Pea Soup, 98, *99*
  Fried Oyster Mushrooms, 133
  Hearts of Palm Calamari with Cocktail Sauce and Lemon-Caper Aïoli, *116*, 117–19
  Pappardelle Bolognese, 185–86, *187*
  Sweet Corn Puree, 79
  Sweet Corn Risotto with Buttered Leeks, Cherry Tomatoes, and Tomato-Sherry Cream Sauce, *164*, 165
  Tomato Béarnaise, 134
  Vanilla-Basil Ice Cream, 227, 264
cauliflower:
  Cauliflower Bisque with Fried Capers, 100–101, *103*
  Cauliflower with Olives and Sun-Dried Tomatoes, *150*, 151
  Pickled Vegetables, 10, *11*, 12
  Roasted Cauliflower Flatbread with Pistachio-Kalamata Tapenade and Frisée, *70*, 74, 75–76
Cavi-art (note), 132
celery:
  Pappardelle Bolognese, 185–86, *187*
  Roasted Vegetable Stock, 269
  Spring Chopped Salad with Whole-Grain-Mustard Vinaigrette, *30*, 31
  Vegetable Stock, 268

chickpeas: Spiced Chickpeas, 128, *129*
Chive Fettuccine with Asparagus, Morels, and Prosecco Sauce, *180*, *181*, 184
Chive Pasta Dough, 175
chocolate:
    Dark Chocolate Rice Pudding with Sugared Pine Nuts and Raspberries, *222*, *223*–24
    Decadent Dark Chocolate Cake with Figs and Hazelnuts, *242*, 243–45
    Fudge-Fig Frosting, 244
    Mocha Sipping Chocolate, 235
clementines:
    Clementine Beurre Blanc, 148
    Roasted Fennel with Clementine Beurre Blanc and Toasted Buckwheat, *146*, 147–48
cocktails, 247–59
    Happy Harlequin, *256*, 257
    Hard Times, *252*, 253
    Parisian Standard, *254*, *255*
    Respectable, 250, *251*
    Sophia, 258, *259*
Cocktail Sauce, 119
cocoa, *see* chocolate
Coconut Cream, 250
coconut oil (note), 148
Coconut Whipped Cream, 238
coffee: Decadent Dark Chocolate Cake with Figs and Hazelnuts, *242*, 243–45
cookies: Oat Florentine Cookies with Mocha Sipping Chocolate, 232, *233*, 234–35
corn:
    Charred Okra Flatbread with Sweet Corn Puree and Cherry Tomatoes, 78–79, *81*
    Creamy Polenta with Roasted Corn and Porcini Mushroom–Bordelaise Sauce, *160*, 161–62
    Polenta Fries, 168–69
    Sweet Corn Puree, 79
    Sweet Corn Risotto with Buttered Leeks, Cherry Tomatoes, and Tomato-Sherry Cream Sauce, *164*, 165
couscous: Israeli Couscous with Champagne Grapes, Haricots Verts, and Marcona Almonds, 56, *57*
crackers: Lentil Crackers, 15
Crispy Shallots, 71
cucumbers:
    Pickled Vegetables, 10, *11*, 12
    Tomato and Watermelon Gazpacho, *96*, 97
    Watermelon Salad with Persian Cucumbers, Cherry Tomatoes, and Balsamic Reduction, *38*, 39
currants: Kale Salad with Currants, Pine Nuts, and Lemon-Thyme Vinaigrette, *50*, 51

Decadent Dark Chocolate Cake with Figs and Hazelnuts, *242*, 243–45
Demi-Glace, 270
    Porcini Mushroom–Bordelaise Sauce, 162
desiccant packs (note), 221
desserts, 211–45
    Banana Bread, 236, *237*
    Cannoli with Candied Kalamata Olives, *214*, 215–17
    Coconut Whipped Cream, 238
    Dark Chocolate Rice Pudding with Sugared Pine Nuts and Raspberries, *222*, 223–24
    Decadent Dark Chocolate Cake with Figs and Hazelnuts, *242*, 243–45
    Fudge-Fig Frosting, 244
    Grilled Marinated Nectarines with Vanilla-Basil Ice Cream, 225, *226*, 227
    Oat Florentine Cookies with Mocha Sipping Chocolate, 232, *233*, 234–35

Pumpkin Parfaits, 238, *239*, 240–41
Roasted Pumpkin Mousse, 238, *239*, 240–41
storing frosting for later use, 245
Summer Berry Galette, *228*, 229–31
Whipped Sweet Lemon Ricotta Cream, 220

eggplants:
    Baba Ganoush, 20
    Fig Caponata with Polenta Fries, *166*, 167–69
    Grilled Garden Vegetable Lasagna with Puttanesca Sauce, 201–2, *203*
    grilling or roasting, 20
    Tagine Flatbread with Eggplant and Minted Spinach, 86–87, *88–89*
egg replacer, 143
    Cannoli with Candied Kalamata Olives, *214*, 215–17
Egyptian Fava Bean Spread, *17*, 22–23
espresso: Mocha Sipping Chocolate, 235

farro, 58
    Butternut Squash Farinata with Arugula Salad and Pomegranate Vinaigrette, *58*, 59–60, *61*
    Mushroom Farro Soup, 104, *105*
    Summer Minestrone with Basil Pesto, 94, *95*
Fava Bean Agnolotti with Parsley and Galio Olio Sauce, *204*, 205–6, *207*
fennel:
    French Lentil Soup with Crispy Kale, *106*, 107
    Roasted Fennel with Clementine Beurre Blanc and Toasted Buckwheat, *146*, 147–48
    Roasted Spring Root Vegetable Flatbread with Leek Pâté and Crispy Shallots, 69, *70*, 71
    Summer Minestrone with Basil Pesto, 94, *95*
    Vegetable Bouillabaisse with Rouille, 108, *109*, 110
    Vegetable Stock, 268
figs:
    Decadent Dark Chocolate Cake with Figs and Hazelnuts, *242*, 243–45
    dried (note), 245
    Fig Caponata with Polenta Fries, *166*, 167–69
    Fig-Hazelnut Jam, 243–45
    Fudge-Fig Frosting, 244
    Hazelnut Syrup, 244
flatbreads, 63–86
    Butternut Squash–Puree Flatbread with Mustard Greens and Fried Brussels Sprout Leaves, 82, *83*, *84*, 85
    Charred Okra Flatbread with Sweet Corn Puree and Cherry Tomatoes, 78–79, *81*
    Flatbread Dough, 66, *67*, 68
    Roasted Cauliflower Flatbread with Pistachio-Kalamata Tapenade and Frisée, *70*, *74*, 75–76
    Roasted Mushroom Flatbread with Spicy Tomato-Pepper Jam and Caramelized Onions, *70*, 72–73
    Roasted Spring Root Vegetable Flatbread with Leek Pâté and Crispy Shallots, 69, *70*, 71
    Tagine Flatbread with Eggplant and Minted Spinach, 86–87, *88–89*
French Lentil Soup with Crispy Kale, *106*, 107
Fudge-Fig Frosting, 244

garlic:
    Acorn Squash Ravioli with Kale and Black Garlic Butter Sauce, 191–92, *193*
    black (note), 54, *54*
    Black Garlic Vinaigrette, 55

Cauliflower Bisque with Fried Capers, 100–101, *103*
Fava Bean Agnolotti with Parsley and Aglio Olio Sauce, *204*, 205–6, *207*
Fig Caponata with Polenta Fries, *166*, 167–69
Kale Spanakopita with Harissa Sauce and Mint Oil, 120–21, *122*, 123
Puttanesca Sauce, 202
Rapini with Black Garlic, Sherry Vinegar, and Toasted Hazelnuts, *126*, 127
Scoty's Marinara Sauce, *274*, 275
Vegetable Stock, 268
Ginger Syrup, 240, *241*
gluten-free flour (note), 234
Gnocchi, *208*, 209
grapefruit juice: Sophia, 258, *259*
grapefruits:
    Melon Salad with Watercress and Oroblanco Vinaigrette, 45, *46*, 47
    Oroblanco Vinaigrette, 47
grapes: Israeli Couscous with Champagne Grapes, Haricots Verts, and Marcona Almonds, 56, *57*
grappa, 155
    Oven-Roasted Romanesco with Onion Agrodolce and Grappa-Soaked Raisins, 152, *153*, 155
greens:
    Hearts on Fire (note), 36
    see also salads
Grilled Garden Vegetable Lasagna with Puttanesca Sauce, 201–2, *203*
Grilled Marinated Nectarines with Vanilla-Basil Ice Cream, 225, *226*, 227
guar gum (note), 227

Happy Harlequin, *256*, 257
Hard Times, *252*, 253
Harissa Potato Chips, 4, *5*
Harissa Sauce, 121, *122*, 123
    Kale Spanakopita with Harissa Sauce and Mint Oil, 120–21, *122*, 123
harissa spice mix, 4
hazelnuts:
    Decadent Dark Chocolate Cake with Figs and Hazelnuts, *242*, 243–45
    Fig-Hazelnut Jam, 243–45
    Peach Salad with Balsamic-Glazed Cipollini Onions, Toasted Hazelnuts, and Mint Vinaigrette, *42*, 43–44
    Rapini with Black Garlic, Sherry Vinegar, and Toasted Hazelnuts, *126*, 127
    toasting (note), 44
Hearts of Palm Calamari with Cocktail Sauce and Lemon-Caper Aïoli, *116*, 117–19
Herb Ricotta, 196
    Grilled Garden Vegetable Lasagna with Puttanesca Sauce, 201–2, *203*
    Tortellini with Sun-Dried-Tomato Ricotta and Sweet Peas, *194*, 195–96
herbs:
    Balsamic-Roasted Mushrooms with Shallots and Toasted Marcona Almonds, 124, *125*
    Herb Ricotta, 196
    Roasted Vegetable Stock, 269
    Vegetable Bouillabaisse with Rouille, 108, *109*, 110
hummus: Smoked White Bean Hummus, *5*, 6

ice cream: Grilled Marinated Nectarines with Vanilla-Basil Ice Cream, 225, *226*, 227
Israeli Couscous with Champagne Grapes, Haricots Verts, and Marcona Almonds, 56, *57*
Italian Butter Beans with Pan-Roasted Kale, Sherry Aglio Olio, and Toasted Pumpkin Seeds, *156*, 157

jams:
    Fig-Hazelnut Jam, *242*, 243–45
    Spicy Tomato-Pepper Jam, *17*, 18

kale:
    Acorn Squash Ravioli with Kale and Black
        Garlic Butter Sauce, 191–92, *193*
    Crispy Kale, 207
    French Lentil Soup with Crispy Kale, *106*,
        107
    Italian Butter Beans with Pan-Roasted
        Kale, Sherry Aglio Olio, and Toasted
        Pumpkin Seeds, *156*, 157
    Kale Salad with Currants, Pine Nuts, and
        Lemon-Thyme Vinaigrette, *50*, 51
    Kale Spanakopita with Harissa Sauce and
        Mint Oil, 120–21, *122*, 123
    Warm Kale and Artichoke Dip, *24*, 25
Kite Hill, 77
kombu, 111
    vegetable stock, 108

latkes: Sweet Potato Latkes with Spiked
    Applesauce, 141, *142*, 143
leeks:
    Cauliflower Bisque with Fried Capers,
        100–101, *103*
    Leek Pâté, *16*, 19
    Roasted Spring Root Vegetable Flatbread
        with Leek Pâté and Crispy Shallots, 69,
        70, 71
    Sweet Corn Risotto with Buttered Leeks,
        Cherry Tomatoes, and Tomato-Sherry
        Cream Sauce, *164*, 165
    Vegetable Bouillabaisse with Rouille, 108,
        109, 110
    Vegetable Stock, 268
lemons:
    Almond Greek Yogurt, 263
    Happy Harlequin, *256*, 257
    Hard Times, *252*, 253
    Lemon-Caper Aïoli, 119
    Lemon-Thyme Vinaigrette, 51
    Parisian Standard, 254, *255*
    Parsley Vinaigrette, 140
    Shaved Brussels Sprouts with Za'atar,
        Lemon, and Pine Nuts, 48, *49*
    Spiked Applesauce, 143
    Whipped Sweet Lemon Ricotta Cream, 220
lentils:
    French Lentil Soup with Crispy Kale, *106*,
        107
    Lentil Crackers, 15
    Lentil Skillet Bread, 14–15, *16–17*
lime juice: Sophia, 258, *259*
limes: Tomato and Watermelon Gazpacho,
    96, 97
Linguine with Balsamic-Roasted Mushrooms
    and Tomato-Basil Butter Sauce, *188*,
    189–90

maple syrup:
    Hard Times, *252*, 253
    Roasted Baby Parsnips with Sherry-Maple
        Glaze and Chanterelles, 158, *159*
Marinated Mediterranean Olives
    with Rosemary-Fried Almonds,
    7, *8*
mayonnaise:
    Lemon-Caper Aïoli, 119
    Lentil Skillet Bread, 14–15, *16–17*
    Rouille, 111
Melon Salad with Watercress and Oroblanco
    Vinaigrette, 45, *46*, 47
mint:
    Balsamic-Roasted Mushrooms with
        Shallots and Toasted Marcona Almonds,
        124, *125*
    Happy Harlequin, *256*, 257

Israeli Couscous with Champagne Grapes,
    Haricots Verts, and Marcona Almonds,
    56, *57*
Kale Spanakopita with Harissa Sauce and
    Mint Oil, 120–21, *122*, 123
Melon Salad with Watercress and
    Oroblanco Vinaigrette, 45, *46*, 47
Mint Oil, 123
Mint Vinaigrette, 44
Tagine Flatbread with Eggplant and Minted
    Spinach, 86–87, *88–89*
Mocha Sipping Chocolate, 235
mushrooms:
    Balsamic-Roasted Mushrooms with
        Shallots and Toasted Marcona Almonds,
        124, *125*
    Chive Fettuccine with Asparagus, Morels,
        and Prosecco Sauce, *180*, 181, 184
    Creamy Polenta with Roasted Corn and
        Porcini Mushroom–Bordelaise Sauce,
        160, 161–62
    dried, reconstituting (note), 162
    Fried Oyster Mushrooms, 133
    Linguine with Balsamic-Roasted
        Mushrooms and Tomato-Basil Butter
        Sauce, *188*, 189–90
    morels (note), 184
    Mushroom Farro Soup, 104, *105*
    porcini (note), 162
    Porcini Mushroom–Bordelaise Sauce, 162
    Roasted Baby Parsnips with Sherry-Maple
        Glaze and Chanterelles, 158, *159*
    Roasted Mushroom Flatbread with Spicy
        Tomato-Pepper Jam and Caramelized
        Onions, *70*, 72–73
    Roasted Vegetable Stock, 269
    Smoked Mushrooms, 52, 55
    Vegetable Bouillabaisse with Rouille, 108,
        109, 110

nectarines: Grilled Marinated Nectarines with
    Vanilla-Basil Ice Cream, 225, *226*, 227
nutritional yeast flakes, 6
    Acorn Squash Ravioli with Kale and Black
        Garlic Butter Sauce, 191–92, *193*
    Artichoke Oysters with Tomato Béarnaise
        and Kelp Caviar, *130*, 131–34, *135*
    Basil Pesto, 272, *273*
    Cappellacci with Spinach Cream Sauce,
        197, *199*, 200
    Chive Fettuccine with Asparagus, Morels,
        and Prosecco Sauce, *180*, 181, 184
    Creamy Polenta with Roasted Corn and
        Porcini Mushroom–Bordelaise Sauce,
        160, 161–62
    Fava Bean Agnolotti with Parsley and Galio
        Olio Sauce, *204*, 205–6, *207*
    French Lentil Soup with Crispy Kale, *106*,
        107
    Harissa Sauce, 121, *122*, 123
    Italian Butter Beans with Pan-Roasted
        Kale, Sherry Aglio Olio, and Toasted
        Pumpkin Seeds, *156*, 157
    Polenta Fries, 168–69
    Tomato Béarnaise, 134
    Tortellini with Sun-Dried-Tomato Ricotta
        and Sweet Peas, *194*, 195–96
    Walnut Parmesan, 267
    Warm Kale and Artichoke Dip, *24*, 25

Oat Florentine Cookies with Mocha Sipping
    Chocolate, 232, *233*, 234–35
oils:
    coconut oil (note), 148
    Mint Oil, 123
    red palm oil (note), 175
okra:
    Charred Okra Flatbread with Sweet Corn
        Puree and Cherry Tomatoes, 78–79, *81*

Oven-Roasted Okra with Calabrese
    Peppers and Pickled Scallions, *136*, 137
olives:
    Candied Kalamata Olives, 221
    Cannoli with Candied Kalamata Olives,
        214, 215–17
    Cauliflower with Olives and Sun-Dried
        Tomatoes, *150*, 151
    Marinated Mediterranean Olives with
        Rosemary-Fried Almonds, 7, *8*
    Pistachio-Kalamata Tapenade, 21
    Puttanesca Sauce, 202
    Roasted Cauliflower Flatbread with
        Pistachio-Kalamata Tapenade and
        Frisée, *70*, 74, 75–76
    Sophia, 258, *259*
onions:
    Butternut Squash–Puree Flatbread with
        Mustard Greens and Fried Brussels
        Sprout Leaves, 82, *83*, *84*, 85
    caramelized, 72
    Cauliflower Bisque with Fried Capers,
        100–101, *103*
    Cauliflower with Olives and Sun-Dried
        Tomatoes, *150*, 151
    cipollini (note), 44
    Egyptian Fava Bean Spread, *17*, 22–23
    Fig Caponata with Polenta Fries, *166*,
        167–69
    French Lentil Soup with Crispy Kale, *106*,
        107
    Grilled Garden Vegetable Lasagna with
        Puttanesca Sauce, 201–2, *203*
    Kale Spanakopita with Harissa Sauce and
        Mint Oil, 120–21, *122*, 123
    Mushroom Farro Soup, 104, *105*
    Oven-Roasted Romanesco with Onion
        Agrodolce and Grappa-Soaked Raisins,
        152, *153*, 155
    Pappardelle Bolognese, 185–86, *187*
    Peach Salad with Balsamic-Glazed
        Cipollini Onions, Toasted Hazelnuts, and
        Mint Vinaigrette, *42*, 43–44
    Roasted Fennel with Clementine Beurre
        Blanc and Toasted Buckwheat, *146*,
        147–48
    Roasted Mushroom Flatbread with Spicy
        Tomato-Pepper Jam and Caramelized
        Onions, *70*, 72–73
    Roasted Vegetable Stock, 269
    Scoty's Marinara Sauce, *274*, 275
    Spicy Tomato-Pepper Jam, *17*, 18
    Summer Minestrone with Basil Pesto,
        94, *95*
    Vegetable Stock, 268
oranges:
    Oat Florentine Cookies with Mocha Sipping
        Chocolate, 232, *233*, 234–35
    Vegetable Bouillabaisse with Rouille, 108,
        109, 110
Oroblanco Vinaigrette, 47

Papas Arrugadas (Spanish Wrinkled
    Potatoes) with Parsley Vinaigrette, 138,
    139, 140
Pappardelle Bolognese, 185–86, *187*
Parisian Standard, 254, *255*
parsley:
    Balsamic-Roasted Mushrooms with
        Shallots and Toasted Marcona Almonds,
        124, *125*
    Basil Pesto, 272, *273*
    Black Garlic Vinaigrette, 55
    Cauliflower with Olives and Sun-Dried
        Tomatoes, *150*, 151
    Fava Bean Agnolotti with Parsley and
        Olio Sauce, *204*, 205–6, *207*
    Herb Ricotta, 196
    Parsley Vinaigrette, 140

Roasted Cauliflower Flatbread with Pistachio-Kalamata Tapenade and Frisée, 70, 74, 75–76
Spicy Tomato-Pepper Jam, 17, 18
Spring Chopped Salad with Whole-Grain-Mustard Vinaigrette, 30, 31
Vegetable Stock, 268
parsnips: Roasted Baby Parsnips with Sherry-Maple Glaze and Chanterelles, 158, 159
pasta, 171–209
Acorn Squash Ravioli with Kale and Black Garlic Butter Sauce, 191–92, 193
Cappellacci with Spinach Cream Sauce, 197, 199, 200
Chive Fettuccine with Asparagus, Morels, and Prosecco Sauce, 180, 181, 184
Chive Pasta Dough, 175
Fava Bean Agnolotti with Parsley and Aglio Olio Sauce, 204, 205–6, 207
Gnocchi, 208, 209
Grilled Garden Vegetable Lasagna with Puttanesca Sauce, 201–2, 203
Linguine with Balsamic-Roasted Mushrooms and Tomato-Basil Butter Sauce, 188, 189–90
Pappardelle Bolognese, 185–86, 187
Pasta Dough, 174–75
tips for making, 177, 178
Tortellini with Sun-Dried-Tomato Ricotta and Sweet Peas, 194, 195–96
pâté: Leek Pâté, 16, 19
Peach Salad with Balsamic-Glazed Cipollini Onions, Toasted Hazelnuts, and Mint Vinaigrette, 42, 43–44
pear: Parisian Standard, 254, 255
peas:
Cream of Fava Bean and Pea Soup, 98, 99
Spring Chopped Salad with Whole-Grain-Mustard Vinaigrette, 30, 31
Tortellini with Sun-Dried-Tomato Ricotta and Sweet Peas, 194, 195–96
peppers:
Calabrese peppers (note), 137
Cauliflower with Olives and Sun-Dried Tomatoes, 150, 151
Fig Caponata with Polenta Fries, 166, 167–69
Grilled Garden Vegetable Lasagna with Puttanesca Sauce, 201–2, 203
Oven-Roasted Okra with Calabrese Peppers and Pickled Scallions, 136, 137
Rouille, 111
Spicy Tomato-Pepper Jam, 17, 18
Tomato and Watermelon Gazpacho, 96, 97
pesto:
Basil Pesto, 272, 273
Basil Pesto Cream Sauce, 272
Pickled Vegetables, 10, 11, 12
Pickling Spice, 12
pine nuts:
Basil Pesto, 272, 273
Cauliflower with Olives and Sun-Dried Tomatoes, 150, 151
Kale Salad with Currants, Pine Nuts, and Lemon-Thyme Vinaigrette, 50, 51
Oven-Roasted Romanesco with Onion Agrodolce and Grappa-Soaked Raisins, 152, 153, 155
Shaved Brussels Sprouts with Za'atar, Lemon, and Pine Nuts, 48, 49
Sugared Pine Nuts, 224
Pistachio-Kalamata Tapenade, 21
polenta:
Creamy Polenta with Roasted Corn and Porcini Mushroom–Bordelaise Sauce, 160, 161–62
Fig Caponata with Polenta Fries, 166, 167–69
Fried Oyster Mushrooms, 133

Hearts of Palm Calamari with Cocktail Sauce and Lemon-Caper Aioli, 116, 117–19
Polenta Fries, 168–69
Pomegranate Vinaigrette, 60
Porcini Mushroom–Bordelaise Sauce, 162
potatoes:
Charred Okra Flatbread with Sweet Corn Puree and Cherry Tomatoes, 78–79, 81
Egyptian Fava Bean Spread, 17, 22–23
Gnocchi, 208, 209
Harissa Potato Chips, 4, 5
Papas Arrugadas (Spanish Wrinkled Potatoes) with Parsley Vinaigrette, 138, 139, 140
Roasted Spring Root Vegetable Flatbread with Leek Pâté and Crispy Shallots, 69, 70, 71
Sweet Potato Latkes with Spiked Applesauce, 141, 142, 143
pumpkin:
Pumpkin Parfaits, 238, 239, 240–41
Roasted Pumpkin Mousse, 238, 239, 240–41
pumpkin seeds:
Butternut Squash–Puree Flatbread with Mustard Greens and Fried Brussels Sprout Leaves, 82, 83, 84, 85
Spiced Pumpkin and Almond Crunch Topping, 240, 241

quinoa: Lentil Skillet Bread, 14–15, 16–17

radishes:
Pickled Vegetables, 10, 11, 12
Spring Chopped Salad with Whole-Grain-Mustard Vinaigrette, 30, 31
watermelon radishes, 10, 11
raisins: Oven-Roasted Romanesco with Onion Agrodolce and Grappa-Soaked Raisins, 152, 153, 155
Rapini with Black Garlic, Sherry Vinegar, and Toasted Hazelnuts, 126, 127
Ras el Hanout, 253
Respectable, 250, 251
rice:
Dark Chocolate Rice Pudding with Sugared Pine Nuts and Raspberries, 222, 223–24
Sweet Corn Risotto with Buttered Leeks, Cherry Tomatoes, and Tomato-Sherry Cream Sauce, 164, 165
Roasted Vegetable Stock, 269
romanesco: Oven-Roasted Romanesco with Onion Agrodolce and Grappa-Soaked Raisins, 152, 153, 155
Rosemary-Fried Almonds, 8, 9
Rouille, 111
Vegetable Bouillabaisse with Rouille, 108, 109, 110

salads, 27–61
Baby Beet Salad with Apples, Candied Walnuts, and Balsamic Reduction, 32–33, 34–35
Bloomsdale Spinach Salad with Black Garlic Vinaigrette, 52, 53, 55
Butternut Squash Farinata with Arugula Salad and Pomegranate Vinaigrette, 58, 59–60, 61
Israeli Couscous with Champagne Grapes, Haricots Verts, and Marcona Almonds, 56, 57
Kale Salad with Currants, Pine Nuts, and Lemon-Thyme Vinaigrette, 50, 51
Melon Salad with Watercress and Oroblanco Vinaigrette, 45, 46, 47
Peach Salad with Balsamic-Glazed Cipollini Onions, Toasted Hazelnuts, and Mint Vinaigrette, 42, 43–44

Shaved Brussels Sprouts with Za'atar, Lemon, and Pine Nuts, 48, 49
Spicy Moroccan Carrot Salad with Chili and Cumin, 36, 37
Spring Chopped Salad with Whole-Grain-Mustard Vinaigrette, 30, 31
Watermelon Salad with Persian Cucumbers, Cherry Tomatoes, and Balsamic Reduction, 38, 39
sauces:
Basil Pesto Cream Sauce, 272
Clementine Beurre Blanc, 148
Cocktail Sauce, 119
Ginger Syrup, 240, 241
Harissa Sauce, 121, 122, 123
Hazelnut Syrup, 244
Lemon-Caper Aioli, 119
Porcini Mushroom–Bordelaise Sauce, 162
Puttanesca Sauce, 202
Scoty's Marinara Sauce, 274, 275
Simple Syrup, 250
Spaghetti Squash Noce Moscata, 144, 145
Spiked Applesauce, 143
Tagine Sauce, 87
Tomato Béarnaise, 134
Tomato-Sherry Cream Sauce, 165
see also pasta
sausage: Pappardelle Bolognese, 185–86, 187
scallions:
Oven-Roasted Okra with Calabrese Peppers and Pickled Scallions, 136, 137
Pickled Vegetables, 10, 11, 12
Polenta Fries, 168–69
Scoty's Marinara Sauce, 274, 275
Fig Caponata with Polenta Fries, 166, 167–69
Linguine with Balsamic-Roasted Mushrooms and Tomato-Basil Butter Sauce, 188, 189–90
Pappardelle Bolognese, 185–86, 187
Puttanesca Sauce, 202
Sweet Corn Risotto with Buttered Leeks, Cherry Tomatoes, and Tomato-Sherry Cream Sauce, 164, 165
shallots:
Balsamic-Roasted Mushrooms with Shallots and Toasted Marcona Almonds, 124, 125
Crispy Shallots, 71
Linguine with Balsamic-Roasted Mushrooms and Tomato-Basil Butter Sauce, 188, 189–90
Porcini Mushroom–Bordelaise Sauce, 162
Roasted Fennel with Clementine Beurre Blanc and Toasted Buckwheat, 146, 147–48
sherry:
Acorn Squash Ravioli with Kale and Black Garlic Butter Sauce, 191–92, 193
Egyptian Fava Bean Spread, 17, 22–23
Fava Bean Agnolotti with Parsley and Aglio Olio Sauce, 204, 205–6, 207
Italian Butter Beans with Pan-Roasted Kale, Sherry Aglio Olio, and Toasted Pumpkin Seeds, 156, 157
Linguine with Balsamic-Roasted Mushrooms and Tomato-Basil Butter Sauce, 188, 189–90
Spaghetti Squash Noce Moscata, 144, 145
Spiced Chickpeas, 128, 129
Sweet Corn Puree, 79
Sweet Corn Risotto with Buttered Leeks, Cherry Tomatoes, and Tomato-Sherry Cream Sauce, 164, 165
Warm Kale and Artichoke Dip, 24, 25
Simple Syrup, 250
Happy Harlequin, 256, 257
Smoked Mushrooms, 52, 55
Smoked White Bean Hummus, 5, 6

Sophia, 258, *259*
soups, 91–111
   Cauliflower Bisque with Fried Capers,
     100–101, *103*
   Cream of Fava Bean and Pea Soup, 98, *99*
   French Lentil Soup with Crispy Kale, *106*,
     107
   Mushroom Farro Soup, 104, *105*
   Summer Minestrone with Basil Pesto,
     94, *95*
   Tomato and Watermelon Gazpacho, *96*, 97
   Vegetable Bouillabaisse with Rouille, 108,
     109, 110
Spaghetti Squash Noce Moscata, 144, *145*
Spiced Chickpeas, 128, *129*
spices:
   harissa spice mix, 4
   Pickling Spice, 12
   Pumpkin Parfaits, 238, *239*, 240–41
   Ras el Hanout, 253
   Spiced Pumpkin and Almond Crunch
     Topping, 240, 241
   Tagine Sauce, 87
   za'atar (note), 23
Spicy Moroccan Carrot Salad with Chili and
   Cumin, 36, *37*
Spicy Tomato-Pepper Jam, *17*, 18
   Roasted Mushroom Flatbread with Spicy
     Tomato-Pepper Jam and Caramelized
     Onions, 70, 72–73
Spiked Applesauce, 143
spinach:
   Bloomsdale Spinach Salad with Black
     Garlic Vinaigrette, 52, *53*, 55
   Cappellacci with Spinach Cream Sauce,
     197, *199*, 200
   Cream of Fava Bean and Pea Soup, 98, *99*
   Tagine Flatbread with Eggplant and Minted
     Spinach, 86–87, *88–89*
Spring Chopped Salad with Whole-Grain-
   Mustard Vinaigrette, *30*, 31
squash:
   Acorn Squash Ravioli with Kale and Black
     Garlic Butter Sauce, 191–92, *193*
   Butternut Squash Farinata with Arugula
     Salad and Pomegranate Vinaigrette, *58*,
     59–60, *61*
   Butternut Squash–Puree Flatbread with
     Mustard Greens and Fried Brussels
     Sprout Leaves, 82, *83*, *84*, 85
   Grilled Garden Vegetable Lasagna with
     Puttanesca Sauce, 201–2, *203*
   Spaghetti Squash Noce Moscata, 144, *145*
   Summer Minestrone with Basil Pesto,
     94, *95*
Summer Berry Galette, *228*, 229–31
Summer Minestrone with Basil Pesto, 94, *95*
Sweet Potato Latkes with Spiked
   Applesauce, 141, *142*, 143

Tagine Flatbread with Eggplant and Minted
   Spinach, 86–87, *88–89*
Tagine Sauce, 87

tahini:
   Baba Ganoush, 20
   Smoked White Bean Hummus, *5*, 6
tapenades:
   Pistachio-Kalamata Tapenade, 21
   Roasted Cauliflower Flatbread with
     Pistachio-Kalamata Tapenade and
     Frisée, *70*, *74*, *75*–76
tea, note, 111
thyme:
   French Lentil Soup with Crispy Kale, *106*,
     107
   Lemon-Thyme Vinaigrette, 51
   Mushroom Farro Soup, 104, *105*
   Roasted Fennel with Clementine Beurre
     Blanc and Toasted Buckwheat, *146*,
     147–48
   Roasted Vegetable Stock, 269
   Vegetable Stock, 268
tofu: Pasta Dough, 174–75
tomatoes:
   Cappellacci with Spinach Cream Sauce,
     197, *199*, 200
   Cauliflower with Olives and Sun-Dried
     Tomatoes, *150*, 151
   Charred Okra Flatbread with Sweet Corn
     Puree and Cherry Tomatoes, 78–79, *81*
   Egyptian Fava Bean Spread, *17*, 22–23
   Harissa Sauce, 121, *122*, 123
   Roasted Vegetable Stock, 269
   Scoty's Marinara Sauce, *274*, 275
   Spicy Tomato-Pepper Jam, *17*, 18
   Summer Minestrone with Basil Pesto,
     94, *95*
   Sweet Corn Risotto with Buttered Leeks,
     Cherry Tomatoes, and Tomato-Sherry
     Cream Sauce, 164, 165
   Tagine Sauce, 87
   Tomato and Watermelon Gazpacho, *96*, 97
   Tomato Béarnaise, 134
   Tortellini with Sun-Dried-Tomato Ricotta
     and Sweet Peas, *194*, 195–96
   Vegetable Bouillabaisse with Rouille, 108,
     109, 110
   Watermelon Salad with Persian
     Cucumbers, Cherry Tomatoes, and
     Balsamic Reduction, *38*, 39
Tortellini with Sun-Dried-Tomato Ricotta
   and Sweet Peas, *194*, 195–96
turnip: French Lentil Soup with Crispy Kale,
   106, 107

Vanilla-Basil Ice Cream, 227
vegetables:
   Grilled Garden Vegetable Lasagna with
     Puttanesca Sauce, 201–2, *203*
   Pickled Vegetables, 10, *11*, 12
   Roasted Spring Root Vegetable Flatbread
     with Leek Pâté and Crispy Shallots, 69,
     70, 71
   Roasted Vegetable Stock, 269
   Summer Minestrone with Basil Pesto,
     94, *95*

Vegetable Bouillabaisse with Rouille, 108,
   109, 110
Vegetable Stock, 104, 108, 268
vinaigrettes:
   Black Garlic Vinaigrette, 55
   Lemon-Thyme Vinaigrette, 51
   Mint Vinaigrette, 44
   Oroblanco Vinaigrette, 47
   Parsley Vinaigrette, 140
   Pomegranate Vinaigrette, 60
   Whole-Grain-Mustard Vinaigrette, 31

Walnut Parmesan, 267
   Spaghetti Squash Noce Moscata, 144, *145*
   Sweet Corn Risotto with Buttered Leeks,
     Cherry Tomatoes, and Tomato-Sherry
     Cream Sauce, 164, 165
   Tortellini with Sun-Dried-Tomato Ricotta
     and Sweet Peas, *194*, 195–96
walnuts:
   Baby Beet Salad with Apples, Candied
     Walnuts, and Balsamic Reduction,
     32–33, *34–35*
   Candied Walnuts, 33
   Pistachio-Kalamata Tapenade, 21
   Walnut Parmesan, 267
watermelon: Tomato and Watermelon
   Gazpacho, *96*, 97
Watermelon Salad with Persian Cucumbers,
   Cherry Tomatoes, and Balsamic
   Reduction, *38*, 39
Whipped Sweet Lemon Ricotta Cream, 220
wine:
   Acorn Squash Ravioli with Kale and Black
     Garlic Butter Sauce, 191–92, *193*
   Artichoke Oysters with Tomato Béarnaise
     and Kelp Caviar, *130*, 131–34, *135*
   Cappellacci with Spinach Cream Sauce,
     197, *199*, 200
   Chive Fettuccine with Asparagus,
     Morels, and Prosecco Sauce, *180*, 181,
     184
   Clementine Beurre Blanc, 148
   Harissa Sauce, 121, *122*, 123
   Leek Pâté, *16*, 19
   Pappardelle Bolognese, 185–86, *187*
   Parisian Standard, 254, *255*
   Porcini Mushroom–Bordelaise Sauce, 162
   Puttanesca Sauce, 202
   Roasted Vegetable Stock, 269
   Tomato Béarnaise, 134
   Tortellini with Sun-Dried-Tomato Ricotta
     and Sweet Peas, *194*, 195–96
   vegetable stock, 108
   Warm Kale and Artichoke Dip, 24, 25
wood chips (note), 52

yogurt: Almond Greek Yogurt, 263

za'atar, 23
   Egyptian Fava Bean Spread, *17*, 22–23
   Shaved Brussels Sprouts with Za'atar,
     Lemon, and Pine Nuts, 48, *49*

CONVERSION CHARTS

Here are rounded-off equivalents between the metric system and the traditional systems used in the United States to measure weight and volume.

WEIGHTS		VOLUME			OVEN TEMPERATURE			
US/UK	METRIC	AMERICAN	IMPERIAL	METRIC		°F	°C	GAS MARK
¼ oz	7 G	¼ TSP		1.25 ML	VERY COOL	250–275	130–140	½–1
½ oz	15 G	½ TSP		2.5 ML	COOL	300	148	2
1 oz	30 G	1 TSP		5 ML	WARM	325	163	3
2 oz	55 G	½ TBSP (1½ TSP)		7.5 ML	MEDIUM	350	177	4
3 oz	85 G	1 TBSP (3 TSP)		15 ML	MEDIUM HOT	375–400	190–204	5–6
4 oz	115 G	¼ CUP (4 TBSP)	2 FL OZ	60 ML	HOT	425	218	7
5 oz	140 G	⅓ CUP (5 TBSP)	2½ FL OZ	75 ML	VERY HOT	450–475	232–245	8–9
6 oz	170 G	½ CUP (8 TBSP)	4 FL OZ	125 ML				
7 oz	200 G	⅔ CUP (10 TBSP)	5 FL OZ	150 ML				
8 oz (½ LB)	225 G	¾ CUP (12 TBSP)	6 FL OZ	175 ML				
9 oz	255 G	1 CUP (16 TBSP)	8 FL OZ	250 ML				
10 oz	285 G	1¼ CUPS	10 FL OZ	300 ML				
11 oz	310 G	1½ CUPS	12 FL OZ	350 ML				
12 oz	340 G	1 PINT (2 CUPS)	16 FL OZ	500 ML				
13 oz	370 G	2½ CUPS	20 FL OZ (1 PINT)	625 ML				
14 oz	400 G	5 CUPS	40 FL OZ (1 QT)	1.25 L				
15 oz	425 G							
16 oz (1 LB)	450 G